PRAISE FOR
CANARY IN THE COAL MINE

"*Canary* is terrific. Salzberg has hit it out of the park. Love the writing style, and the story really draws you in. Pete Fortunato is a formidable character, strong enough to open a new series. Flawed, lovable, ballsy, smart. As with Salzberg's prior works, he has a knack for making his heroes real, which makes their jeopardy real, too. So, say hello to Pete Fortunato, a modern PI who thinks on his feet and has moves like classic noir that reads like the noir version of *Midnight Run*."

—Tom Straw, author of the Richard Castle series
(from the ABC show) and *Buzz Killer*

"Salzberg writes hardboiled prose from a gritty stream of conscious. Peter Fortunato is an old school PI to be reckoned with."

—Sam Wiebe, award-winning author of
Invisible Dead and *Never Going Back*

"Charles Salzberg's *Canary in the Coal Mine* is everything a reader wants in a great crime novel, and then some. The rat-a-tat cadence of the noir masters, seamlessly blended with the contemporary sensibilities of an author thoroughly in control of his craft. Private Investigator, Pete Fortunato is the thinking-person's Marlowe; worldly, tough, cynical and smart. I liked this book so much I read it twice. No kidding. It's that good."

—Baron R. Birtcher, multi-award winning
and *Los Angeles Times* bestselling author

CANARY IN
THE COAL MINE

BOOKS BY
CHARLES SALZBERG

Henry Swann Mystery Series
Swann's Last Song
Swann Dives In
Swann's Lake of Despair
Swann's Way Out
Swann's Down

Stand Alone
Devil in the Hole
Second Story Man
Canary in the Coal Mine

Novellas
Triple Shot (Twist of Fate)
Three Strikes (The Maybrick Affair)
Third Degree (The Fifth Column)

Non-Fiction
On a Clear Day They Could See Seventh Place:
Baseball's Worst Teams
From Set Shot to Slam Dunk:
The Glory Days of Basketball
in the Words of Those Who Played It

CHARLES SALZBERG

CANARY IN
THE COAL MINE

Down & Out Books
3959 Van Dyke Road, Suite 265
Lutz, FL 33558
DownAndOutBooks.com

The characters and events in this book are fictitious. Any similarity to real persons, living or dead, is coincidental and not intended by the author.

Cover design by JT Lindroos

ISBN: 1-64396-251-5
ISBN-13: 978-1-64396-251-1

"What is ordered must sooner or later arrive."
—James Fenimore Cooper, *The Last of the Mohicans*

"Cold empty bed, springs hard as lead
Pains in my head, feel like old Ned
What did I do to be so black and blue?"
—Harry Brooks, Andy Razaf, and Fats Waller,
"Black and Blue"

Part One
New York City

"Doubt, of whatever kind, can be ended by action alone."
—Thomas Carlyle, *Past and Present*

1
This Could Be the Start of Something Big

I wake up with a bad taste in my mouth.

It's not the first time this has happened and it won't be the last. I like to think of it as my personal canary in the coal mine. That taste usually means trouble on the horizon. Sometimes it's someone else's trouble. Sometimes it's mine. Sometimes it's both. Those are the times I have to watch out for.

Once I rouse myself from bed—it's never easy when I've had a rough night—I launch into my usual routine. Shower, shave, brush my teeth, my pride and joy, especially the two phony teeth implanted on the upper left side replacing those knocked out in a particularly vicious fight I didn't start, at least that's the way I see it. The way I usually see it. It was a pickup softball game. A guy came into second hard and late and spiked my shortstop in the leg. It was bad. So bad, it took eleven stitches to close the wound. Someone had to do something and as usual I was the first one out there and the one who threw the first punch. That's the drill for most of my fights. I never start them, well, hardly ever because being provoked doesn't count. But when I do throw a punch I always have good reason. The fights usually end with me bloodied but unbowed. You might say I have a temper but I prefer to think of it as a short fuse and an obsession with justice. No one gets away with anything on my watch. I win a few. I lose a few. There's always a price to pay and I always make my point. But let's face it there are no real winners when it comes to violence. Everyone, even the winner, loses something. That's just the way it goes.

These phony teeth of mine match the others perfectly. A dentist who owed me a favor—I provided him with all the information he needed to divorce his cheating wife and avoid being taken to the cleaners—planted them and swore no one could tell the difference. So far, he's been right. I like to think those are the only phony things about me. Everything else, for better or worse, is me, all me. I don't apologize for it. Take me or leave me. I don't care.

Lately, I've had to curb the physical stuff. Now that I'm well into my forties, things are starting to fall apart. They say it's the legs that go first, but in my case, it's my shoulder. I displaced it throwing a punch at someone who deserved it, someone who'd had a little too much to drink and insulted a woman I was with. The embarrassing thing is I missed. Turns out that's what did the damage. Missing my target. I had my arm in a sling for almost a month. It's pretty much healed now though I sometimes feel it in damp weather. The doc warned me it could go out again any time. "Try to stay out of fights, Pete," he said, then added, "though knowing you that's not very likely."

He was right. I'm combative. It's my nature. I've never run away from a fight and I probably never will. If you don't stand up for yourself, who will? I just have to be a little more careful now, which means choosing my battles more wisely.

I stop at the local diner for my usual breakfast: two cups of black coffee—neither of which take that bad taste out of my mouth—then head downtown to my office in Greenwich Village. Well, let's be honest here. It's not really my office. It's the office of a friend who runs a small real estate firm here in the city. He has an extra desk he rents me for only a couple hundred bucks a month, which includes phone service and a receptionist, if you call the person who takes up space at a desk up front a receptionist. I mean, shouldn't a receptionist be able to take a proper message? Shouldn't they be able to direct someone to your desk, even if it's in back, half hidden behind a pillar? But there's a hitch—there always is. When business picks up and they have to hire another broker, it's arrivederci, Pete. Fortunately, in the two years I've been here that's only happened once, and then just for a couple months.

New York City real estate is like having a license to print money, but the competition for listings is fierce and how anyone but the crème de la crème makes a living is beyond me. But I can't say being without an office puts much of a dent in my business, since it's always been pretty much touch and go. Thank goodness for that bank overdraft protection thing which has kept the wolves from my door more times than I'd like to admit.

I'm a PI. I have a license that says so. I take it out and look at it every so often, just to remind myself I actually have a profession. *Profession.* I say the word aloud. It's a strange word. It makes me think of the "world's oldest." I've done pretty much everything in my life except for that, though some might not make much of a distinction between what I do and what they do. They do it on their back. I do it on my feet. That's pretty much what sets us apart. It's like that Sinatra song. You know the one. Puppet, pauper, pirate, poet, pawn and king. Only with me substitute menial jobs like shoe salesman, night watchman, doorman—one summer the year after I graduated college—hot dog vendor, dog walker, even a short stint as a waiter. I was the world's worst. Half my salary went for broken glassware and plates. Once, I actually had to pay for a guy's meal out of my own pocket to keep him from ratting me out to the owner and getting me fired. Turned out it wasn't a very good investment. The next day I got canned anyway. I also spent a short time as a cop. More on that later.

This job as a PI stuck by process of elimination. The only real talent I have for anything was as a ballplayer, and after I washed out of the game because of injuries that pretty much made it impossible to throw or swing a bat, then trashed my way through that bunch of other jobs, I realized I was suited to do little else. My new profession meets a laundry list of criteria.

- I do not have to wear a suit and tie.
- I do not have anyone telling me what to do, where to be, and when to be there.
- It gives me an opportunity to use my brain, brawn (not that I'm brawny, but even now I'm still pretty solid, topping out at 170 pounds on my five-foot-ten-inch frame, but I've always been a physical guy willing to use what muscle I had), and ingenuity. But not too much of any of the three.
- It doesn't take too much concentration since like half the population of the world, I've got ADHD issues. In other words, I lose interest very quickly.
- I make my own hours.
- I mind someone else's business while I can ignore my own.
- The job fits my cynical, paranoid personality which makes me suspicious of everyone and supports a strong belief in Clare Boothe Luce's claim that no good deed goes unpunished. I believe there is evil lurking in everyone's soul, especially mine, though I do my best to fight against those darker urges. Other traits I own up to include being lazy, combative, argumentative, and stubborn. I love getting up in everyone else's business, which gives me the perfect excuse to avoid mine.

I didn't grow up watching cops and robber shows. My drug of choice was sports, especially baseball. I loved the game not only because I was good at it but because although it appears that for long stretches of time nothing is happening there's always something going on. Even if it isn't discernible to the eye. Baseball is not just a game of physical skill. It's a game of thought, analysis, contemplation, and anticipation. Unlike other team sports, there is no time limit. It takes as long as it takes, and in this sense, it mimics life. No one knows when it's going to end. Theoretically, a game can go on forever, ending only when one team has scored more runs than the other. It is a game of nuance. It is a game that can be won with power, or speed, or defense, or a combination of these attributes. It can be won on the mound, at the plate, or in the field. It can be won by a score of one nothing or twelve to eleven. It can end as a result of a timely hit or an untimely error. It is a game of ebb and flow. It is unpredictable. Just like life.

I'll take a thinking player over a naturally talented one any day of the week. Baseball is a game like chess. The best ballplayers are always several steps ahead of the game. They're thinking about what they'll do long before they actually do it. "If it's hit to me I'll fake the runner back to second then go to first." That sort of thing does not show up on the TV screen nor does it appear in the box score. But that's what wins and loses games.

Baseball imitates life: Long stretches of nothingness, then short bursts of action, which comes as a logical conclusion of those stretches of nothingness. This is much how our lives unfold. At least it's the way mine does.

I thought I'd make it as a major league ballplayer, but I never got the chance to prove it. I was a pretty good high school pitcher and when I wasn't pitching, I played shortstop with middling range, a good arm, and a better than average bat, although I lacked power. I told myself I'd grow into it, though I never did. I threw the ball in the mid-eighties, not very fast by today's standards, when young players can now flirt with a hundred on the gun. But I had a decent curve and was working on what I hoped would be a better than average changeup. I figured by the time I got to the minors I'd ramp it up, adding a few miles per hour to the fastball. I was good enough to earn a partial scholarship to a small upstate New York college.

But before I got halfway through my first college season, I developed arm trouble. In those days, more than a quarter century ago, Tommy John surgery wasn't what it is today and it certainly wasn't for college kids without a buck to their name. Even if I wanted it, who was going to pay for it? My father was lucky to make the rent each month and if it hadn't been for that athletic scholarship, I would have wound up working some soul-sucking civil service job.

Once I accepted the fact I'd never pitch again, I had to shift gears, away from the idea of becoming a professional athlete. They let me keep the scholarship so long as I maintained my grade point average. I was certainly no A student, but when I put my mind to it, I can do almost anything, no matter how unlikely. I sure as hell wasn't the best student in the world, but I wasn't the worst either, and somehow, I made it through to graduation. The first to do so in the Fortunato line. My mother's family was a bunch of brainiacs. She went to college and might have gone further if she hadn't met my father. That was the first thing he screwed up in her life. It wouldn't be the last.

I'd like to say I'm choosey about the kinds of cases I take, but that would be a lie. It's not that I don't lie, by the way, it's just that I don't lie frivolously, which makes it difficult to know whether what comes out of my mouth is the truth or a lie. That's not necessarily a bad thing. In fact, in my business it probably qualifies as a plus.

It's that time in New York when the city isn't quite sure what season it wants to be. A few days before Halloween, people are already gearing up for Thanksgiving, then Christmas. Always one, sometimes two holidays ahead of itself. One day in late August, I was shocked to see plastic pumpkins lined up on display in a CVS pharmacy. As if life isn't disorienting enough.

The weather doesn't help. Today, when I look out my window,

the sky is cloudless and that shade of deep blue so beautiful it makes you want to cry. But it's deceiving because when I get outside the temperature is hovering in the low forties. But like the city itself, the weather can break your heart by promising something it just can't seem to deliver. Tomorrow it's supposed to be pushing seventy, at least that's what the weather people are forecasting. And as if that isn't disorienting enough, the next day it's supposed to drop back to the fifties with overcast skies and intermittent showers. It's that schizo time of year when you never quite know what to wear. As a result, I always seem to be dressed one or two days ahead or behind the weather.

I usually roll into my office around ten, which I think is a pretty decent time considering the erratic hours I keep. Sometimes it's because I'm on a job, sometimes it's because I suffer from debilitating bouts of insomnia. When that strikes either I lie in bed thinking about all the things I could have done different in my life, and there are plenty, or I get up, get dressed, and roam the streets. In this city, there's always plenty to keep things interesting. So yeah, New York really is the city that never sleeps. At least that's true for some of its citizens. No matter how late or early it is I'm never the only one walking the streets. But I'm probably the only one who has no idea where he's going.

Obviously, not everyone is in agreement about arriving at a decent hour thing, because half a dozen other desks in the office are already filled with folks either working the phones or staring blankly into their computer. I park myself at my desk way in the back, near the bathroom, and as soon as I do, Philly, my friend and boss man of the real estate firm, appears in front of me.

"I wasn't sure you were coming in today, Petey," he cracks. He flashes a goofy grin after the words tumble out of his mouth like a waterfall. He's a born and bred New Yorker so he talks as if he's in a race to finish a sentence so he can move on to the next one. Sometimes, he speaks so quick the words stick to each other and he is this close to being unintelligible. Unlike others who have to ask him to slow the fuck down, I, being a born and bred New Yorker, too, can understand him without much effort.

When he speaks, he bares his teeth, which are a dull yellow and seem to be in a life-or-death struggle for room in his mouth. But his nose, well, that's another story. Unlike mine, which has been broken too many times to count, his is straight and in perfect harmony with the rest of his face. You might suspect he's had work done on it, but no, Philly was born this way. He is, no doubt about it, a handsome man—except for those teeth, which I keep advising him he ought to get fixed—and he knows it. He's been married three times, each one of them a stunner, and if he ever gets divorced from his present wife, Marnie, I have no doubt there'll be a fourth waiting in the wings. He can afford it, though.

"What are you talking about?" I say, tapping my watch for emphasis. "This is fucking early for me."

"I've been here since eight, my friend. That's early."

"You're not going to tell me about the damn bird, are you?"

"What bird?"

"The one who gets the worm."

"I don't need any bird to tell me when to get to work, Petey."

"What can I say, Philly, other than you're a better man than me."

"Damn straight. You'd give everything in your bank account to change places with me, Petey, and you know it."

"That wouldn't be much, Philly, and you know it."

He shrugs. "Maybe that'll change. There was a broad in here earlier looking for you."

"Yeah?"

"That's right."

"She actually asked for me?"

"Yeah. By name, not the usual 'where's that scumbag owes me money?'"

"What'd she look like?"

"That's the first thing you ask?"

"I yam who I yam."

He smiles. There are those teeth again. I want to give him the name of my dentist but I know it won't do any good, so why bother?

"You and Popeye. She looks like you'd want to get to know her and spend a lot of time with her. If I weren't so blissfully married, she'd be at the top of my list for number four."

I resist asking, *how long's that gonna be for?* and say instead, "That good, huh?"

"Yeah. That good."

"I hope you didn't try to sell her an apartment."

"She didn't look like she needed one."

"Did she tell you why she wanted to see me?"

"Nope. But she did give me this." He pulls a business card out of his pocket and tosses it on my desk. "Said you should call her. If I were you, I'd do it ASAP. She reeked of money and folks with money don't like to be made to wait."

I look at the card then bring it up close to my nose. It smells like lemons. The name on it is Lila Alston. I like the sound of that. And the smell of lemons. Her name reminds me of those in one of those pulp crime novels. Like Velma. Or Bubbles.

As soon as Philly dismisses himself, I dial the number. A woman's voice answers. I take a shot.

"I believe you were looking for me, Ms. Alston."

"If you're Peter Fortunato that would be correct. But it's Mrs. Not Ms. At least for the moment."

"Then I'll take a wild guess and say this has something to do with your husband."

She laughs. It's short and it's raspy and it's sexy. Very sexy. "That's correct. And it appears I may have found the right man...for a change."

"Would you like to meet in person or continue this over the phone, Lila?"

"I liked it better when you were more formal, Mr. Fortunato. At least until we get to know each other a little better."

I can't wait. I'm already getting the beginnings of a hard-on.

"Got it. So, phone or meet up, *Mrs.* Alston?" I'm hoping

she'll agree to the latter. I have to see for myself what this chick looks like because Philly is only prone to exaggeration when it comes to real estate.

"I suppose a face-to-face meeting would be more advantageous. This is a rather...odd situation and it might take some explaining."

"I specialize in odd situations, Mrs. Alston."

"I suspected as much."

"By the way, how did you come to get in touch with me?"

"I went down a list of private investigators until I found a name I liked. It happened to be yours. *Fortunato*. It has a rather nice ring to it."

"Yeah, just like the sound of a cash register. So, you know nothing else about me?"

"I didn't say that, Mr. Fortunato. I didn't say that at all."

2

If You've Got the Money, Honey, I've Got the Time

We meet at a coffee shop on the corner of Lexington Avenue and 70th Street. Presumably, it's near Lila Alston's home, though she refuses to fill me in on any personal details, especially where she lives.

"There'll be plenty of time for that, Mr. Fortunato," she purrs when I ask her where she lives. And for some reason I want to believe her.

Philly is right. She is a looker. Fair-skinned with flaming red hair. She has a face that looks as if it really could launch a thousand ships. It's a face straight out of one of those upscale fashion magazines. More angles on it than a pyramid. She stands around five-seven, taller in heels, as I find out when I stand to greet her. She is wearing a pair of tight, faded blue jeans and a light blue sweater layered over a white T-shirt. Her nails are painted the same color as her shoulder-length hair, which is restrained by one of those purple scrunchies. If she were in a James Cain, Jim Thompson, or Mickey Spillane novel, someone, at some point in the book, would inevitably refer to her as Doll Face or Kewpie Doll.

Considering the package she comes wrapped in, I'm pretty sure she's trouble times ten. Yeah, yeah, I know that's a sexist remark, especially when it comes to this Me-Too age we're in.

But honestly, I don't much care. Trust me, there are plenty of other reasons not to like me.

I order my go-to sandwich: turkey club, with coleslaw and Russian dressing. All she asks for is a glass of iced coffee, which she sweetens with two packets of Splenda and then pretty much ignores.

"Not hungry?" I ask, when the waitress leaves to fill the rest of my order.

She shakes her head. "I never eat lunch. It seems like a useless meal to me. A big breakfast more than holds me over till dinner. Besides, I can use the time."

I can't help but wonder what her idea of a big breakfast is. A celery stick? A carrot? A bite of

"To meet with people like me?"

She cocks her head to one side and smiles.

"I hardly ever meet with people like *you*, Mr. Fortunato."

I get her point. She's up there and I'm down here and never the twain shall meet.

"I think we know each other well enough for you to call me Pete."

"I'll stick with Mr. Fortunato for now. You're Italian, aren't you?"

"Half."

"What's the other half, if you don't mind my asking?"

The truth is I do mind people asking personal questions in an annoying attempt to get to know me, but I answer anyway. "The Chosen People."

"Jewish?" She stirs another packet of Splenda into her iced coffee. "I never would have guessed."

"Why's that?"

"I don't know. You just don't seem..."

"To be the type to secretly control the world's monetary system?"

"I don't appreciate being mocked, Mr. Fortunato. There's absolutely nothing wrong with being Jewish, unless you're one of those…" She pauses.

"Self-haters."

"That wasn't what I was going to say."

"But it's what you meant."

"You have no idea what I meant," she says. Her voice is wrapped in a thin layer of indignation, which is okay by me. I don't mind getting a rise out of people. It puts them off their game and me on mine.

"Let me guess. Some of your best friends are Jewish."

"You're mocking me again, Mr. Fortunato."

"Am I? You know, I've been trying to rid myself of that nasty habit but obviously I've got some work to do. But don't worry, Mrs. Alston. I'm really not much of anything. I have no mob ties and I haven't been in a synagogue since my best friend Harry Stein's bar mitzvah. My mother and her family were assimilated Jews who ate pork and shellfish and whatever else was put in front of them. And my mother learned to cook Italian food better than my fraternal grandmother. And my father, he was a boring Italian insurance salesman who drank like an Irishman. Everything was pretty mixed up in my family. So mixed up, there are times I have no idea who or what I am."

"I didn't mean to open a can of worms," she deadpans—I suspect that in her life she's opened up plenty of cans and not all of them had worms in them. "But perhaps you ought to keep that sort of information for your therapist."

"No can. No worms. No therapist. So," I say, as I spread a healthy amount of Russian dressing on each side of all four rectangles of white toast, "what's your story?"

She laughs. "Is everything just a story to you?"

I take a bite of my sandwich. "Yeah. Pretty much."

"Well, my story is that I'd like to hire you to prove my boyfriend innocent."

"Innocent of what?"

"You won't be shocked, will you?"

"Nothing shocks me anymore," I say, taking a bite of my

pickle. And this is the truth and nothing but the truth. The last time I was shocked was when I learned that those big birds don't deliver babies.

"Of murdering my husband."

"Whoa!" I say, putting down my sandwich. "I think you started at the end of your story. Wanna back up a little?"

"Well, I suppose I am getting a little ahead of myself. I mean I'm not one hundred percent sure Donald is actually dead. But he has been missing for almost a week and under the circumstances…"

"Donald's your husband?"

"He is."

"And he's missing so you presume he's dead?"

"Well, I can't be sure but there are indications that might be the case."

"Indications?"

"We'll get to that later."

I think she's smiling when she says this. In fact, I'm pretty sure of it. This is one ice-cold bitch and you know what, I'm starting to fall in love.

"You reported this situation to the cops?"

"You mean his disappearance?"

"Yeah."

"Of course. But they haven't done a thing so far as I can see. I don't think they're taking it seriously."

"But you are?"

"Yes. I am."

"But you're not hiring me to find *him*?"

"No, I don't really care if he's lost and even if he is I don't care if he stays lost." She hesitates a moment. "That doesn't make me sound like a very nice person, does it?"

"Hey," I say, throwing my hands up in the air, "I'm the last person to judge anyone else."

"I don't believe that for a moment, Mr. Fortunato. You look like the type who's judging people all the time."

I smile. She's right, of course. Am I that transparent? Oh, what the hell, why not just let that pass?

"What makes you think he's dead?"

"Because I don't believe he took a sudden, unannounced vacation to the Bahamas and I believe it's inevitable that if he doesn't show up fairly soon the police will come to the conclusion that he's no longer with us, which might well be the case. And when they do reach that conclusion, there will be two obvious suspects."

She says this so matter-of-factly it's like she's talking about last night's bridge game. I make a note to myself. This chick has ice water running through her veins.

"You being one of them, I presume."

"Yes."

"And the other?"

"Travis."

"Your boyfriend?"

"Sort of."

"That's a strange answer, Mrs. Alston."

"My life is very complicated, Mr. Fortunato."

"Mine, too. Just not Dr. Phil kind of complicated."

She stirs another packet of Splenda into her iced coffee—it's her third—but she still makes no move to drink it. I want to ask her if she's afraid of cancer or that if she ever has kids that they'll wind up with two heads and three arms. But wisely, for a change, I keep my mouth shut.

"We aren't really involved anymore."

"When did that end?"

"Oh, maybe a week or two ago." She smiles. "Maybe a year."

This chick is something else.

"You and your husband fought?"

"No." She spits the word out like she can't wait to get rid of it. Like it's radioactive. "He didn't mean enough to me to fight with him."

"You end it, or did he?"

19

"What do you think?"

"Yeah. Stupid question. Your husband know about him? This guy Travis."

She laughs. It's a short laugh. Not the kind of laugh that comes from finding something funny. The kind of laugh that comes from the place of ridiculous or absurd. But wherever it comes from she seems pretty jolly for someone whose husband is missing, according to her most likely dead, leaving her and her boyfriend the most likely prime suspects. "You presume Donald and I are married in the happily ever after way."

"Not after you've told me you found yourself a boyfriend."

She ignores my crack. "We don't even live under the same roof anymore. Donald and I have been physically separated for almost six months now. That's why it took me a while to realize he was missing."

She makes a fist. Reverses it. And checks her fingernails which, from where I sit, look perfect.

"Let me guess. Separated and heading for a divorce but you signed a pre-nup, so the only way you'll actually cash in is if he's dead...and you didn't kill him. Do I have that right?"

She smiles and runs her hand through her thick, wavy red hair. Somehow, she's managed to come up with another kind of smile that says *You really don't want to get involved with me* and *What are you waiting for?* At the same time. "I believe you're way smarter than you look, Mr. Fortunato."

"It's my secret weapon."

She shrugs.

"Dead or alive I don't stand to benefit financially. Over the years I've managed to sock away enough so I don't have to worry. So," she says with more than a hint of sarcasm in her voice, "I'm afraid you—and the police—can strike money as a motive."

"A motive for what?"

"To have anything to do with Donald's disappearance or..." She leaves the rest of the sentence hanging there and so do I.

"So, will you take the case, Mr. Fortunato?"

"Not until I know exactly what the case is."

"I guess it's to either find my husband or..."

"The corpus delicti."

"Precisely."

"Got a preference?"

She shakes her head and her hair does that shampoo commercial thing of gently wafting back and forth, as if it's in slow motion. How the hell does she do that? I can only imagine it comes with the genetic package.

"Not really."

"You haven't asked how much I charge."

"I knew you'd get around to it when the time came."

She shrugs and stirs her still untouched iced coffee with a straw.

"The time has come. Five hundred a day plus expenses."

"Those are uptown prices, Mr. Fortunato. Don't you think that's a little steep for someone who leases a desk in a real estate office?"

"We're in the midst of inflationary times, Mrs. Alston. As for the office, I'm a thrifty guy, so why pay top dollar for a desk I'm hardly at? I'm an outside kind of guy. As for my rate, if you're looking for a bargain, look somewhere else. I'm too good at what I do to be cheap."

I did mention that lies come easy to me, didn't I?

"I have no trouble paying for quality, Mr. Fortunato. And I wouldn't respect a man who doesn't respect himself. Would a week in advance be satisfactory? And as a bonus, if you succeed before the week has ended, you may keep the difference."

What kind of person uses the word satisfactory? I didn't think I'd seen or heard that word since I got three of them on my fourth-grade report card. But somehow, coming from her, it's sexy, not pretentious.

"You got yourself a deal, lady."

She pulls her checkbook from her purse and writes me a

check for $2,500. Just like that. I examine it real close when she hands it to me. It looks legit. It even has both her and her husband's name on it. No address, though, which strikes me as a little odd. But it's dated today. She spelled my name right. And as if she wasn't hot enough, I would fall in love with her after seeing her perfect penmanship.

We sit around another half hour or so while she fills me in on everything she thinks I need to know about Donald. His haunts, his friends, his job—he operates a hedge fund or something like that. I tend to tune out when it comes to big business. I'm tempted to ask her what a hedge fund is but I don't want to embarrass myself any more than I already have. And, I don't want to waste the time, since in the end I really don't give a shit. I can look it up on the internet if it's important. No one is stupid today, unless they want to be. Besides, I probably know enough to get by. It's about using someone else's money to make more money, something I don't need to know about. He works mostly from home, she tells me, though he does have a small office he shares in midtown.

She provides me with a few photos of her husband, who's in his early fifties, distinguished-looking, trim, salt-and-pepper hair, well-groomed, not particularly distinctive from any other wealthy businessman, not that I have all that much experience hanging around those folks.

My final question, or at least what I think is going to be my final question, is the obvious one: "When was the last time you saw him?"

"We had brunch, a week ago Sunday, at The Smith, the one across from Lincoln Center. And please don't ask me what we spoke about because, to be honest, that place is so noisy I could hardly hear myself think."

"Why'd you meet with him?"

"We had business to discuss."

"What kind of business?"

"That would be the none of your business kind."

"You make things difficult for me, Mrs. Alston, it's going to wind up costing you a lot more than twenty-five hundred. It wouldn't have been to give you some money, would it?"

She stares at me, or rather right through me. This is a chick you do not want to tangle with...or cross. But silence gives me the answer.

"How much?"

"How much what?"

"How much money did he give you?"

"I don't see where that's relevant."

"I don't usually give out trade secrets, Mrs. Alston, but one way to trace someone is to follow the money. If he gave you a large sum, then it was either check or cash."

For the first time, she takes a sip of her iced coffee before she answers, "Cash," she says, looking up seductively.

"Then he had to get that cash from somewhere. Probably the bank. And if it wasn't the bank, then we've got what we call in the detecting business, a lead."

"It was ten thousand dollars," she says, like that's the kind of chump change that gets handed over to people like her every day of the week. Well, come to think of it, maybe it does.

"What bank?"

"He has a couple."

"One not big enough to hold all his dough, huh? Which ones?"

"Chase and Wells Fargo, I think."

"What was it for?"

"If you must know it was my monthly allowance."

"I used to get twenty bucks."

She smiles. "Inflation."

"Did he say where he was off to when he left you?"

"I believe he said he was going to see his girlfriend."

What? The rich must have very different rules from the rest of us. How fucking civilized...

"Why the hell didn't you tell me he had a girlfriend upfront?"

23

"You didn't ask."

"Yeah, well, I wouldn't think that's the kind of information I'd have to ask for. Who is she?"

"Her name is Susan something or other."

"You know damn well what her last name is."

"You don't miss a trick, do you, Peter?" She smiles mischievously. It finally occurs to me that this is all a game for Lila Alston. And she's enjoying every minute of it. I know the type. They like to shock. They like to get a rise out of folks like me. Or at least she thinks I'm folks like that.

"It's Lane. Susan Lane."

"How long have you known about her?"

"Oh, I don't know. Several months, probably."

"How did you find out about her?"

She smiles that all-purpose, predatory smile of hers. I'd like to say it doesn't work on me, but it does.

"Is that really important?"

"It might be."

"Let's just say he wanted me to know, and leave it at that."

"Have you ever met her?"

She smiles. "We're not that progressive."

"Where does she live?"

"What makes you think I know that?"

"I think you know a lot about her, including where she lives and what she does for a living, and maybe even where she has her hair and nails done."

"She's a shop girl," she says dismissively, with a wave of her hand.

"What's that supposed to mean?"

"She works in one of those fancy, high-end designer clothing shops on Madison Avenue."

"It's an honest living," I say, but I refrain from asking Lila just what it was she does for an honest living because I don't want to risk thinking any less of her than I already do. Besides, ten grand a month would be more than enough for most of us.

I write down all the information down in my small notebook, knowing that fancy designer shop on Madison Avenue is going to be my first stop.

"One more thing before you leave, Mr. Fortunato. Do you happen to own a gun?"

"I have a license for one, but I rarely carry it around with me, if that's what you're asking."

"Why is that?"

"Why is what?"

"Why don't you carry it around with you?"

"Because I've got a temper and I'm afraid I'll use it. If I use it someone's going to get hurt. Someone gets hurt, there are complications. Besides, I don't need a gun to protect myself outside the home. Why do you ask?"

"Curiosity."

"You think I'm going to need it?"

"Do you?"

She pauses. Followed by the beginnings of a smile. "Oh, I certainly hope not."

We're done. I pick up the check. I figure I can afford to with that twenty-five-hundred-dollar check burning a hole in my pocket. Besides, she doesn't offer. I have the distinct feeling paying is something Lila Alston just isn't used to doing.

Our meeting over, Lila Alston goes her way and I go mine. But there's something about this thing, about Lila Alston, that just doesn't make sense.

Maybe that explains why that bad taste in my mouth is starting to make a comeback.

3
Just a Gigolo

As soon as I step inside the store it feels like some magic portal has opened and sucked me into another world. It's a world I'm unfamiliar with. A world of money, beauty, and power. Maybe it's because me and money, me and fashion, me and opulence, me and power don't mix well. Or maybe it's because we never had a chance to try out our relationship.

I spot the woman I peg as Susan Lane as soon as I walk through the door. She's standing near the back of the store, in front of a rack of expensive dresses. I know they're expensive because there isn't much to any of them. It seems like the less fabric there is the more expensive the dress is. Nothingness magically translates into $omethingness. It appears as if rich people like to pay more and get less. I'm guessing it's one of the things that sets them apart from the rest of us.

The woman I take to be Lane is talking to a customer, a middle-aged matron dressed as if she's on her way to high tea at the Plaza. They're standing in front of a rack of jackets, which Lane is taking out one at a time to show. She has short blonde hair and is wearing an expensive-looking, tight-fitting blue dress, straight off the shop's racks, I assume. She's a few inches shorter than Lila, small-waisted, and looks to be in her mid to late thirties. She's very attractive, in that wholesome, middle

American, Delta flight attendant way. Not in the same league as Lila, but pretty enough and far more accessible to folks like me.

"You Susan Lane?" I ask, approaching her after her customer heads out of the shop carrying a fancy shopping bag filled with merchandise she's just purchased.

She looks up from rearranging the jackets and gives me a look as if I'm Kreskin or some other two-bit mind reader. "Who are you and how do you know my name?" she asks, her hands planted firmly on her hips. That's what she says, but what I hear is *Who the hell do you think you are?* This is what I've heard most of my life and with good reason. It's a question I've even asked myself at various times, usually after I've left one job for another. Especially after my short-lived experience as an upstate cop and was floundering, wondering what I would do next.

"I'm looking for Donald Alston and I was told you might be able to help me find him."

She looks me up and down, while giving me the skunk eye. Like I haven't seen that before.

"You didn't answer my questions and I'd still like to know who you are."

"Pete Fortunato. You can call me Pete or Petey, but never Peter, for the same reason guys named Richard don't like to be called Dick."

Under most circumstances this might elicit a chuckle or at least a smile. Not this time.

"Okay, so now I know your name but I still don't know who you are and why you're looking for Donald Alston and most of all, why you're bothering me." She drops her hands, knitting her fingers together as if in prayer.

"I'm a PI, Ms. Lane, and from what I understand you know him well enough to call him Donald or Don or even Donnie."

Her voice lowers to a whisper, even though we're the only ones in the store. "This is a place of business. I can't stand around talking to you. I've got clients to wait on."

I look around and don't see any, but I get her point. Laying eyes on the likes of me might scare any decent woman away and with her what I imagined would be a hefty commission.

"Got it. How about we meet for a drink after work so we can discuss this more privately? What time you get off?"

Her hands swing back to her hips, which she thrusts forward at the same time her lips curl into a sneer. Trust me, I've seen that expression before, too.

"You're assuming I have something to say to you."

"If you care about Donnie, or if you want to stay out of trouble, you might want to talk to me. As for telling me something I need to know, well I rarely have trouble getting people to talk to me. It's a gift and between you and me the real problem is once people get going, it's almost impossible to shut them up."

This time, she cracks what I take to be a smile. She doesn't want to, I can tell. But she does anyway. It means I've pierced her armor ever so slightly and this is the opening I'm looking for.

"What makes you think I give a damn about Donald Alston?"

"At this particular time, that might not be something you'd like to admit to."

"Why not"

"Because he's missing."

"Missing? What do you mean missing?"

"Gone. Vanished. Disappeared. Poof." I wave my hands in the air like a magician. "No one knows where he is and what condition he's in."

The expression on her face suddenly makes the trip from curious to worried, indicating to me that she really doesn't have any idea where he is. Not exactly what I want to hear.

"What do you mean by condition?"

I shrug. "You tell me."

Her face flushes. "All right. Six thirty," she says. "I'll meet you at six thirty. Sharp. I don't have a lot of time to spend frivolously."

I hear the tinkling of a bell. I turn to find someone entering the store. A well-dressed, silver-haired woman who looks like she's just been released from the beauty salon after a thorough going-over.

"I'm sorry, but I have a customer. There's a small bar and grill over on Lexington. I'll meet you there."

She doesn't give me the name or the address. Evidently, she has confidence in my ability as a private dick to find it on my own.

I have a couple hours to kill and I'm not far from the Met, so I decide to kill them there. I'm not exactly the museum type, but there is an exhibit of vintage crime scene photos I want to see. Evidently, crime is now considered art. Or at least the depiction of it is. Several of the photographs are by Weegee, who chased crime calls on his police radio, snapped black and white photos then developed them from the trunk of his car. After browsing through that exhibit, I go upstairs to check out a replica of the *Psycho* Bates house on the roof. This is the kind of museum that engages my adolescent mind.

When I arrive at the bar around a quarter past six, it's already filling up. Guys in suits and ties. Women in business wear. All there to unwind after work. I grab a table near the back so we can have some privacy. I order a brew to keep me company while I wait. Susan Lane is a few minutes late. Just a few, but enough to make me worry she might not show up. If that happens, what do I do next? Do I go back the next day and keep going back till she'll speak to me?

Fortunately, I do not have to plan my next move because she suddenly I look up and she is here, standing over me. She puts her purse on the table and sits across from me.

"I hope you don't mind if I leave my purse on the table. It's so easy for someone to just grab it in places like this."

"I'll watch it like a hawk," I say.

The waitress service is spotty so I go to the bar myself and fetch Lane's Cosmo, one of those pastel-colored girly drinks, and another brew for me.

When I return, she reaches for her purse.

"Your money's no good here," I say.

"What makes you think I was going to pay?" she says.

I nod toward her purse.

She smiles and pulls out her lipstick, then places it on the table. She removes a compact and sets it carefully beside the tube of lipstick. I get the point.

"Wishful thinking," I say. "It gets me hot when a woman pays."

"Don't worry, that's not going to happen here, so you can skip that cold shower tonight."

"Too bad. I'm not such a bad guy when you get to know me."

"I don't think that's going to happen either."

"Harsh," I say. "So, when was the last time you saw him?"

She ignores my question. "Who sent you? His wife?"

"You think answering a question with another question is going to work?"

"There are some things I need to know before we continue this conversation. One of them is who hired you."

"I can't divulge that information. It's in the PI bylaws."

"I didn't think people like you had laws. Or obeyed them."

"We have 'em, we just tend to ignore them whenever it suits us. We're a reckless bunch."

She sips her Cosmo. "You don't have to answer. She's the one who hired you. I don't know why she bothered. She doesn't give a fuck about him, you know."

"She?" I repeat, playing dumber than I am.

"You prefer I give her a name?" She shakes her head. "His wife. That's all you're going to get from me."

"I understand they're separated, heading for legal Splitsville."

"If I had a nickel for every man who's told me he's separated, just waiting for the divorce papers to be signed, I wouldn't have to work at that damn store for fifteen bucks an hour plus commission."

"So, I've been misinformed?"

"You'd have to ask her or her husband. If they did divorce, she'd get practically nothing. They have a pre-nup."

"You seem to know an awful lot about their situation."

"I know what I know. You've obviously met her. Do you really think divorce is in the cards for her?"

"I don't really care one way or the other. I was hired to do a job and that's what I'm doing. You still haven't answered my question."

"Remind me again."

"When was the last time you saw Donald Alston?"

She takes another sip of her drink. Her eyes drift up toward the ceiling, as if the answer is written up there. "It's been at least a month."

"That long?"

"I hate to be the one to break your heart, but Donald and I aren't seeing each other anymore. Not that it was ever any big thing. It's been over for weeks. And it wasn't because he was married."

"Something like that doesn't bother you?"

She shrugs, stirs her drink, then finishes what is left. "Not really."

"Funny, because I was told you were with him last week."

"Do you believe everything you're told?"

"Sometimes," I say, as I reach for her empty glass.

"Well, in this instance I'm afraid you were misinformed."

"It's from an impeccable source," I say.

"You call his wife an impeccable source? Unless she had me followed how would she know?" She locks eyes with mine. "You wouldn't be the one following me, would you?" She taps her glass with her red plastic stirrer then shakes it in my direction. "I could use a refill."

Loose lips sink ships, so I make my way back to the bar and return with another drink for her. I still have half my beer left, and as of six months ago two is my limit. Any more than two and I begin to turn a little hostile. Then a lot hostile. And that's when I get into the kind of trouble I'm trying hard to stay out of.

"I've got better things to do with my time than tail girlfriends for angry wives," I say as I set the drink in front of her. "Could she have been referring to someone else, another woman maybe?"

"You'd have to ask her, but I doubt Donald was into *dating*." The word comes out coated with a heavy dose of sarcasm. "He had some business problems to deal with and he was focused on that. It was probably one of the reasons we didn't work out."

"What kind of business problems?"

"You'd have to ask him."

"I will when I find him. What were the other reasons?"

"That's none of your business."

"Actually, it is. And if it's not mine it will be the cops' once they get involved."

"Who's going to call the police?"

I shrug. "A good citizen maybe?"

I can see she's weighing her options. Me or the cops? Finally, she makes her mind up. "He had personal problems and if you think you're going to get any more from me, you're wrong."

"So, you're telling me you have no idea where he is?"

"Look, I don't know that he's actually missing. All I know is what you've told me and why should I believe that? Some stranger shows up and starts feeding me a line? You think that hasn't happened before? Donald is an adult. I'm sure he knows where he is. Maybe he just took off to be alone. Or to get away from her." She leans forward. "And you know something, I wouldn't put it past that bitch to have done something to him. She is a bitch, you know."

"I don't know. But thanks for the warning. I've only met her once and she was perfectly civil with me. But if he's not missing, or if she's done something to him, why would she hire me to find him?"

"You'd have to ask her, not that she'd tell you the truth."

"You've met her?"

"His wife?"

"Yeah."

She makes a sound. It's supposed to be a laugh, a derisive one like, *What, are you kidding?* But it doesn't come out that way. It comes out more like the kind of snort a pig makes.

"No. And I don't want to. What do you think, we'd hang out together and swap horror stories about Donald?"

"What kind of horror stories might you swap?"

She smiles. "You're slick."

"Thanks for the compliment."

"I didn't mean it as a compliment. I'm not going to sit here and discuss that. First off, it's really none of your business. You were just hired to find him, right?"

"Finding out as much as I can about him is the way I get it done."

"You'll have to find someone else willing to give you that kind of information because it's not going to be me."

One thing about me, I don't give up easy. It's that competitive thing. I always had it when I played the game and I still have it. It sometimes gets me into trouble—I've got the scars to prove that—but it often gets me what I want. There's always a price to pay, but if it gets too steep, I just back off and look for another way to get what I want.

"You know her boyfriend, what's his name?"

"Travis?"

"Yeah, that's him," I say, while congratulating myself for being slick.

"Kind of."

"What does that mean?"

"I had the misfortune to meet him once and let me tell you it was not a pleasure."

"Why's that?"

"He's a thug."

"What's that supposed to mean?"

"I'm sure you know what a thug is, Mr. Fortunato. I'm

guessing you've had plenty of experience with them. Let's just say he's not a very nice man. Wait. Let me amend that. He's a wannabe thug. In fact, he's more than that. He's an asshole."

"Sounds like you're not a fan."

"You could say that."

"If you've never met Lila Alston then how did you meet him?"

"I'd rather not say."

"You've got a lot of secrets, Ms. Lane."

"More than you'll ever know, Mr. Fortunato."

"You wouldn't happen to know what he does for a living, would you?"

She laughs. "A living. That's a good one. Does leeching off women count as a living?"

"Sure. I suppose that takes a certain talent. But does he have an actual job? You know, the kind with a paycheck."

"Does the phrase, 'would you like fries with that?' mean anything to you?"

"He works at McDonald's?"

She laughs. "From what I've heard they have standards at McDonald's. He's a would-be actor and part-time bartender at some dive bar over in Hell's Kitchen."

"Know the name of it?"

"Do they actually have names?" she says, raising her eyebrows like Groucho Marx. "No, I don't. I think it's on 46th and 9th. There are a bunch of them over there and every one of them looks like the next. Just go up and down the block and ask for Travis. Eventually, you'll hit the right one."

"I have to say you don't sound very worried about Donald."

"I told you, he's not my problem anymore. But don't get the wrong idea. It's not that I want to see anything happen to him. He's not a bad guy and he never did anything bad to me. It's just that I don't give a shit. I have enough problems of my own. If you ask me, all three of them deserve each other."

4

Who's Been Sleeping in My Bed?

Like most nights, I hardly get any sleep. I used to count hours, but when I saw I was averaging no more than two, three a night, on a good night, I gave up. It only adds to the anxiety. I never know why I can't sleep. I've suffered from insomnia since I was in my teens and though I've wrestled with all kinds of explanations, I know, in the end, it really doesn't matter why.

I've tried all the usual suspects. Counting sheep. Warm milk. Self-hypnosis. Earplugs. Blindfolds. White noise. No noise. Melatonin. Nothing seems to help. And so, I catch sleep whenever it catches me. As a result, my day often has no shape. Day is night. Night is day. I've learned not to lie in bed in the dark, eyes wide open. If sleep does not come within a reasonable amount of time, I get out of bed. I read. I pace the floor. I switch on the TV. Thank god for twenty-four seven programming. It's an insomniac's best friend.

The causes for my lack of sleep defy the usual suspects: a bad day; too much to drink or eat; too much on my mind. Tonight, I should sleep like a baby, knowing I'm employed for a change. That I have money jingling in my pocket. But it doesn't work that way. I don't waste much time trying to figure out what the reason is this particular night, but as a result I'm moving a little slower than usual today.

It isn't till late morning that I'm able to make out it of my apartment to begin my search for Travis Chapman, who I hope will ultimately lead me to Donald Alston.

Susan Lane is right. There are more than half a dozen bars on that short strip of 9th Avenue, one more low-rent than the next. It could be worse, but fortunately it's the third one I visit, appropriately named, Dive Bait, that's the charm.

It's just before noon and the joint is empty except for two losers of indeterminate age who sit slumped over at either end of the bar. For all I know, they could be left over from last night. They're both nursing mugs of beer, neither apparently aware of the other's existence. For some people it's never too early (or late) to start drinking. I know. I used to be one of them. I never considered myself an alcoholic. I just liked the feeling it gave me right up until the fifth or sixth drink. It helped get me through the days or nights. Every so often when I seemed to be overdoing it, I'd lay off for weeks at a time, with every good intention of stopping all together. But it never seemed to work out that way. My only concession now is to make sure I never approach that magic number. In my case it's three.

"I'm looking for Travis Chapman," I announce to the bartender as I slide onto a middle stool, equidistant from the other two patrons, not that they're even slightly aware of my presence.

"He ain't here today," he mumbles in response. He's middle-aged, paunchy with his long gray hair tied back in a ponytail. He's wearing a stained powder blue T-shirt at least a couple sizes too small, with the name of the bar emblazoned across the front. He wipes down a row of glasses he's just removed from a sink of soapy dishwater, occasionally holding one up to the light to see if he's missed a spot. Not that I figure anyone who bothers drinking here would care. Pick up. Dry. Put down. Pick up. Dry. Put down. It's like he's on autopilot. Maybe if I watch him long enough I'll be lulled into the arms of Morpheus?

"Day off?" I ask.

He holds one of the glasses up to the light and examines it.

"Travis don't have no day off. Mr. High and Mighty comes and goes whenever the hell he feels like it. Boss loves him, so he gets away with murder."

"Why's that?"

"Why's what?"

"Why does the boss like him so much?"

"He's a good-looking dude. Asshole fancies himself an actor. Like he's James fucking Dean or something." He shrugs and holds another glass up to the light. Even from my angle I can see it's smudged, but he just shrugs then puts it down on the "clean" side.

"He's a chick magnet, man. And it's chicks who bring in the dudes, and the dudes bring in the dough. It's a business, pal. Look at me. What do you see?"

He taps his belly and doesn't wait for my answer. "This is why I'm doing the day shift, man. If I pocket ten bucks in tips today I'll be lucky."

"Life is unpredictable. Perhaps things'll pick up."

"And perhaps fucking Angelina Jolie will be the next one to walk in that door and slip me her digits."

"When was the last time you saw Travis...or Angelina Jolie?"

"Very fucking funny." He puts down the glass he's working on and stares up to the ceiling, as if searching for divine answers. "Come to think of it, haven't seen him in a few days. Maybe he finally got one of those parts on a soap he was always yapping about."

"Know where he lives?"

He nods. "Yeah, I know."

"Wanna share that with me?" I ask, sliding a Jackson across the bar. He grabs it, folds it in half, then jams it down into his jeans pocket.

"Usually, I wouldn't give out that kinda information but you know what, fuck him, man. He'd do it to me in a heartbeat. I ain't even gonna ask you why're you're looking for him. Know why? 'Cause I don't give a fuck. And if it turns out he owes you money and you have to mess up that pretty-boy face of his to get it, well, I'd just consider that a public service."

"Not on your Christmas list, huh?"

"I seen him stick his grubby little paw into the tip jar once too often. Stealing from strangers is one thing, man, stealing from the people you work with, well, it don't get no lower than that. Fuckin' scumbag." He picks up another glass, doesn't even look at it before he puts it down in the clean pile.

I take out a pen and pad and jot down the scumbag's address then slip the bartender another ten. It's not because I feel sorry for him and it's not because I want to be a big shot. I have no respect for someone who'll sell someone else out for dough. It's more like an investment. Down the line, I might need more information from this dude and this will leave a good taste in his mouth.

Turns out I don't have to go far. Travis's apartment is in a rundown, turn-of-the-last-century tenement a couple blocks up from the bar just off 9th Avenue. I punch the buzzer next to his name a couple times, but there's no answer. There's no one around so I pull out my one and only credit card, the one with the five-hundred-dollar limit that has long since been reached, slip it in between the doorjamb and the lock, jiggle it around a little, hear a click, turn the handle, and the door pops open.

I'm in.

The hallway reeks of a deadly combination of urine and cigarette smoke. I know why. If I can get in so easy so can the homeless guys in the 'hood, always look for a safe, warm spot. Once they gain entrance, they make themselves at home, probably behind the staircase. There might even be one of them there now, but I'm not going to check.

According to the nameplates in the vestibule, Travis occupies apartment 3B. I climb the two flights and punch the doorbell. Nothing. I rap on the door a few times. Still nothing.

I rap one more time and call out, "Hey, Travis, you in there?"

All I hear is the echo of my own voice bouncing off the

paint-chipped, graffiti-covered, dingy walls.

I press my ear to the door and pick up the faint sound of music. Maybe he's home but can't hear me over the music? More likely he's using an old urban security trick: leave the radio playing so prospective burglars will think someone's home.

I consider my options. I can turn around and leave or I can resort to self-help. If I leave, I may be missing something that will point me in the direction of Donald Alston. At the same time, something seems off, though I can't quite put my finger on what it is.

Before giving my credit card another workout, I twist the doorknob. The door opens. That bad taste in my mouth is getting stronger. It should be a warning to get the fuck out of there, but it's not. I shout out Travis's name again.

No answer. I go inside and quickly and silently close the door behind me.

I pass a bathroom on my right. The door is slightly ajar. I nudge it open the rest of the way with my foot. I stick my head in. Shaving stuff on the sink. A sliver of soap in the soap dish below the medicine cabinet. A used towel crumpled up on the floor, its twin hanging from a rail next to the sink. Something else catches my attention. A very faint aroma of lemons. The same scent on Lila Alston's business card.

I move forward, passing through the kitchen. Dirty dishes are stacked up precariously in the sink. An open Diet Coke can is on the counter. Flies buzz around a half-eaten sandwich sitting next to the can of Coke. Next to the sink is a small oven, next to that a half refrigerator. Up against the wall opposite the sink and oven there's a bathtub covered by a wooden plank which doubles as a kitchen table.

The living room is decorated in early dumpster. A frayed, faded blue couch. A couple folding chairs with items of clothing hanging over them. A bookcase with only a few books in it. A coffee table covered with newspapers and magazines. *Backstage. Variety. Entertainment Weekly. People.* The printed detritus of a wannabe star.

As I move closer to the back of the apartment the sound of music grows stronger. Finally, I reach what must be the bedroom. I push open the door with my foot and enter. There's a sour smell filling the air. I know exactly what it is. I smelled it the first time when I was an upstate deputy. An old guy, living alone, died in his shack at the edge of town. He'd been dead more than a week, but no one noticed, no one missed him. We got the call to do a wellness check from his great niece who'd been trying to reach him. No one was surprised he was dead. No one cared. Not even his great niece when she found the bank owned his house and the land it was on.

The music is coming from a portable radio sitting on the nightstand next to the bed. A man's body, fully clothed, wearing a pale blue, button-down shirt and tan slacks, is lying on top of the bed. A sport jacket is draped across a chair beside the bed. The corpse's eyes are closed and his head, angled slightly toward the door, as if he'd heard something and turned his head to see what it was. His head is nestled in a blood-soaked pillow. His mouth is open like a fish gasping for air.

I recognize him immediately from his photo.

It's Donald Alston.

5

Cashing In

The first thing that crosses my mind is, *Good work, Fortunato, you just worked yourself out of a job.*

I return to the bathroom and unroll a foot and a half of toilet paper. I go back into the bedroom and, using the toilet paper so as not to leave any prints, I crack open the window to air out the room. I pull out my phone and snap a few photographs of the body and the room. It might mean trouble if they're found on my phone, but at the same time it might come in handy if I have to prove I had nothing to do with the death of Donald Alston.

I move to the other side of the bed and lean in close enough to see the bullet hole in Alston's left temple. There's dried blood running down the side of his head and onto the bedsheet. His left arm is dangling over the side of the bed, his fingers inches away from a Glock pistol, not unlike the one I carry. I lean in close enough to catch the unmistakable odor of gunpowder.

The scene laid out in front of me has all the signs of a suicide. But something isn't right. For one thing, Alston's watch is on his left wrist which means he was right-handed. If so, it would be almost physically impossible to shoot himself where the entry level of the bullet is near the back of his left temple.

But the obvious question is: what the fuck is Donald Alston doing in Travis Chapman's apartment?

All sorts of possible reasons skip through my mind.

He was there to confront Travis about his affair with Lila. Maybe. But if so, why commit suicide here? What makes more sense is that they argued, Travis lost his temper. Either he owns the gun or Alston came with one. They struggle for it. Alston is the loser. Travis panics. He tries to make it look like Alston took his own life.

But how likely is it that Alston would be lying on Travis's bed when the argument takes place? And as far as I can see, the only blood in the room is on the pillow beneath Alston's head. This means this is where he was shot.

It looks more like an execution than a suicide.

I wrap the toilet paper around my hand and pick up Alston's right wrist by the sleeve of his jacket. I smell his fingers. No sign of gunpowder. I do the same with his left wrist. None on that hand either.

The scene is clumsily staged. It's either a panicked, stupid afterthought or a calculated move allowing the killer to buy time. If I'm not fooled, the cops won't be either. It won't take long before they figure out it's a setup. And if they find me here, guess who suspect number one is going to be?

I check my watch. I've been in Chapman's apartment for close to twenty minutes. It's obviously not a good idea to hang around much longer. But before I leave I want to take one last look around. It's not because I'm interested in solving the case. I'm off the clock now. It's because I can't help myself. It's because I have the curiosity of a cat.

There's a dresser opposite the bed. I open the three drawers, using what's left of the toilet paper so as not to leave prints. Not much in there, except for a couple pairs of socks, some underwear, and a couple T-shirts.

I check the closet. A couple pair of shoes on the floor, a couple dress shirts on hangers, a few sport jackets, a couple pairs of jeans and a pair of dressier pants, all on hangers. Curious how the rest of the apartment is a mess but Travis seems to take good care of his clothing, which means he puts a lot of stock in the way he looks. Considering his aspirations of making it as an actor, or a gigolo, maybe both, this isn't surprising. There are a few empty hangers, which probably indicate that he's taken clothing with him, wherever he's gone. Running scared, probably. There's a top shelf in the closet, but I can't see what's on it, so I drag over a chair, again making sure I don't leave prints, and stand on it. Dust has left a rectangular outline where I figure Travis kept his luggage. There's also a shoebox, pushed back against the wall. I don't want to disturb any dust surrounding it, so I flip open the top. It's filled with newspaper clippings, programs, and photographs, probably from showcases Travis has appeared in over the years. I close it up and step down.

I've found Donald Alston in little more than a day which means I can keep all the dough, making it by far my biggest payday ever. There's nothing else I can do here, so there's no reason to risk sticking around any longer.

Once outside, I cross the street, take out my phone, and dial 911. I identify myself as a concerned neighbor. I tell the operator there's a strange odor coming from apartment 3B and I think there may be something wrong. When she asks for my name I hang up.

I stick around until a squad car rolls to a stop in front of Travis's building. As soon as two burly cops climb the stoop and disappear into the building I take off. I've done my civic duty and hopefully covered my ass. Now it's the cops' problem. Not mine.

The next step is to call Lila Alston and give her the news. I should be in a good mood. I'm not. Something keeps gnawing at me. It doesn't figure that Travis would off Lila's husband in his own apartment. No one is that dumb. You never shit where you eat. If you're gonna do something like this, do it someplace else, someplace that doesn't immediately tie the murder to you. Or at least get rid of the damn body. It's more likely that Travis isn't involved and someone is trying to make it look as if he is.

It occurs to me maybe that someone is Lila Alston. Not everyone can commit murder and not everyone can afford to hire someone to murder for you. But Lila Alston? Well, she looks to me like she might be capable of both.

If Lila did kill her husband she needed someone to find the body and it couldn't be Travis because that would lead directly back to her. And it couldn't be her, because the first suspect on the hot seat is always the spouse. So, why not hire some patsy and hope he'll follow the breadcrumbs leading to the "lost" husband? Only when he finds him, he's settling in for the "big sleep."

Lila is certainly smart enough to make sure she has an alibi and hiring the patsy, which would be me, would also deflect suspicion from her. After all, who hires a private dick to find their husband when they know their husband is dead? And if that was the plan then those two proverbial birds could be taken care of with one stone. And that stone would be me.

With her husband and her lover out of the picture, Lila is in the clear. Pre-nup or not she winds up being one very wealthy widow. This seems like the most logical conclusion. But what if it's someone else. What if neither Travis nor Lila pulled the trigger? Then who did?

Few of us get through life without making enemies. Certainly not me. I'm sure Donald Alston made his fair share, especially since he worked in the money business. No one works that game without pissing someone off. Maybe an investor who feels cheated? Maybe an investor who was cheated?

Right now, my first (second and third) priority is to remove myself from being in the middle. I know eventually the cops'll figure out I'm involved. They'll trace my 911 call and it won't be long before they realize I've been in the apartment. Despite how careful I've been chances are I've left some kind of forensic evidence.

The question I'm now grappling with is should I let the cops find me or should I walk in under my own steam? I might be able to help the cops, at least point them in the right direction and save them some valuable time. But why should I? If Lila Alston is setting me up, I need an ace in the hole. And the quicker I put distance between me and this clown car of wackos the better.

The next morning, I deposit Lila's twenty-five-hundred-dollar check. I look at the bank receipt long and hard, trying to create a mental picture of a checking account bulging at the seams. When I've had enough I go home hoping I can grab a couple hours' nap to make up for those lost hours I didn't get last night.

I'm lying on the couch, the blinds drawn, a white noise machine purring in the background, when my cell buzzes. It's my friendly banker, Rob. He is "very sorry" to inform me that the check I deposited earlier today has bounced higher than the Empire State Building and by the way, not only am I out the two and a half grand but also another twenty-five-buck penalty for the bounce. He's very sorry, but those are bank rules, not his. However, if I do want to upgrade my account, which would mean keeping a balance of ten grand, this kind of thing wouldn't happen because I'd qualify for draft protection which means I'd never be overdrawn again. I tell Rob he must not be acquainted with my banking history or else he'd know that if you toted up my entire deposits for the year, they would hardly add up to ten grand. He laughs. Not at me, I hope, but because he thinks I'm joking around. I'm not.

And when I hang up I realize I finally have an explanation for that bad taste in my mouth.

6
Extra Innings

It's times like these when I develop an almost uncontrollable urge to punch someone or something. Yeah, I know. It's not going to solve anything. But I also know it's gonna make me feel a helluva lot better.

That's why I have been "invited" to attend anger management classes. Okay, it's not really an invitation. It's the result of a very strong recommendation from my lawyer after a dust-up I swear I did not start. In fact, it was one of those rare times when I was the guy trying to act as peacemaker. It just didn't turn out that way.

I was in Central Park one Sunday morning, watching a softball game on the Hecksher Fields, adjacent to the merry-go-round. I'm sitting there trying to ignore a heckler who's getting on one of the pitchers, a tall, lanky Hispanic with a tricky delivery that skirts illegality. Usually, I don't mind a little trash talk, but this guy was getting out of hand. In a booming voice, he kept at it, making no effort at all to steer away from obnoxious, border-line racist catcalls. It's not even ten thirty and he's already drinking a can of beer wrapped in a paper bag. And I can tell it's not his first. After a while, I can't help myself. It's not so much for the player on the field, though being an ex-player myself I can certainly empathize, because I figure he can take care of himself. It's because he was starting to annoy the hell out of me. He had broken one of my cardinal rules: He was seriously impinging on my enjoyment of the morning.

Finally, I lean over and say, "Hey, pal, how about turning it down a little. I think the pitcher pretty much gets the point."

He turns to me and says, "What the fuck business is it of yours, fathead?" Believe me, I've been called much worse, but he didn't stop there. "You don't fucking like it, move. This ain't the only game in town, man."

"I know, friend, but it's the only one I'm watching. And because of your big mouth I'm not getting a chance to enjoy it."

"Fuck you, man," he says, spraying me with a mouth full of beer.

I'm on the edge and I know it. The younger me wouldn't have bothered with words, but I'm trying to limit my physical interactions so I say, "Hey, pal..." But before I can finish the sentence he reaches over to push me away. You put your hands on me, you're taking a very big chance. Of course, he doesn't know this. I push him back and when I see he's about to swing at me, I beat him to the punch. Literally. Then, all hell breaks loose. We've got ourselves a genuine, honest-to-god, good old-fashioned melee. Someone calls the cops. Both of us get pinched. I have to get a lawyer and she takes one look at me, realizes this is not my first rodeo, and strongly suggests I offer to take anger management classes as part of a deal to drop all charges. It seems I've got a bit of a reputation as a brawler that has somehow made it to the official record. Well-earned, I admit.

"I think it'll go much easier on you if we're the one to bring it up," she says. "It's not the first time you've been involved in a violent altercation, which establishes a pattern of bad behavior. If we admit to that and offer a solution, I think the judge will go easy on you. She might even put you on probation for a year or so."

"I've never been convicted of anything," I argue. "Why should I volunteer to go to one of those ridiculous groups where you stand up and tell how your father beat you and your mother paid no attention to you and that's why you're so fucked up and full of anger."

"It doesn't matter. It's on the record that you have a bit of a temper which, by the way, you just proved by the way you just responded to me. You can't even hide it very well."

Point taken. Discussion over. So, now I have to go to a class once a week, Tuesday evenings, where I learn things like how to recognize when you're angry.

- You rub your face frequently.
- You tightly clasp one hand with the other, or make clenched fists.
- You become rude and lose your sense of humor.
- You start to raise your voice.
- You develop cravings for things you think might relax you, like tobacco, sugar, alcohol, drugs...

And then there are the emotional symptoms of anger:
- A desire to "run away" from the situation.
- Irritation.
- Anxiety.
- A feeling or desire to last out verbally or physically.

I've never scored so high on a test in my life.

I have to keep an "anger journal," (I filled my first notebook in less than a week) as well as practice and then employ a comprehensive list of tips that are supposed to tame my out-of-control temper.

- Think before I speak. High degree of difficulty.

- Once I'm calm I'm supposed to express my anger, verbally, of course, and calmly. This, I might be able to fake.
- Don't hold a grudge. Huh? What is there to live for if you can't hold a grudge?

There are more but reciting them just depresses me which makes me angry. You see the dilemma, right?

I don't think much of this crap, because as far as I'm concerned, my anger is always justified. But still I attend the classes and actually take notes, just in case the time comes when it becomes a real problem.

Most of the time, I'm able to restrain myself. I've been in enough trouble in my life to know there are other less destructive ways of dealing with anger and frustration. The easiest and least destructive way, at least for me, is to have a couple drinks at my neighborhood bar. Sure, the drinks are usually watered down, but to compensate for that the bartender, Sid, doesn't mind me bitching about everything under the sun.

Sid's the perfect listener because he doesn't really hear anything you say. I'm sure if you quiz him the next day about a conversation you know you had with him he'll just lay this blank stare on you, which makes me wonder sometimes if he even knows who I am. But I'll say this for him, he's very adept at faking it in the moment. And most of the time that's all I need.

That's where I find myself the next evening. Sitting on a barstool nursing my third drink, hoping tonight I'll stick to my limit. And Sid? Well, he has the night off so I'm on my own recognizance.

The more I drink the more pissed off I get. I'm so pissed, I get alarmingly close to starting a fight with the guy next sitting next to me over, if you can believe it, the Mets versus the Yankees. Do I really give a fuck? No. But you wouldn't know it from the argument. I know it's really not about baseball, although I also know this guy doesn't know what the fuck he's talking about. Finally, when things look like they're starting to get a little out of hand, the bartender, I don't even know his name, has to intervene.

"Hey, pal," he says, "whatever's bugging you why don't you just deal with it instead of making the rest of us miserable?"

He has no idea how close he is to the truth. That's exactly what I want: to make everyone else in the world as miserable as I am. But I also know this can only end bad for me and maybe worse for the guy on the stool next to me. I've been getting into bar fights since I was seventeen and I've got the procedure down pat, so that the poor slob next to me doesn't have a chance.

The last thing I want tonight is to get into a fight, because this time I'll be lucky if I get community service and have to pay any damages.

So, I go home, take a cold shower—not by choice but because something is wrong with the damn boiler again. I try to sleep, but my insomnia kicks in. All I can think about is finding Lila Alston and wringing her pretty little neck until cash spurts out of her mouth like an ATM. The more I think about this the less the possibility there is of finding sleep. Finally, I give up and switch on the TV. I find an old gangster flick on Turner Classics and stay up till dawn watching one vintage movie after another.

The next morning, I set off to tracking down Lila Alston. It isn't hard. Public records are just that: public. And in this day and age it's practically impossible to go completely off the grid, even if you want to. There's always some telltale detail that gives you away. With Lila it's her phone number. I got a guy who can hack into almost anything and the phone companies are a piece of cake. But I don't even have to go that route. Instead, I call a buddy of mine who works for one of the big carriers. Once I give him the number from Lila's business card it takes him less than two minutes to provide me with her address.

Lila Alston lives in a pre-war building on Madison Avenue, on the northwest corner of 88th Street. The doorman asks who I'm there to see and I tell him.

He gives me the fisheye. Like what the hell am I doing in this neighborhood and what possible business could I have with someone as classy as Lila Alston? If he only knew.

He's paid to be polite, though, so he answers, "I'm afraid she's not here, sir. She left just a few minutes ago."

"You wouldn't happen to know which direction she went in, would you?"

He sizes me up. Pervert? Stalker? Troublemaker? I can tell he isn't likely to help me so I make up a story. I tell him I work with her husband, Donald, and he's sent me over with some papers to sign pertaining to their divorce. It's a story with just enough detail to be the truth and not so much detail to make it look fishy. I know from experience that doormen know everything that's going on in their building, so I know not to give up easily.

"Look, man," I plead, "I don't get these papers signed I'm gonna be up shit's creek. The truth is, I'm hanging on by a thread. I fuck this up, you can find me on the unemployment line."

Appealing to his working-class roots and we're-all-in-this-together-so-let's-stick-together attitude works. He leans over and whispers, "She went across the street to the bank. I haven't seen her come out yet so she might still be there. But you didn't hear this from me."

"Thanks, man, you just saved my ass. I really appreciate it." I put my finger up to my lips, "and I promise you, man, this goes no further." I think momentarily about slipping him a fiver, but I know that would only peg me as a liar.

I cross Madison Avenue and peer into the bank window. There she is, sitting in one of the cubicles, talking to a bank officer. I wait, leaning up against a parking meter a few feet down from the bank entrance. Less than ten minutes pass before she emerges. She's texting on her phone so she doesn't see me until I'm practically in her face.

"Fancy seeing you here," I say. She looks up, startled. At first, she's smiling but that disappears pretty quick when she realizes who I am and, no doubt, why I'm there.

"Mr. Fortunato, what are you doing here?"

"I think it was Freud who said there are no coincidences, Mrs. Alston. And so, I think you know exactly why I'm here."

"I'm too busy now to play games, Mr—"

"Me, too," I interrupt. "But I'm sure we both have a couple minutes, time enough for us to go back into the bank and you make good on that rubber ducky check you gave me."

"Rubber check?"

"Yeah. Far as I know it's still bouncing all the way down to Foley Square."

She wrinkles her brow, as if she's baffled. Me? I'm baffled she thinks I'm stupid. "I don't understand it. There's no way that should have happened."

"It did. But no real harm done. We'll just fix it and everything will be fine." I take her by the crook of her elbow and steer her back toward the bank. I can practically feel a breeze from the wheels turning in her head.

She snaps her fingers. "Oh, my, I know what the problem was," she says, making a sudden stop.

"I'm happy for you, but it doesn't matter—"

"Of course, it does. It's so silly. I must have used an old set of checks. I'm so sorry."

"For the record, I've heard that story before."

"It's not a story…"

"Sure, it is. But I like stories, especially if they come with a happy ending. And that's what we're going to do right now: make this a happy ending. And then we're going to have a little chat, Mrs. Alston."

"You can call me Lila," she says. Her voice dripping honey. Suddenly, we're besties.

"No. Not yet. Maybe after we get to know each other a little better."

"Are hundreds okay?"

"Sure. I love the idea of flashing a roll of real C-notes instead of my usual Missouri bankroll."

This is the Upper East Side in the middle of the day, so there are very few people in the bank. She chooses one of the three tellers, while I lean against a counter a few steps in back of her. The view from there isn't half bad.

"Would you like to count them?" she asks, handing me a bank envelope stuffed the cash, as we head toward the door.

"After all we've been through, I doubt you'd shortchange me."

She smiles. "You're right. That's definitely not my style."

I don't ask her what her style is because I think I already know. And to be honest, I don't intend sticking around long enough to find out what that style is.

"Are we done?" she asks, hiking her pocketbook over her shoulder.

I flash a smile. "Not even close. We've got things to discuss. There's a Starbucks over on Lex. My treat."

"When's the funeral?" I ask, stirring an extra sugar into my three-buck cup of designer coffee as we sit at a table opposite the counter of what is a throwback coffee shop with a window that's decorated by lines of old-time Coca-Cola bottles. She's sipping from some concoction called a Skinny Peppermint Mocha. It's like we're two kids out on a first date, only I'm not tongue-tied and know exactly how this date is going to end.

"You mean Donald's?"

"You burying anyone else this week?"

"That's not particularly funny."

"It wasn't a joke."

Her expression turns serious and I'm back in Mrs. Immediato's third grade class waiting for that free pass to the vice principal's office. "The funeral is Friday. We need a few days for his family to arrive in town."

"You know, all things considered, you seem to be taking this very well."

"What's that supposed to mean?" There's a sharp edge in her voice, like I've hit a nerve.

"Your husband was just murdered and you don't seem very upset."

She nails me with her eyes. "You have absolutely no idea how I feel."

"So, why don't you tell me?"

"I don't have to justify my feelings to you. Or anyone else, for that matter."

"You're right. You don't."

There's a moment of silence and I'm not the one who's going to break it.

"If you must know, I'm devastated," she says, stirring her drink with a straw.

"Surprising, since you didn't sound that close when you hired me to find him and then left me holding the bag."

"I have no idea what you're talking about."

"You knew your husband was dead before you hired me."

"No, I did not," she says with more emphasis than seemed necessary. "If I did why would I hire you?"

I stir another teaspoon of sugar into my coffee, which still has a faintly bitter taste. I pretty much drink coffee now because it's a long-held habit, not because I enjoy it. And never, ever, after four p.m. "You tell me."

"There's nothing to tell. I had no idea where Donald was or if he was alive or dead. That's why I hired you in the first place."

"And I did what you hired me to do."

She looks surprised. "You mean you're the one who found him?"

"That's right."

Her eyes drop to the table.

"The police didn't tell me that," she says. If I hadn't already made up my mind about her, I would actually have believed her. Instead, all I could do was wonder if she had any acting classes in her past.

"The police don't know yet."

"You mean you didn't report it to them? You haven't even

spoken to them?"

"Oh, I reported it all right, they just don't know I was the one who did. But they will. It won't be long before they're knocking on my door. They're not stupid. And for the record, neither am I."

"You think I know more than I told you?"

"A lot more."

She shakes her head.

"Your husband's found dead in your boyfriend's apartment. And surprise, I'm the one who finds him. That doesn't read setup to you in big, blinking neon lights?"

"You don't have a very high opinion of me, do you?"

"Should I?"

"I'm not anywhere near as evil and calculating as you make me out to be. Although sometimes I wish I was."

"Maybe I misjudged you. Maybe I'm wrong. But there's something else."

"What?"

This is what's known as playing the trump card, hoping it will shake things up. "You were in that apartment recently, weren't you?"

"What?"

"You heard me. You visited Travis's apartment recently."

"When?"

"The day he was killed."

I don't know this for sure, but that doesn't stop me from saying it.

"What makes you think that?"

I tap my nose.

"I have no idea what that's supposed to mean."

"You're a big fan of lemons, Mrs. Alston."

She gives me one of those quizzical looks that's supposed to make me think she doesn't know what I'm talking about. But she knows.

"The perfume you wear. It's got a lemony scent. There was a

hint of that scent in Travis's apartment. The cops won't be aware of it, it certainly faded by the time they combed the apartment, and even if they did smell it, they wouldn't make anything of it, they wouldn't connect it to you. But I am."

"You think you're pretty smart, don't you?"

"Smart enough."

"Of course, the scent was there. Why shouldn't it be? I left a bottle of my perfume in Travis's bathroom the last time I was there. That's where you smelled it, right? In the bathroom? But that doesn't mean I was there yesterday. And it certainly doesn't mean I had anything to do with Donald's demise."

"That's a pretty cold, fancy word for murder."

"I graduated Harvard, Mr. Fortunato. I'm actually familiar with, as you call them, some fancy words. Would you prefer I dumb it down for you?"

"I didn't graduate some fancy college, but somehow I managed to make it through and I'll let you know when I have to consult a dictionary. So, when was the last time you were there?"

"I don't remember exactly. Maybe a week ago. Maybe more. As you know, it's not exactly the Ritz and I didn't enjoy spending time in that horrible apartment."

"I'm having a tough time picturing you there at all."

She shrugs. "On occasion it was convenient. But I didn't make a habit of it. So, what are you going to do now?"

"Do?"

"In terms of contacting the police."

"I'm not looking to get involved in this but I think it's probably too late for that. I'm sure they'll track me down eventually."

"You mean you're not going to inform them yourself."

"Let them earn their salary. Two questions. Who do you think killed your husband and where do you think Travis is?"

"In terms of the latter, I haven't the foggiest idea. In terms of the former, well, it wasn't me and I very much doubt Travis would be capable of something like that, although he probably is stupid enough to do it in his own apartment and leave the body for somebody else to find."

"I take it Travis is not a fellow Harvard alum."

"Hardly. I couldn't even swear he graduated high school."

"So, what do you see in him?"

"Did. The past tense, Mr. Fortunato. Did."

"Pardon me. *Did* you see in him?"

"He had certain areas of expertise."

"Such as?"

"I don't think I want to get into that. In the end, he served a purpose."

"What purpose would that be?"

"Use your imagination," she says.

"You mean to make your husband jealous."

"Donald had long since shown any interest in me and me in him. If you want to know the truth, I think he was playing for the 'other team,' if you know what I mean."

"Your husband was gay?"

"It's possible he had those tendencies."

"He had a girlfriend."

She laughs. "You can't possibly be that naïve."

"Switch hitter?"

She flashes a surprisingly good facsimile of a Mona Lisa smile.

"So, you're telling me you think he was having an affair with Travis?"

"Oh, my. Affair? That's a pretty formal word for what they might have been doing."

"Travis is gay, too?"

"Travis is an opportunist. He sees an opportunity and he grabs it. That was true of me and it might have been true of Donald. It would explain why Donald was in Travis's apartment, wouldn't it?"

"I suppose…"

She wipes her mouth with a napkin. I can see she's ready to wrap things up. "But as you said, all this is really none of your business. You did what you were hired to do—and very efficiently, I might add. And now that you've been paid, I don't really see why any of this should concern you. And why you and I should have anything more to do with each other."

"You've got a point, Mrs. Alston. But all that could change if somehow, I find myself in the middle of this. Because if that happens, it's every man...and woman...for themselves."

"Oh, I don't think you have anything to worry about."

"Really? Well, I do."

She looks at her watch. "I'm late for a hair appointment, Mr. Fortunato. I'm sorry for the inconvenience, but you've got your money now, so I believe our business is completed. I wish you the best of luck."

"Really?"

She smiles. "Well, to be honest, I couldn't care less."

7
Uninvited Guests

I'm not expecting company but here they are. Two of New York's finest knock, knock, knocking at my door.

It's a little after eight p.m. the very evening of the very day I had collected my pay from Lila Alston. I know what they're here for and they don't have to introduce themselves as cops. I know exactly what cops look like. How they act. How they think. Why shouldn't I? I used to be one. Not for long. A blink of an eye, really. And in a universe far, far away—a small town in upstate New York where you're likely to find snow on the ground all the way up to May. They call it "lake effect" snow, but to me it was just too much snow too late in the season. Eight months as a deputy. I carried a gun and I had a badge and a peaked hat. I got the job through the process of elimination. No one else wanted it. And so, a few courses in law enforcement, some weapons training, and the promise of more of both got me the job. What ended the job is something I don't like to think about, so I don't. But let's face it, if it hadn't ended me, I would have ended it.

"What took you so long?" I ask as I hold the door open just enough so I can get a good look at them.

"You were expecting us, Mr. Fortunato?" says the taller of the two.

I shrug. "You or someone like you."

"My name's Detective Divicek," he says. I expect him to hold out his hand for to shake but then I realize this isn't a social call.

I don't know if they go by height or something subtler, but this one, the taller of the two, Divicek, is obviously the alpha. Somewhere in his mid to late forties, he's dressed in an ill-fitting, shiny dark suit that looks like something my dad would have worn on one of his insurance calls. He's a couple inches over six feet and lean, and he has close-cropped gray hair and those gaunt, angular, chiseled facial features I associate with men from Eastern European countries.

"This here's Detective Murphy," he says, nodding toward his partner, who appears to be the yin to Divicek's yang. He's shorter than me, no more than five-six and built like a frigging fireplug. He's obviously spent way too much time in the gym (actually, for me any time at all in the gym is way too much time; I get my rippling muscles honestly), because it looks like his chest is bursting out of his suit jacket. Unlike his partner he's put some time and thought into his expensive-looking dark suit, because it's actually tailored well enough so that he doesn't look like a gorilla all decked out in a suit.

"Pleased to make your acquaintance, guys," I say. I've never invited a cop into my apartment and there's no reason to make an exception here. If they want it, they'll ask for it. In the meantime, I'm very comfortable dealing with them on one side of the door and me on the other.

"That's a lie," says Murphy. "And I hope that's not gonna be a trend."

"Yeah. You're right. Just being polite. Anyone ever tell you you've got an attitude, Detective?"

"Yeah. All the fucking time."

He's got that little man's chip on his shoulder. It's a chip I can appreciate. Not because I'm especially little— at five foot eleven, I'm considered a tad above average—but because I'm usually the guy who winds up out-of-step.

"You gonna keep us standing in the hall or are you gonna invite us in?" says Divicek.

"Or maybe you'd like to join us down at the station."

"What's your pleasure, gentlemen?" I say, just trying to jerk their chain a little because there's no way I want to leave my apartment. Especially to that destination.

"We're here, so why not get down to it?" says Murphy.

I wave them in.

"Sorry about this," I say, indicating the apartment mess. "But I'm afraid the maid didn't make it in today."

Actually, for once the place isn't in such bad condition. It never gets too bad and that's not that I'm all that neat, it's because I don't own much. Minimal furniture. You know. The usual stuff. Couch. A couple chairs. Small all-purpose table where I eat and set up my laptop. A couple bookcases. Big screen TV. A Pullman kitchen. All in one room. I've lived here almost three years now. Ever since I split from Kate, my girlfriend of seven years. We're still sort of friends. Or maybe I mean friendly. It just wasn't a good idea for us to be together anymore. If we did, we wouldn't be friendly anymore. I guess you could say that to preserve the relationship we had, whatever that was or would be, I had to move out.

"That's okay, we ain't from the health department," says Murphy. I peg him as the wise guy. The comic relief. You know, like Falstaff. Only I didn't think this was going to wind up being very funny.

I don't bother offering them something to drink. I know they wouldn't accept it. Might be considered a payoff. That's what we were taught when I was in the department upstate. You accept anything, you're compromised. Even a Coke. But why bother getting busted for the small shit when you can risk it for something bigger?

They sit on the couch, which does double duty as my bed. The one thing I do every morning when I get up is strip the sheets, fold them up, and put them in a drawer. Then I reassemble the couch. Not doing that would be a sign I've given up. I've been tempted several times to do just that, but I'm not quite there yet. I figure so long as I'm able to put my bed back together I'm not too far gone. Besides, there's even a practical reason for making it. I read somewhere it's not wise to confuse the mind if you suffer from insomnia. A couch is for sitting. A bed is for sleeping. And never the twain shall meet.

"Fortunato," says Murphy. "What kinda name is that? You a wop?"

"Half wop, half kike," I say, just to be outrageous.

"Really," says Murphy. "Sicilian? A paisan?"

"Jersey."

I drag a chair over from the table and sit facing them.

"So, you're an ex-cop?" says Divicek.

They've obviously done their homework, which means I didn't just pop up on their radar.

"That was a long time ago."

"How long?"

"How long ago or how long was I on the job?"

"Both," says Murphy.

"Listen, boys, why waste my time and yours? I know you've done your homework. You know it was nine years ago, that it was a small, shithole town outside Syracuse and that I worked there for less than a year."

"Why'd you leave?" asks Divicek.

"Got tired of taking orders," giving an answer that's the truth but not the whole truth.

"It wouldn't have been something else?" says Murphy.

The little shit is starting to get on my nerves. I know the type. He's the guy on the bench who lacks talent but loves getting under the skin of those who do by talking trash, trying to get under our skin. Sometimes it works, but only if you let it. If you're smart, you tune them out. Eventually, they shut the fuck up. If they don't, if they ever do make it out onto the field, there's a good chance they'll find a slide that comes in a little too high, or a pitch a that's a little too close.

I know he's trying to piss me off. See, if he can shake me up and, like a can of soda, I'll explode. Not a chance. Not with all these calming techniques at my disposal. But what the fuck? I'll play along.

I throw up my hands. "You got me. Truth is, I didn't look good in blue."

"Fucking wise guy," says Murphy under his breath. A few years back I might have taken a swing at him, but now I'm better than that.

"Listen, boys, it's getting close to my bedtime so why don't we cut the niceties and get down to why you're here. It's about Donald Alston, right?"

"Bingo," says Murphy.

"What were you doing at Travis Chapman's apartment the other day?" asks Divicek, who's back to taking the lead.

"Whose apartment?"

"Let's not play games," says Divicek.

"What game is that, Detective?" I make sure the word *detective* is dripping with irony and disdain. I'm pretty good at doing both.

"We know you were the one who called it in."

"Called what in?"

"Don't try our patience, Fortunato," says Divicek.

"But I'm kind of enjoying it."

"Do you think you'd fucking enjoy it if we locked you up for obstruction of justice?" says Murphy, who obviously has less patience than his taller partner.

"Or maybe worse?" says Divicek.

"You can do that?" Again, irony.

"Yeah. We can do it," says Murphy. "So, let's cut the crap. We know you called it in because we traced your cell."

"Oh, yeah. I remember now. I called in a smell, right? But that doesn't mean I was actually in the apartment. You got any proof that says otherwise. My prints? DNA?"

Divicek ignores my question and I know why. There is no way they can nail me on actually being in the apartment, though all three of us know I was there.

"Okay, so what were you doing in the hallway?" says Divicek, his face turning red. Anger? Frustration? Probably a little of both.

"I was on a job."

"What kind of job?"

"Missing persons."

"Who was missing?"

"Who do you think?"

"Listen, asshole," says Murphy, pounding on the coffee table for emphasis. Good thing there's nothing breakable on it. In fact, there's nothing on it at all. "Let's cut the crap. Just answer the fucking question. Who were you looking for?"

I'm getting bored. There's something on the tube I'd rather be watching. Check that. There's anything on the tube I'd rather be watching. I'm tired of them being in my space and in my face. So, I tell them what they already know. "Donald Alston."

"Well, good work, pal. He ain't missing anymore," says Murphy.

"I'm very good at what I do."

"Who hired you?" asks Divicek.

"You know that's privileged information."

"We wouldn't want you to betray your high moral standards," says Murphy.

"I wouldn't want to mislead you boys on that score. It's debatable whether I have any standards at all."

"His wife, right?" says Divicek.

"Why don't you ask her?"

"We did."

"Then why are you wasting my time?"

"Look," says Divicek, softening his tone. I have to smile at his attempt to play both good cop and bad cop at the same time. "We're not accusing you of anything, Pete." Nice touch, using my first name, like we're best buddies. "We just want to find out who killed Donald Alston. You help us out and we'll be out the door."

"I'm sure you'll find the killer. The NYPD always gets their man, right?"

"That's the fucking Mounties," says Murphy, out of the side of his mouth.

"Why don't you make it easy on yourself and on us?" says Divicek.

"I'll do my best, boys."

"That's good. You answer a few more questions then we'll get out of your hair," says Divicek.

"What's left of it," I say, trying to lighten the mood a little. But either nobody picks up on it or they just don't give a damn. The latter being the more likely.

"Listen, you…" says Murphy who can't quite contain himself. But before he can finish the sentence Divicek places his hand on his partner's shoulder.

"How about it, Pete? Let's get this over and call it a night, okay?"

The buddy-buddy approach will not work with me. But truth is, I'm getting bored by this pointless back and forth. I'm actually getting a little sleepy, which doesn't mean I'll fall asleep any easier, but I always figure that when it comes on I ought to be close to a bed. So, why not tell them everything I know and be done with it? I have my money—in cash—so I have no skin left in this game.

"Okay, boys, I'll tell you what I can, but you understand I have no intention of incriminating myself."

"Understood," says Divicek, the beginnings of a smile appearing on his face. He pulls out a small notebook and Murphy does the same. "Why don't you start at the beginning."

"That's all there is. A beginning. Mrs. Alston hired me to find her missing husband. I find he's got a little something on the side. The something leads me my employer's boy-toy. Turns out to be Travis Chapman. I figure maybe he knows where her husband is, so I track him down. I knock on the door. No answer. The door's open and there's this smell coming from the apartment that makes it all the way out in the hall. So, I call it in, like the good citizen I am. End of story."

Murphy laughs.

"You got a problem with that?"

"You expect us to believe that's all there is?" says Divicek.

"We know all about you, Fortunato," says Murphy. "Some washed up ballplayer hurts his arm and has to get a real job. Gets himself hired in a small town as a deputy and washes out of that, too."

"You don't have a very high opinion of me, do you, Murphy?"

"You got that right."

"Look," Divicek says, "we're not here to bust your chops or to trade insults with you. We got better things to do with our time. We know you didn't have nothing to do with this thing. But we also know you know more than you're telling us."

I shrug.

"So why not save all of us a lot of time and just give us everything," adds Murphy.

"I already did."

"So, you're telling us you never set foot inside that apartment?"

"That's right."

"And if we find prints that match yours?"

"Then I'm lying. But you won't."

"What makes you think we haven't already?" says the combative Murphy, who's not willing to give an inch. Man, what I wouldn't give to have this guy in a poker game. I'd own everything damn thing he has. I can't suppress a smile because I love the idea of that.

"You had my prints or anything else that ties me to being inside the apartment I'd be answering these questions at your house, not mine. You know that. I know that." I glance up at the clock over my refrigerator. "Look, it's getting late. You know everything I know, so how about we call it a night."

"We find you're lying to us, Fortunato..." says Murphy, starting to turn red in the face.

"I don't think he'd be stupid enough to lie to us, Dennis," says Divicek.

"Yeah? You think this guy is smart?"

"Smart enough he wouldn't pull that on us."

"I ain't so sure," says Murphy.

Me? All I can do is smile. Playing pitty-pat with these two morons is an unexpected bonus. But all good things must come to an end.

"Look," says Divicek, as he gets up from the couch, and not easily. I can tell he's either got knee problems or arthritis. Maybe both. "You think of anything else, you give us a call, okay?" He hands me his card.

"You got it, chief," I say, not even looking at it as I toss it on the coffee table.

Murphy gets up, too. "You think you seen the last of us, pal?"

"It's a small world after all, my friend. I wouldn't be surprised if we bump into each other again. It's not something I'd look forward to, you understand, but it wouldn't surprise me."

When I say it, I mean it, because I know there's no way I'm free and clear. I'm pretty sure I haven't heard the last of Travis Chapman, Donald Alston, and Lila Alston. And these two cops aren't about to forget about me. I'm much too much of a challenge to them. They're like me. None of us like to lose.

8
And the Beat Goes On

I'm right back where I started from. Familiar territory. Unemployed with no idea where my next buck will come from. Or when.

Despite my name that seems to promise great wealth, I'm no heir to a family fortune. I'm still making monthly payments to my ex-wife, which continues either until she remarries or one of us kicks the bucket. I don't expect either of those options, especially her remarrying, to happen any time soon. The same way I don't expect hell to freeze over. My credit card, I've only got one, is in a constant state of being maxed out. And here's a newsflash for you: when most months you barely make the minimum payment, the debt grows larger not smaller.

Lila Alston's money will keep me afloat and the wolves from the door for another month or two. But only if I don't blow it on something totally unnecessary. The chances of that happening? Too high to contemplate. My former shrink—who I visited only because my ex-wife insisted on one last ditch attempt to save a marriage that never should have happened in the first place—would have said it was part and parcel of my overall self-destructive behavior. "You understand, Pete," my therapist once said, and this in front of my ex-wife, which only provided her with that much more ammunition to use against me, "that when you do things like that," fill in the blanks as to what she was referring to, "you're punishing yourself, don't you?"

"Not to mention everyone else around you," my wife muttered.

"For what?" I asked, knowing full well that following up would only make things worse.

Not that there weren't plenty of things that deserved punishment. Give my ex a pen and a large yellow legal pad and she would have come up with quite a list, I'm sure.

Out of the corner of my eye I could see (or was it a sixth sense?) my ex-wife shaking her head and rolling her eyes. It was something I didn't actually have to witness because I'd been on the receiving end of that disapproving reaction way too many times. Once I said something it got locked securely in her vault only to appear later at some future date when she could use it as a weapon to either get what she wanted or simply to piss me off. It always worked. I believe she got some kind of perverse pleasure out of seeing me lose my shit, as if it reinforced all the bad feelings she had about me. But looking back, I can also see that it was a pretty effective way of controlling me and ultimately getting what she wanted.

I could see the shrink straining to come up with some kind of pithy, brilliant response but evidently, she thought better of it and remained silent. I don't know if it was because she knew the list was so long we'd spend the rest of the session on it, or that she realized the monumental futility of trying to answer the question.

I disappear into my little cubicle in Philly's real estate office every day, rain or shine. I do this if for no other reason than to get myself out of the apartment, while at the same time allowing me the illusion that I'm actually getting some work done. I get there by ten, ten thirty, sit in front of my laptop surfing the web or playing video games till about noon when I head out to lunch. Back by one thirty or two, then I put in another couple hours playing on the computer before calling it a day.

This is what I laughingly call my life.

Over the course of a week, there are a handful of calls. One telemarketer trying to induce me to take an all-expense paid trip to Florida with the only string attached my having to listen to a sales pitch for a condo. Usually, I hang up. This time, desperate to make it appear as if I might be doing some meaningful business, I hang on for the whole spiel. The second call is from my ex-wife berating me for not being on time with my monthly payment. That call gives me some satisfaction, since I'm able to threaten her with the specter of going back to court to renegotiate the terms of our divorce, since I'm the one who's only one step away from applying for food stamps. This isn't quite true, of course, but it is close enough to true for me to surprise even myself when she backs off.

Friday afternoon, just as I'm about to pack it in for the weekend, I look up to find a guy standing in front of my desk. Youngish, early thirties maybe, unshaven, wearing faded blue jeans, a black T-shirt, and a rumpled brown leather bomber jacket, he has what I take to be a desperate look on his face. It's a look I recognize immediately. It's the look I've seen countless times, right before someone tries to hire me for some particularly lurid and dishonorable task.

"You Pete Fortunato?" he asks.

"That's me. What can I do you for?"

His eyes dart back and forth, like he's on something. Maybe drugs. Maybe alcohol. Maybe caffeine. Maybe fear. Whatever it is, it's making me nervous. He keeps looking over his shoulder, like he's afraid someone's watching him.

"You got somewhere we could maybe have a little more…privacy?"

I spread my hands out in front of me, indicating what is virtually an empty office, except for a lone sales agent on the phone near the front of the office. Either Philly's sales agents are out showing apartments or they've whacked a few hours off the normal work day and left early for the weekend.

"It is what it is, my friend."

"Yeah, well, I don't feel comfortable talking out here…in the open." Watching his eyes dart back and forth as he occasionally looks over his shoulder is making me dizzy. I gotta get this guy someplace where he can relax.

Philly has a room in back he sometimes uses for private meetings. Using it isn't one of the privileges I'm paying for. But, what the hell? Philly is gone for the weekend and since no one else in the office pays much attention to me or what I do—I suspect most of his staff don't even know who I am or why I am here, sitting behind a desk in the back of the room—I figure I can use the conference area. The door might be locked, but if it is, the key is likely somewhere in Philly's desk. If not, I'm pretty confident my unofficial skeleton key, the lone credit card in my wallet, will get me into the room.

"There's a conference room back there," I say, jerking my thumb over my right shoulder like I am hitching a ride. "Lemme see if it's open."

The door is unlocked, so I escort my nervous visitor, who continues look over his shoulder toward the front of the office, as if someone is watching us from the street.

There is a long conference table in the room. I take a seat at the head of it and he sits to my immediate left, close enough to make me uncomfortable.

"So, what's going on?" I ask, as I lean back in my chair, hands folded behind my head.

"I need to hire you," he says, his knee bobbing up and down like a jackhammer.

"First off, why don't we start with your name?"

He hesitates a moment.

"And please don't waste my time with any John Smith crap."

He hesitates another moment before he says, "Travis. Travis Chapman."

Jesus Christ. This is Lila Alston's boy-toy?

He smiles. "You know who I am, don't you?"

"Yeah. I know exactly who you are."

"You're the guy she hired to find Donnie, aren't you?" He doesn't wait for an answer. "Which means you're the guy that broke into my apartment and found the body, right?"

"I don't know what you're talking about."

"Hey, man, don't bullshit a bullshitter. I know all about you. If you're into playing games, I'll just find someone else."

I'm tempted to have him do just that, but two things stop me. One, curiosity. Two, and this is by far the more important of the two reasons, I need the work.

"For what?" I say.

"I'm in trouble, man. Big trouble."

"I'll say. Cops find a stiff in your apartment, that's pretty much the dictionary definition of big trouble, my friend."

He shakes his head. "That ain't all of it, man."

"You mean there's more than the cops tagging you as the killer?"

He nods his head, yes.

"Why's that?"

"We're not there yet, man."

"It may not look like it, Travis, but I've got things to do. What the fuck is it you want from me?"

"I told ja, I wanna hire you."

"To do what?"

"To get me out of a jam."

I shake my head. I lean forward. "I think you need a good lawyer for that, my friend."

"I don't need no lawyer. I didn't kill the dude. Why would I?"

"There are probably a hundred reasons, Travis. What's that book, *Eight Million Ways to Die?* Maybe I should write a book, *Eight Million Reasons to Die.* You don't want me to start counting them off, do you?"

"Fuck you, man."

"Yeah, well, maybe. But if you're hiring me to get you off the hook, I don't think that's in the cards. If you are innocent, I was you I'd turn myself in to the cops. They're not rocket scientists but they'll figure it out quick enough."

That's what I say, rather convincingly, I think, but the truth is this is probably the last thing I'd do if I were in his shoes. In fact, I'd probably do just what Travis is doing. Look for help. Or get the fuck out of town. Thing of it is, I don't see someone like me as his savior. Anyone's savior, for that matter.

"That ain't happening," he says. And I'm sure he has his reasons, none of which concern me at the moment. What does concern me is me getting him the hell out of my office, which is the first step toward me getting him out of my life.

"Look, why don't you get to the point. Just tell me what this is all about. I can say, get lost, and we can both get on with our lives."

"It's not that simple."

"Why not? And by the way, what was Lila's husband doing in your apartment in the first place? And if you weren't there, how'd he get in?"

He ignores my question and is silent for a moment. Like he's considering whether to explain why Donald Alston had a key to his apartment. Finally, seeing he has no choice, he says, "It's not important."

"Okay. Next question would be why?"

"We had this thing going..."

"You mean you and he...?"

"No, man. Get your fucking head out of the toilet. Not that kind of thing."

"What kind of thing then?"

"It was a business thing."

"What could you and he possibly be in business?"

"I don't know if I should talk about that now."

"If not now, Travis, never. Because I'm heading out the door..." I play my bluff which isn't really a bluff, and start to get up. But before I get far, he grabs my arm and won't let go. He has a powerful grip—a quick image of him spending hours working out in a gym flashes by—and without much effort he pulls me back down into my chair. I don't like being manhandled. I promise myself, anger management or not, the next time he lays a hand on me, I lay him out.

He lets go of my arm and I sit back down as does he. He cradles his head in his hands. He isn't going to cry, is he? When he finally looks up at me again, he has this crazy look and his eyes are practically spinning in their sockets. You know, that *Exorcist* kind of thing.

"Okay, man. I guess I gotta tell you everything."

Suddenly, like one of those wind-up toys, he runs out of steam. His body slumps. His mouth shuts. He closes his eyes.

Something big is going to be revealed. Something I probably shouldn't even know. But I can't help myself, and so I say, "What's going on, Travis?"

9
A Not So Modest Proposal

Travis says he isn't comfortable in a space that makes him feel "vulnerable." For one thing, he thinks the room might be "bugged." I try to explain to him this isn't the Oval Office and besides, I'm pretty sure Philly wouldn't bug his own conference room—having nothing to do with ethics and everything to do with cost. But it isn't worth the effort or the time to convince Travis, so now we're sitting at a table in the back of some poorly lit dive bar on 10th Avenue. A couple more avenues to our left and we'd be swimming in the Hudson with the rest of the fishes.

Two untouched, once frosty now just sweating glasses of beer sit in front of us. I can tell Travis isn't going to start the conversation—he seems to be in some kind of trance, staring at some mysterious point over my shoulder—so I get the ball rolling.

"How the hell did you get mixed up in something like this?" I ask.

His head snaps up and he seems to come out of whatever state he was in.

"He made me an offer I couldn't refuse." He smiles when he says it. At least he has a sense of humor. Or maybe he's dead serious. I'm not sure which, but what I am sure of is that I'll find out soon enough.

"Like what?"

"All this shit is confidential, right?" he asks, his hand flapping back and forth between us, as if we've just sealed some unspoken contract.

"You mean like if I'm a priest or a shrink?"

"Yeah. You're a private dick, right? And you got rules about this kind of stuff, right? Like a code? Like you don't give up your clients? Am I right?"

"Yeah. Sure," I say, though there is no such code and even if there was, what would be the chances of me sticking to it, especially if it put me in a jam I couldn't get out of? And even if there actually is a code, what's he gonna do if I break it? Sue me? Yeah, right. That'll do him a lot of good.

"So, from now on, this is just between you and me, right? I mean, I'm officially invoking the code. Or do we need some kind of signed thing? Or do I have to pay you something first? Like I could give you a symbolic dollar or something."

I wave my hand over the table, as if I'm a magician getting ready to pull an imaginary rabbit out of an imaginary hat. "Code invoked. Let's start at the beginning. How did you and Alston meet?"

"I met him at this midtown bar, near the theater district."

"Where you work?"

"No. Different bar. I'd been in this off-off-Broadway showcase thing. Not far from here, as a matter of fact. No big deal. Just a showcase. I figured maybe an agent would show up and…"

He focuses on my fingers tapping on the table like I'm Buddy Rich and realizes he might be losing me, so he'd better pick up the pace.

"I was at the bar, having a toot before heading home. This dude sits down next to me and says something like, 'You were pretty good in that play. Maybe the only good thing.' It wasn't anything big, you understand. I had a pretty small part. More than a walk-on, but less than like a supporting role kind of thing. But he was right. I was pretty good. It's my job to make something out of nothing and I thought I'd nailed it that night. Too bad no one was coming to see it...I couldn't believe he'd been in the audience...I mean there were what, maybe twenty-five people there. And most of them were friends of the actors, the writer or the director. Actually, it was a piece of shit, if you ask me..."

"Travis," I snap my fingers in front of his face a couple times. "I don't give a shit about your acting career. Just tell me what happened, okay?"

"Yeah. Right. Sure. Anyway, he starts the conversation and, you know, he's asking me things like how long I been an actor? Did I do something else for a living? Where was I from? Do I have anything else lined up? That kinda thing. He buys me a couple drinks. Nice enough guy, I guess. I mean, he kept paying, so what the hell, right?"

"Was he trying to pick you up?"

"You know, at first that's what crossed my mind. But I'm pretty tuned into that kinda shit, and the vibe wasn't there, if you know what I mean."

I don't. All I care about is to keep him talking until he tells me what I need to know.

"He had a point to all this chatter?"

"Yeah. He had a point, all right. Finally, he gets down to it. He asks me what I do for a living. I tell him I tend bar. He wonders if I'm looking to pick up a little extra cash. I say, sure. Listen, I could always use some extra cash. So, I ask him what he has in mind."

He stops and licks his lips. He takes a swig of beer. "You know, I wonder if they got any pretzels or some kind of snack stuff. I just realized I haven't eaten since breakfast. That sound you hear is my stomach growling."

"I'll get you something to eat, Travis, as soon as you tell me what you want to tell me."

"Okay, man. But come to think of it, I think I'm gonna need more than just pretzels or nuts."

"I'll buy you a whole fucking dinner, man. Just get on with it."

"Yeah. Okay. So, I ask what kind of job he has in mind. Remember, he was well-dressed, but in a business way, not like in a mobbed-up way. You know the difference, right?"

My head drops. "Yeah, I know the difference," I say even though I don't know what the fuck he's talking about. I just want to keep him talking because eventually I figure he's going to get to the point and then I can turn him down. Because the idea of working for this doofus kinda turns my stomach. Besides, I don't see the idea of getting involved with someone who's had a stiff found in their bed in their apartment is any kind of a genius move.

"Anyway, the guy looked legit and I figured it wasn't likely to be something, you know, like illegal. 'Cause if it was, I don't think I would have gotten involved. I mean, you've seen those *Dateline* things, right? Where the husband hires someone to kill his wife or vice versa? There's no way I wanted to get involved in something like that."

Chapman is an actor, probably capable of many things, but I don't see potential killer as one of them. Even if it is something he's willing to try, I don't see him being able to pull it off without literally or figuratively shooting himself in his own damn foot. Nope. That *Stranger on a Train* shit is definitely out of the question.

Nevertheless, I ask, "Is that what this was?"

"Nah. Not strictly speaking. He didn't want her dead." He smiles. I can tell he's giving it a beat for dramatic effect. Probably something he's learned in acting class. Turns out, I'm right. Not necessarily about the acting class but about the dramatic effect.

"...He wanted to pay me a grand to hook up with his wife."

"You mean, have an affair with her?"

"Yeah. That's right. An affair."

What the fuck is this all about?

"Why?"

"That's what I wanted to know. I mean, who the hell pays someone to have an affair with his own wife?"

Curiouser and curiouser.

"What'd he say?"

Chapman shrugs. He knows he's got me hooked and he's loving every minute of it. A big, fat smile is on his face. The kind of smile you want to wipe off just for the satisfaction of seeing it gone. But that's before my anger management classes. Now, it's a whole different, more patient, more accepting me.

"He wanted to divorce her but he didn't want to have to give her half of everything. So, he said if he could prove she was having an affair he could pretty much shut her out. It might have been something in a pre-nup, but I'm just guessing about that part. What do I know about divorce?" He takes a hit of his beer. "What do I know about people with money?"

"It's a no-fault state, Travis."

He looks at me wide-eyed.

"What's that mean?"

"It means you don't need a reason for getting a divorce in this state and his wife stepping out on him wouldn't affect the settlement one way or another."

"Really?"

"That's right."

He runs his hand through his thick, dirty blond hair. "Well, I didn't know that. I thought you had to find your husband with another chick. Or a dude. Or like if he beat you up all the time." He shrugs. "Made sense to me at the time. I ain't no lawyer."

"So, you agreed to do it?"

"Well, I mean, not right away. There was a little more back and forth. I even got him to raise the amount and even give me a per diem. Like, you know, for expenses."

"I know what a per diem is, Travis."

He smiles. His top teeth are straight, but the bottom are crooked. Like he'd run out of dough before the whole job could be completed. Maybe he figured no one sees the bottom teeth anyway. I know how those things go. Dental work is expensive.

But he's an actor and probably got them done for those movie close-ups while I'd earned mine legitimately, the result of not ducking quick enough.

"I don't care about the money part," I say. "I want to hear about the back and forth part."

"Man, why's that important?"

"Travis, my friend, you got somewhere else to be?"

"Not really."

"Then let's do it my way. Tell me about the conversation. Everything you remember."

"Okay," he begins, lifting his beer and taking a couple quick swigs, as if that will lubricate his answers. "He wants me to romance her. Those were his exact words. 'Romance her.' I ask him to be more specific. He says, like take her out for a drink, dinner—he says he'll pay for everything. Then, after a while, he says things should progress to where I should sleep with her. But he wants it to be more than just a one-night stand. He wants it to be like a real relationship. He even said, 'If she falls for you, all the better.' Can you believe that, man? His wants his fucking wife to fall in love with me." He smiles. "Not that that wasn't a distinct possibility," adds Mr. Charm.

"And he claimed it was all about the divorce?"

"Yeah. Only I guess it wasn't."

"How's that?"

"You'll see."

"Does he tell you how to do it?"

"You mean, like the details?"

"Yes. The details."

"Like you want the blow by blow?"

"Travis…"

He shrugs. "Okay. Okay. He left that shit up to me. He said he'd get me her schedule, but that I should come up with how and when. He said I should think of it as an improv kind of thing. It had to look natural, he said. Because his wife is no dummy. He said he knew I could pull it off from what he saw up there on stage."

His chest puffs up as if there's someone behind him with a bicycle pump.

I can't decide whether I'm dealing with a bunch of nitwits or that I'm missing something important and there's an element of devious genius involved. Either way, I'm curious enough to see where Travis thinks I come in.

"Didn't this seem a little strange to you?"

"Sure."

"Then why'd you do it?"

He rubs his thumb and forefinger together.

I get it. Join the club.

"So, it was all about money."

"You got it, pal. The dough was much too good to pass up. You've been to that hole I work in, right?"

I nod.

"Do you blame me?"

I don't. Who am I to judge? I'm a private dick, for god's sake. I dig into people's lives. I root through their garbage. I spy on them. I hope to find them in compromising positions and then I expose them for who and what they are. I'm a fucking junkman and I work in a junkyard. I see people at their worst. So bad, it sometimes even makes me feel better about myself. Nothing surprises me anymore. And I, too, get paid for it. Although, I have to admit, sometimes I wonder if maybe I wouldn't do it anyway. Just for the fun of it. That's when I know it's time for a drink. Or two.

"He gave me her usual schedule, you know, like where I'd likely bump into her. Then he gave me a few photographs of her. You know, so I wouldn't pick up the wrong chick. And let me tell you, she's real easy on the eyes, right? I mean, come on, this looked to me like it was going to be a pretty good gig."

"So, you made contact with her and moved in from there."

He nods. "It was easy, man. I mean, it wasn't like she didn't make herself available. But things didn't quite work out the way they were supposed to."

"What's that mean?"

"I mean, you've met her, right?"

"I have."

"So, you know she's no dumb blonde in a short, tight skirt."

"She's a redhead, Travis."

His face tightens. "I know that, man. It's a joke. You know, playing on the stereotype. Anyway, it didn't take her long to figure it out."

"Figure what out?"

"That I was working for her husband."

"How'd she pick up on that?"

"She was playing around. Saying things like she was much too old for me. And she grabbed my wallet. You know, to kind of check out my driver's license, and she found his business card."

I shake my head. This guy is even dumber than I thought.

"You kept his business card in your wallet?"

"Yeah. Who thought she'd ever see it? You ever willingly give your wallet to anyone?"

I ignore his question. The last thing I want is to get involved in a lifestyle discussion with Travis Chapman. "How'd she react?"

He shrugs. "Kinda surprised me. I mean, at first I tried to talk myself out of it."

"How?"

"I made up some cock and bull story about wanting to know something about her husband, so I went to his office and snatched his card off his secretary's desk."

"She believed you?"

"Not for a second. She knew it was bullshit. Asked me where his office was and I drew a blank. I wasn't prepared…That was my bad. As an actor, you always gotta be prepared. You always gotta be ready for the unexpected. You have to watch your partner…"

Did I really want an acting seminar?

"Travis!"

"Oh, sorry…"

"How'd she react?"

"Surprised the hell out of me. I mean, she didn't blow up or anything like that. She didn't tell me to get the fuck out of there, which is what I woulda done. She didn't go running back to her husband and read him the fuckin' riot act. Well, maybe she did, but she certainly didn't tell me she was going to. Instead, she told me she wanted things to continue the way they were."

"Even though she knew it was a setup?"

He nods. "Women, right? And get this. She even said she'd pay me to keep me my mouth shut and continue to make it seem like we were into each other. Pretty sweet, right? Getting paid off from both ends."

He has a big, fat smile on his face, obviously enormously proud of himself. As if he did anything special to make it happen. I know he's just dying for me to ask how she was between the sheets or if they're still getting it on, which I doubt considering what an ice princess she is. But damned if I'm going to give him the satisfaction. Not that I give a fuck.

"So, she didn't want her husband to know she knew about him hiring you?" I ask, trying to get my head wrapped around this whole whacky situation. This was getting complicated. Suddenly, everyone had skin in this crazy game. Everyone was screwing everyone else. Literally and figuratively. And I can't figure out why. It's like some silly French farce. It doesn't make sense. It's like something out of one of those James Cain novels that when you read it you think, *Now why didn't I think of that?*

"Pretty incredible, right?" he grins, giving me a good look at those choppers.

"Among other things."

"Well, hold onto your hat, Petey-boy, because it gets even crazier."

If he calls me that one more time, anger management be damned, I am going to haul off and belt him in his most important asset: his face.

"Do tell," I say, trying to control my temper. There's very little about this guy I like and he's not making it any more likely that's going to change.

"Okay, I gotta back up a little. You know, like fill in some information I left out."

"Be my guest," I said, "but make it the abridged version. I don't have all night."

Normally, I'd be losing interest about this time, but this is crazy enough to do the opposite. This shit is so off the wall, so bizarre, that it captures my attention. All of it. And besides, it's not like I have anywhere else to be.

"Be patient, man. I'm getting to it. Okay? So, here's where we're at. This dude hires me to seduce his wife. Wifey figures it out, but for some reason she wants to keep the parade marching on."

"Did you ask why?"

"To be honest, man, I didn't fucking care. Not after she offered to match what he was paying me. A classic case of double-dipping."

"That didn't make you suspicious?"

"Sure, it did. I ain't no dummy, man. But that kinda dough means I don't have to work in that pit tending bar. It means I can pay for my classes, maybe even get my ass out to the coast. Look, I asked, just out of curiosity, you know, but she just smiled and said, 'It's none of your business, darling. You're either in or out.' She's one cool cucumber, man. Anyway, I figure, what the hell? It's a damn good payday and all I gotta do is hang out with this chick every so often. Believe me, I've had worse gigs. Way worse."

This time, I couldn't help myself from asking, "Did you continue to sleep with her?"

He smiles. "That's a very personal question, man."

"Then give me a personal answer."

"Nah. that pretty much ended."

He seems disappointed. "I mean, I coulda kept going, you

know." He rams his fist into the air a couple times. "But she wasn't into it and I'm not one of those guys who forces himself on women. Don't have to. And with all this Me-Too stuff anyone who does is an idiot. All she wanted was for us to be seen together. I think she believed her husband had someone watching us. Maybe someone like *you* was on our trail." The *you* came out as an insult but am I gonna get all hot and bothered by something this asshole says? Not a chance. Besides, I know who and what I am. Maybe that's what keeps me up most nights.

"She wanted him to think it was still working. I think she got a thrill outta it. She was like this fucking puppet master…"

I really don't need Chapman analyzing the situation for me. Or anything else for that matter. So, I cut in.

"How long did this go on?"

"Couple weeks, maybe."

"Okay. So, how do I fit in?" I ask, hoping to move this thing along. Let's be honest. I didn't see Travis being much of a payday for me.

"Relax. We're almost there. Hey, what about that food?"

"When we're actually *there*, Travis," I said, suddenly realizing I didn't have to sit here all night, listening to him babble about something that didn't concern me and probably never would. This whole thing didn't do much to remove that bad taste from my mouth. I'd almost been stiffed once, by Lila Alston, and the sooner I could extricate myself from these wackos, the better.

"I'm fainting from hunger, man," Travis whined.

Jesus Christ. I'm dealing with a fucking child. Suddenly, it's like he's the Energizer Bunny losing energy and I gotta recharge his battery. But if I don't, I could be sitting here all night. So, I go to the bar, grab a bowl of peanuts, bring it back, and drop it in front of him.

"Eat."

"You said dinner, man."

"Consider this the appetizer. Now, finish up."

He grabs a handful of peanuts and stars popping them in his

mouth one at a time.

"After a while, things started to fall apart."

"How so?"

"Alston kept pressuring me."

"About what?"

"He wanted all kinds of information about his wife."

"About you and her?"

He shakes his head.

"Nah. At this point I don't think he could care less about that."

"What kind of information was he after?"

"He didn't say exactly. He just kept asking me all these questions about her. Some of them were trivial, some of them were kind of personal. Like he wanted to know if she ever talked about him. Or if she had any other 'friends' she hung out with. And he wanted to know how she spent her money."

"Did he mean friends like you?"

"You mean like lovers?"

"Yeah."

"No. I don't think he was interested in that. Besides, I think it was only me. I mean, I couldn't swear to it or anything, because she's not exactly the kind of chick you can trust. But," he taps his gut, "this tells me it was only me."

"Did you tell Alston everything he wanted to know?"

He smiles. "You may think I'm a moron, Fortunato, but I'm not. I'm not one of those MENSA freaks but," he taps his head, "it's not all oatmeal up here. I realized I was in a pretty unique situation. Playing both ends against the middle. And I knew if I played my cards right, I could make it last a while. And the longer it lasted the more," he rubs his thumb and forefinger together, "there was for me. They might have thought they were dealing with a patsy, but they weren't. When you come right down to it, we were all playing each other. The idea was that everyone should get what they want. But that's not always the way it goes, is it? Besides, knowledge is power, right? The more

I knew the better position I was in. I tell him everything he needs to know then the golden goose stops laying those eggs. And where does that leave me? I'll tell you where. Back tending bar in that fucking shithole."

"Did you lie to him?"

"That's the beauty of it. I never actually lied to him. I didn't always tell him everything, but I never lied to him. I mean, come on, how many times does someone like me find himself in a sweet spot like that? I figured if I worked it right, I could squeeze more dough out of both of them, without the other knowing what was going on. To pull that off, sometimes I had to play dumber than I am. Just another role, Petey."

I don't like that Petey stuff, but I'm too hooked by his story to disabuse him from using that name, which might be misinterpreted into that we're friends. One thing I am not, and that's Travis Chapman's friend.

He pops another peanut into his mouth.

"You know, after a while, it actually became kinda fun. Like I was some kind of weird secret undercover agent."

"Being in the middle isn't always the safest place to be. You're a sitting target for both sides. And if they both come at you…"

"Tell me about it. But remember, I'm an actor. I'm used to playing roles. Had a small part in one of those *Law & Order* spinoffs. Lying is what it's all about. But you gotta be convincing. Let's face it. We're all selling something. Only bottom line is, we're not selling can openers, we're selling ourselves. The more convincing you can be, the better the performance. Besides, I had an exit strategy."

"Like what?"

"If I could keep it rolling long enough, I was going to ditch the city and head out to the coast. I figured if I strung them along, I could save up some serious coin. Enough to get me out there, set me up in a place out there, maybe even get a cheap set of wheels…"

I'm getting anxious. I can tell because my right leg keeps

jerking up and down like a jackhammer. I've known plenty of guys like Travis. They're all about the drama. They're deeply and ever-lastingly in love with themselves. They're fascinated by whatever they have to say. They need to hold onto the attention as long as possible. See me. Hear me. Love me. That's what, in the short run, makes guys like Travis irresistible to women. They hope the self-love of guys like this will magically transfer into love for them. And maybe then they can love themselves. Only, it never does. That's when they come to guys like me for help.

I want him to shut the fuck up already. I need to get out of there and to do that I have to shut Travis down.

"I get how you got involved with them, Travis, now let's get to the point where I come in."

"Yeah, yeah. First off, I gotta tell ya, I ain't never been in any real trouble before this. I mean, you know, when I was a kid, petty ante shit. Like a little boosting from the neighborhood five and dime. Tipping a few cows. Slamming a few mailboxes. Kid stuff like that. And maybe I took advantage of people from time to time. Like making promises I know I can't keep. Saying I'd do things I don't do. And okay, maybe a little more serious teenage shit like B and E, just to see if I could get away with it. And maybe I've got a bit of hustler in me, okay? I cop to that. But every actor has to have that. Life's a con, man. You get away with what you get away with and then you don't. I mean, that's what we're all about, right? Illusion. Making someone believe something that ain't. Let's face it, the best actors, Brando, Pacino, DeNiro, they're nothing more than con men. Good ones, sure. That's where I want to be someday. We make you believe something that's not true. We make you believe we're someone we're not. You know what I mean, right?"

I nod. They might not be deep thoughts, but I'd have trouble arguing with most of what he's saying.

"But nothing serious like this has turned out to be." He pops a few more peanuts into his mouth, like he's an elephant in the circus.

"What did Alston want you to do, Travis?"

He puts his head down. I know exactly what he's doing. He's practicing his lines. Figuring out how he's going to say what he's going to say. Like he's prepping for a performance. Finally, after a few seconds, he lifts his head. He's ready.

"He said business wasn't going so good."

"What business was that?"

"He invested money for people and some of his investments weren't doing so good. He was scared shitless people were going to find out and ask for their money back, money he didn't exactly have."

"Bernie Madoff shit?"

"I guess," he says, with a blank look on his face, as if he has no idea who Madoff is.

"So, what does that mean, 'didn't exactly have'?"

"Ever been overdrawn on the bank? Ever write a check you didn't want cashed because you knew it was going to bounce? Well, that's the way it was with Alston."

"So, he needed money."

"Yeah."

"How did he plan to get it?"

"He had a few ideas."

"Like?"

Travis runs his hand slowly across his face, starting on his left cheek and ending up on his right. I know what this means. He has an answer but he isn't necessarily going to tell it to me. It's my job to get what he doesn't want to give.

"Look, Travis," I say, trying to empty as much contempt from my voice as possible, "you want me to help you, I have to know everything. I'm not going into a situation that can blow up in my face. You don't want to come clean, fine. But if not, this conversation is over and you can find yourself someone else."

"I can make things tough for you."

My face hardens. I stare straight into his eyes. If there's one thing you don't want to do with me, it's challenge me. I don't react well to threats. I never back down from a fight, and it's not going to happen with this pretty-boy punk.

"You think you're the first person to threaten me? There's something you ought to know about me, Travis. I don't mind getting my hands dirty. I get hit, I hit back. And twice as hard as I get hit. You want to be friends, fine. I can be a good friend, even a great friend. But what you don't want is me as an enemy. Know why?"

He remains silent, but I can see from his face I've got him on the defensive.

"Because I don't give a fuck. And when you don't give a fuck it means you have nothing to lose. You? Well, you obviously have something to lose, my friend, which is why you came to me in the first place, isn't it?"

He nods. I can see he thinks I'm his only chance to get out of whatever shit he's in. I won't tell him that's unlikely to be true and, if it is, how hopeless that makes it for him.

I expect him to ask me to try to help prove he didn't kill Donald Alston, but that isn't it at all. What he wants from me is a lot more complicated. And a lot more dangerous.

He throws up his hands.

"Okay. I'm sorry. I didn't mean to piss you off. I just gotta know I can trust you."

I lean back, knitting my hands at the back of my neck. "You don't have a choice, my friend."

He hesitates. He's thinking. I can practically hear the wheels grinding. "I guess you're right. It started when he asked me if I wanted to partner up with him."

"Partner up? In what?"

"Some deal he got himself involved in."

"What kind of deal?"

"With the guys."

"What guys?"

Travis rolls his tongue across his lips. "He wasn't specific."

He's lying. He knows what guys.

"Dammit, Travis. Either you tell me everything so it makes sense or find someone else to torment."

"No. You're my guy. You're already mixed up in this. Whether you like it or not..."

"Lucky me," I mutter. "How do you figure I'm already mixed up in this?"

"First off, you're working for Lila."

"*Worked* for Lila. I've been off the clock for nearly a week now."

He shrugs. "Same difference. You're the one who found the body."

"How do you know that?"

"I'm no idiot."

"That's debatable," I mutter under my breath, though certainly loud enough for him to hear it. But he doesn't react. He probably wasn't listening. He's trying to figure out what he can say and what he can't. It's going to be a long evening if I let him get away with that shit.

"Okay, say I was in your apartment and I did find the body. How do you figure it involves me in anything? I was just doing what I was paid to do—find Alston. I found him. I got paid." I brushed my hands together. "Case closed."

He smiles. "You can say 'case closed' all you want but that doesn't mean it's over. Not with these guys."

At first, I think he means the cops, but from the look of fear on his face, I realize he's talking about someone else.

"Again with the guys. What guys?"

He takes his forefinger and bends back his nose.

"The mob?"

He cocks his head to one side.

"What the hell was Alston involved in?"

"I'm guessing it was some kind of money laundering thing."

"Guessing?"

"I don't know for sure."

"For who?"

"He didn't tell me and I didn't want to know."

"How was he laundering the money?"

"He had a few ways, but I didn't really have that conversation with him. It was none of my business."

"What did he need you for?"

"He hired me to do certain tasks."

"What kind of tasks?"

He leans forward and his voice lowers. "I don't think I'm going to talk about those things now."

"Why not?"

"Because I'm smart enough not to give you anything you can hold over my head. And it's probably in your best interest too, not to know too much."

I throw up my hands. "Look, Travis, this is mumbo-jumbo bullshit. I've got things to do. Why not just tell me what you want to hire me for and let's end this thing?"

"I'm afraid for my safety. I know things…"

"I'm not a bodyguard, Travis. Go to the fucking cops if you want protection."

"You're an ex-cop, aren't you?"

"How do you know that?"

"I've done my due diligence."

I doubt he even knows what that phrase means. It suddenly strikes me: This has Lila Alston's fingerprints all over it. She would not have hired me without knowing what she was getting. Or without checking me out. This is totally fucked up. Everyone is talking to everyone else and I'm the only one no one is talking to. If I'm smart, I get up and walk the fuck out of here.

"If you've done it then you know I was a deputy in a small town upstate and it was for less than a year. Hardly long enough to get my uniform dirty. Trust me, that doesn't make me a cop."

"You were trained, right? You know certain, let's say, 'techniques.'"

I smile. I know what he thinks he means. He's watched way

too many of those superhero movies where the good guy kicks
ass against four or five bad guys. I've been a brawler, sure. But I
never got into it unless I figured I had a good chance of coming
out on top. I may have a temper, but I'm also smart enough to
pick my spots. At least now I am.

"I wasn't a very good student," I say, trying to tamp down
expectations.

"You're a tough guy, Fortunato. I know you've gotten into
your fair share of scrapes. You don't take shit. That's what I
need. Someone who's not afraid to stand up to shit. I've got
good reason to believe that I'm in…jeopardy."

"From who?"

"From the same people who took out Donald Alston."

"You're telling me you didn't have anything to do with that
and you know who did?"

His eyebrows shoot up. "Are you kidding? Me? Murder
someone? That's ridiculous. Why would I? What would I have
to gain? He was the golden goose, man. Why would I kill the
golden goose?"

"His body was found in your apartment, Travis."

"That doesn't mean shit. In fact, it proves I didn't have anything to do with it."

"How's that?"

"Would I be dumb enough to kill the dude in my own
apartment and then take off? Look, I'm no rocket scientist, but
I've got street smarts. I know the score, and there's no way I'd
do anything like that."

"So, why was he even there?"

"That's irrelevant to this conversation. He was there and he
got killed. And if I was there with him, I'd probably be dead,
too."

"So, who did do it?"

"Fuck I know."

"You just said you knew who took him out."

"No, I didn't."

Yes, he did. But I'm not going to sit there wasting my time trying to get him to say who did it. In fact, the less I know, the better.

"Are you going to help me or not?"

"Not."

"Why not?"

"Because I don't see what's in it for me."

"Money."

"Money's not much use to me if I'm not around to spend it, Travis."

"Who says you're not going to be around?"

"There's already been one murder. And you're practically pissing in your pants, which tells me that might not be the end of it."

He's silent for a moment. I'm starting to enjoy the quiet when he pipes up again.

"So, you're really not going to help me?"

"No."

"But I don't know where else to turn."

I shrug. "Sorry, pal. Not my problem."

A panicked look crosses his face. He really is scared. For a second, just a split second, I feel sorry enough for him to try to help him out. But that would be stupid, and I might be a lot of things but stupid isn't one of them.

10
Going to Fist City

On my way back to my apartment I begin to have second thoughts. I know I've done the right thing, not letting myself get dragged into whatever mess Travis has gotten himself into. It's *his* mess, not mine. Nevertheless, I'm starting to sense the beginnings of that bad taste in my mouth. I don't know why, since I've got that cash from Lila and I just turned down Travis's offer to work for him. Maybe part of it is fear that I'm not really free and clear of Travis, a dead man named Donald Alston, and his scheming wife, Lila. And walking away as if none of it ever happened isn't likely to change that.

One thing's for sure: I know I'm not done with the cops. As long as there's an unsolved murder, I'm still on the hook. They know I was on the scene, but they don't know why and they don't know for how long. I'm pretty confident they don't suspect me of the murder—they'll be hard-pressed to come up with a motive that makes any sense—but I'm also pretty sure they believe I know more than I've told them. And it wouldn't be the first time the law went after the easiest target instead of the best. Look, I wasn't much of a cop during those eight or nine months I was on the force up there in *Hicksville, USA*, but I did learn that cops, especially the good ones, have a sixth sense when it comes to crime. It's rooted deep in their DNA.

They know when something's not right. They know when someone's lying. They know when someone's holding back the truth. It's a stink most of us can't pick up. But they can. The good ones, and there some very good ones (along with the mediocre ones like me), who are adept at finding the missing parts that make the puzzle come together. Not all of them and not all the time, but enough to add to reasons for my insomnia. Not that it needs a reason. My only hope is they solve this thing quick. Only then will I be completely off the hook and able to get on with my life, such as it is.

But having Travis Chapman in my life complicates any shot at a normal existence.

For the next few days, I go about my business, which pretty much means trying to drum up work. I call a couple attorneys I know, hoping they'll throw something my way. No matter how small. I'll be happy to take scraps. I just need something to help cover the rent and pay a few bills. A couple who have been pleased with my work in the past tell me to call back in a week or so. But I can tell from their tone they're just trying to let me down easy. I let a couple bail bondsmen know I'm not above taking a skip-trace job. Or, god forbid, the lowest of the low: a repo gig. Still, no luck.

I even bite the bullet and as a last resort put up an ad on Craig's List, knowing if I do get any nibbles, it will likely either be from some crazy person having no idea what private investigators really do, or the kinds of cases I hate: getting the goods on straying spouses, which turn me into little more than a professional Peeping Tom. And then there are the jobs that are clearly illegal. Listen, in my day I've skirted plenty of laws, but it's almost always for a good reason—at least it's a good reason in my mind—which probably means I'm pretty nimble about being able to rationalize stepping over the line. Besides, it's a line that seems to be in constant motion making it that much tougher to know when I've crossed it. In the business I'm in, I'm not dealing with Boy and Girl Scouts. I'm dealing with those who are on the edge. Desperate souls who have no one else to turn to. Like me, at this very moment.

It's been nearly a week since my meeting with Travis and I'm at my desk at the back of the real estate office working late Friday evening. Working late is really a euphemism for not having anywhere else to go. It isn't that I have all that much to do, but when you spend most of the day looking for creative ways to procrastinate, things do start to pile up. Namely, paperwork I've neglected for much too long. For instance, my New York PI license is up for renewal. The form has been sitting on my desk for almost a month, but I keep putting it off because I don't have the required four hundred bucks to spare. Mostly, I'm staring out into space trying to figure which Peter I can steal from to pay Paul when both of them are as broke as I am.

It's close to eight p.m. by the time I finally accept the fact that I've long since stopped being productive. I know this because I've been playing video poker for the past hour—and I'm on a losing streak. Thank goodness it's only for fun. I figure I'll pack it in for the day, grab a burger at the local pub, then head home and see what I can find on Netflix that might help put me to sleep. I know I'm just lying to myself because in the last three nights I've gotten maybe a total of less than a dozen hours of sleep. I've got a half full container of Ambien in my medicine cabinet, but I don't want to use it. That would be giving in and then it's a slippery slope, a slope I don't want to find myself on. Besides, I've read about all these crazy things people do when they're on the pill. Like I need that. Like my life isn't crazy enough without some drug making it worse. And yeah, I've tried all those so-called natural soporifics. They may work for someone else, but they sure as hell don't work for me.

I shove all my papers into my desk drawer—with the PI renewal on top—then prepare to lock up the office for Philly, one of the few responsibilities he's given me in the event that I'm the last one out the door. "Pete," he said, his tone more serious than usual, "I'm going to entrust you with this key to the office, so you can come and go as you please during non-office hours. But if you screw up and forget to lock up when you leave, or turn off the lights, or give the key to anyone else, even once, you and me are going to have a problem. And you know what that means, right?"

"Office privileges canceled," I said, running my forefinger across my throat.

"Exactly."

I lock up and as I'm sliding the keys back into my pocket, I sense the presence of someone standing behind me, close enough to be in my space. This is not the kind of New York City neighborhood where I should worry about my safety, and it's a busy enough street that there are always people strolling by, especially this early in the evening. But it's getting dark, it's starting to rain and so the sidewalks are a little less traveled than usual.

"Fortunato?" a raspy voice asks.

I turn to find a large man, a good six inches taller than me, outweighing me by at least fifty pounds, standing practically on top of me. He's wearing a black leather jacket, a black T-shirt, and black jeans. His dark hair is pinned back in a ponytail, his face obscured by a thick, black bushy beard. He has a red kerchief tied around his neck, an earring in one ear and a tattoo of a small dagger on the left side of his neck.

This is not a reassuring look. Especially with his kisser.

He obviously has no sense of personal space because he's close enough for me to smell garlic on his breath. I start to reach for the Glock strapped to my side but stop myself before I get too far. I realize he's right up on top of me so there's no way I'll be able to get it out in time. Besides, this guy's twice my size and it's very likely he's carrying, too.

Still, I've got to reclaim some of my space, but when I go to push him away, I find he's a rock. It's like his feet are planted deep in the pavement. I'm pretty sure I'm quick enough with my hands to get in the first blow, but he looks like he can take a punch, he's most likely taken plenty of them, and with his ridiculous size advantage, going right to fist city doesn't seem like the wisest choice

"We can do this the hard way or the harder way," he growls. "Either way, you're gonna feel it, Fortunato."

There's no point trying to bluff my way out of this by telling him he's got the wrong guy. I can try to talk my way out of it but I don't know what *it* is. I decide it's best to play along and see what he wants.

"Who's asking?"

"You don't get it, do you, asshole?" he hisses. "This ain't no conversation. I ask questions, you give answers."

"Look, I've had a tough day. It's late. All I want to do is get something to eat, go home, and pass out. Why don't you just tell me what you want and we can both get on with our lives?"

"You're coming with me," he says. His jaw jutting forward, his hands stuffed into his jacket pockets makes it pretty clear saying get lost is not an option. But I'm not quite ready to give in yet. Besides having that anger problem, I also have an aversion to being told what to do and when to do it. Yeah, yeah. I know. Just another annoying trait that can and does get me in trouble. And that's why I say, "Look, I don't know you, so I think I'm just gonna walk away and pretend this never happened."

"That would be a bad idea."

"Yeah? What you gonna do out here in the middle of the street? There are cameras all over the place, man." I tip my head in the direction of where I think a camera might be, attached to a stop light at the corner. I have no idea whether there really is one there, but neither does he.

I start to turn away but he grabs me by the shoulder. His grip is powerful enough to nail me in place.

"I don't think you wanna do that," he hisses.

I can feel my temperature rising. I know this is when I should kick in those anger management techniques. But it just isn't my nature. I'm the guy who runs toward the fight not away from it.

That shrink my ex-wife and I went to would probably have said it's all part of my self-destructive streak. I want the fight just to prove that I don't run away from it. Maybe so. But it's who I am and sometimes you gotta give in to who you are.

I puff up my chest. "I don't like anyone putting hands on me, man. Not even my friends."

He doesn't flinch. He doesn't let go of me. Instead, he flashes this creepy, self-satisfied smile. At that moment I realize that in many ways we are the same person. I'm looking in the mirror at someone who's just as fucked up as me. Only trouble is, I'm his mini-me and if we do start to tangle, no matter how good I am at it, I'm gonna get my ass kicked. He knows it and I know it. All I can hope for is that he doesn't want a violent confrontation right there in public and that he's got enough self-control to avoid it. If he doesn't, even if I go down, I'll get my shots in. Bottom line: no one wins. I don't know why I need to save face by making tough-guy noises. But I do.

"This here ain't no negotiation, asshole." He doesn't raise his voice. In fact, he does the opposite, which makes it that much more menacing. "You're coming with us. Now."

He cocks his head toward a car double-parked across the street. I see a guy in the driver's seat looking in our direction. When he sees me staring at him, he opens the door and gets out slowly. His hands tapping on the hood of the car, he stands on the sidewalk side watching us. He's a big guy, too. Maybe bigger than Ponytail. He's wearing a black, thigh-length leather jacket and black baseball cap. He's also got a bushy, dark beard that hides his face.

This does not look good for me. Stupid is forever and I'm still tempted to take a shot at the guy in front of me and take off. But these guys aren't the giving up kind. Eventually, they'll grab me. And when they do, it won't be pretty. Best to go with the flow. At least for now.

"I am partial to doing things the easy way," I say.

"Good choice."

Somehow, that doesn't make me feel any better. I don't see much choice. I'm not stupid. Getting into a car with two goons almost twice my size, isn't a smart move. Confronting Ponytail and probably getting my ass kicked, even if I do get in the first blow, doesn't seem too smart either. The lesser of two evils rule seems about right here. Only I'm not sure which is the lesser, so I substitute the most expedient.

The rain has picked up. Hatless, wearing only a light-weight windbreaker, I'm getting soaked. With Ponytail behind me, his hand gripping my shoulder, we cross over to their car. Like I'm his elderly grandmother, he guides me across the street with his meaty hand clenching my elbow.

"Just get in the damn back seat and shut the fuck up," he says, finally loosening his grip of my shoulder.

I slide into the back seat which is littered with fast food wrappers, Chinese food containers, and old copies of the *New York Post* and the *Daily News*. It reminds me of my apartment after a particularly bad week of getting almost no sleep.

"You guys ever consider getting a maid in here once a week?"

The driver turns his head and I see him up close for the first time. His eyes are jet black. He's got badly pock-mocked skin and tattoos of a teardrop under his right eye and a small dagger on his neck. Ponytail looks tough, but this guy looks even tougher. I realize I've made the right decision. I know guys like this. I've tangled with them all my life. They don't have an off switch. They're sent to do something, they do it. How they do it is whatever they have to do to get it done. Consequences mean nothing. When you don't consider consequences, you can do just about anything. And you will. Especially if you're getting paid for it.

"It's not like you're fucking moving in," says Teardrop. I detect a slight accent, probably Eastern European. These guys are not Mafia. Something else. Something more dangerous.

"Give you any trouble?" Teardrop asks.

Ponytail shakes his head. "Nah, he's a real pussycat. Let's

go. *He* don't like to be kept waiting."

I wonder who *he* is, but I'm not going to waste my breath asking because I know they won't tell me.

Teardrop shifts into gear and we pull away, heading east.

"Mind telling me where we're going?"

Ponytail twists around in his seat.

"Shut the fuck up," he says.

Teardrop spits out a staccato laugh, three quick bursts, then it's over.

When we reach First Avenue, we hang a left, heading uptown. We haven't gone more than a few blocks when Ponytail turns halfway around, reaches out his hand, palm up, over the seat and says, "Okay, let's have it."

"It?" I say, even though I know what he's talking about. He'd have to be an idiot not to notice the slight bulge on my left side.

"Your piece, asshole. Unless you want me to take it from you." He glares at me. "I can use the fucking exercise."

I reach under my jacket, unhook my holster, pull out my Glock 42, the smallest pistol they make, and using two fingers, hand it over to him. I can't even remember if there are bullets in it.

"This thing cost mucho dinero, guys. I hope you're gonna take good care of it." I wait a beat. "And that I'm gonna get it back when we're done."

Ponytail doesn't answer. He simply grabs the pistol from me, examines it for a moment, then jams it into the side pocket of his leather jacket.

Teardrop takes a quick look, shakes his head, and snorts. "Lady gun."

That hurts. But he's right. I carry it more to make me feel like I'm the real deal than for protection. The only time I've used it is at a firing range. I have a vague recollection of one time when I was three sheets to the wind and was tempted to use it in a bar brawl. When I got home, I took out all the cartridges and hid them in my sock drawer. Suddenly, I'm reminded there's another item on my to-do list: it's been almost five years and my license renewal is pending. Another three hundred and forty bucks I don't have.

Ponytail turns back to me and wiggles his fingers in one of those "come hither" gestures.

"What?" I say.

"Your cell. Hand it over."

"Come on, man, what do you need that for?" I ask, knowing full well why they want it. But giving it up will cut off my last possible link with the outside world.

"Just fucking give me the fucking phone," he says.

I pull it out of my pocket and hand it to him. Before he puts it in his pocket, he looks at it, then turns back to me.

"Cute. Real cute," he says.

"What?"

"You know what. You got the fucking phone on record."

"Really? I don't know how that happened. I mean, I don't even know how to work the damn thing. Honest. It's a smart phone, man, which I guess means it's a lot smarter than I am."

"I ain't gonna argue with that," he says, as he fiddles with the phone, turning off the record function.

"I'm gonna get it back, right? All my contacts are in there. Like who the hell remembers phone numbers anymore?"

"Who knows? Maybe you won't need them," he says, flipping me the bird. Teardrop laughs.

I half expect them to blindfold me or pull a bag over my head so I don't see where they're taking me, the result of watching too many kidnap movies. But they don't seem much concerned with me knowing where I'm headed. Or is that they know it's not necessary because I'm not coming back?

As we reach the UN, Teardrop opts for the tunnel instead of the open avenue. When we emerge, rain is coming down harder, but Teardrop doesn't make a move to use the wipers. I wonder if it's a machismo thing or maybe they're busted. From the condition of the inside of the car, I wouldn't be surprised. Either way, it's not good. I'm afraid we're gonna wind up hitting something or someone. Wherever we're headed, I'm anxious to arrive in one piece.

The further we drive the more I can feel that ball of anger welling up in the pit of my stomach. It's a familiar pattern. It begins the size of a ping-pong ball and grows to the size of a baseball. If I don't do something about it, it'll keep growing. It'll travel up from my gut until it explodes out my mouth or my fists. I try to stop it by trying to remember those anger management routines. Trouble is, I can't seem to remember any of them and even if I do, I'm pretty sure they won't do me any good.

We cross 57th Street. Above us looms the 59th Street Bridge. They've renamed it the Ed Koch Bridge, after our former beloved mayor who loved asking, "How'm I doin'?" though he never seemed to care what the answer was. To New Yorkers like me, it's still the Queensboro or 59th Street Bridge.

My first apartment, a walk-up where I lived for almost a year after returning to the city from my self-induced exile upstate, is only a few blocks away. I found it right after I moved back to the city after leaving that rinky-dink police force. But let's face it. The word "leaving" sounds like I had a choice in the matter, which I didn't. It's what I tell anyone who asks, but that doesn't mean it's the truth. At best, it was a mutual parting of the ways. At worst, well, let's just say things didn't quite turn out the way I thought they would, and it was suggested that I might be in the wrong line of work. They weren't wrong. I'm not one who takes to authority easily. Or, at all.

Back in the city and I had no idea what I was going to do with myself. What little dough I had wouldn't last long in a city where a cup of designer coffee is three bucks. It was a rent stabilized apartment I sublet from a friend who hated the cold and was moving down to Miami. A few months later he called and said he wasn't coming back. The only piece of luck I think I've ever had. I wound up taking over the lease. I felt out of place living there, because the apartment was only steps away from Sutton Place, home to plenty of old money. I had neither old nor new money. But I did have a swanky sounding address.

As we head up the ramp to the bridge, Ponytail cranks up the radio and some foreign-sounding music with an incessant, insinuating heart-thumping beat reverberates in the damp, dead air of the car. It's got a slightly Eastern European feel to it, but I'm stumped as to its derivation. I'm tempted to ask, not because I really need to know or care, but because maybe a little idle conversation will loosen these guys up a little.

Meanwhile, I notice the front window beginning to fog up, making it even tougher to navigate on the slippery streets. I'm tempted to suggest Teardrop use the defogger but I'm afraid that by the time the words come out of my mouth it'll just come off sounding like an angry demand. And that, I know, will get me nowhere. So, I keep my mouth shut. If we crash, we crash. And if we do I like my chances in the back seat better than being up front.

At 72nd Street, the light turns red and we stop. This is my chance. But before I can make a move toward the door handle, Ponytail looks back and says, "Don't even try it, fuck head. Even if you get out the door I'll blast your fuckin' head off."

I can tell he means it, that this is no idle threat. In fact, I think he'd like to do it. Just to keep in practice. I shrug, sit back, and continue staring out the window. I give up planning an escape. Instead, I'm imagining what I'm going to do to these assholes if I ever get one of them alone. That's what I'm doing. For some reason this does a lot better calming me down than counting to ten does.

We continue north on First Avenue. At 96th, we hang a right, heading toward the entrance to the FDR Drive. Once we're on the Drive we could be heading anywhere north, as far as Canada even. This is not what I consider a good development.

As we turn onto the Major Deegan highway, that ball in my gut begins to grow again. For me, anxiety often turns into anger.

For a split second, I consider smashing the window, reaching out and opening the door, then rolling out onto the highway. It's a crazy idea. An idea that can't possibly work. But I can't stop my mind from going there. I start counting to ten. Slowly. My body starts to bob almost imperceptibly back and forth, like the old Jews I used to watch davening when my maternal grandfather dragged me into the synagogue in a vain attempt to let me connect with that half of my heritage. My mother's family gave up trying to get me to church. I'm sure it was the half-Jew thing, which didn't go over so well with my father's family. As far as they were concerned, I was halfway to purgatory before I was even born. My mother's side was more stubborn—maybe that's where I get it from. They didn't give up so easy. Every Jewish holiday became a battleground.

I take deep breaths, hold them for a moment, then let them out very slowly. I try to think of something pleasant to calm my nerves. Only thing is, nothing pleasant comes to mind. What does come to mind is meeting each of these guys alone and bashing their heads in. I'm pissed and getting more pissed by the minute. I know me well enough to know I can only keep my mouth shut for so long.

The further we get from Manhattan the less chance there is of me making it back in one piece. Guys like this are very good at making things disappear. My mind wanders to where my final resting place might be.

"Hey," I say, trying to out-shout the music, "maybe you can turn that down a little? I can't hear myself think back here."

No response.

I lean forward, my head between Ponytail and Teardrop, and ask again.

Still nothing.

I tap Ponytail lightly on the shoulder. He doesn't turn around. Instead, he reaches out and cranks up the volume even higher as I watch Teardrop smirk in the rearview mirror.

It's been raining the whole time we've been on the road, but only now do the wipers start to move. Slowly, they scrape across the window, sometimes stopping for several seconds, as if to catch a breath. They're only making things worse: moving the water from one side of the windshield to the other, leaving thick streaks in the window.

After passing Yankee Stadium, the very spot where I was supposed to make a name for myself as a pitching phenom, turning the team into a dynasty again, we turn off the Major Deegan and onto the Bronx River Parkway. After a couple miles, we exit onto the Morris Park section of the Bronx. I haven't been in this part of the city often, but since it's not all that far from Manhattan, I'm able to relax a bit. I'm guessing we're almost where we're going. We turn off Pelham Parkway, cross Neill Avenue then onto Rhinelander where we hang a right and pull up in front of a nondescript, red-brick, three-story building. Although there's an open parking spot maybe twenty feet behind us, Teardrop simply double-parks in front of the entrance to the building. I'm pretty sure the last thing these guys are worried about is getting ticketed.

The rain has turned into a fine mist and the fog has settled, making it difficult to see more than a block or two. The rain-slicked streets reflect light from the streetlamps. It's an eerie scene, like something out of 19th century London.

"Okay, fun's over," says Ponytail. He steps out of the car while Teardrop, after cutting the engine, remains seated. He picks up a copy of the *New York Post* lying on the seat, opens it, and starts to read. Ponytail comes around to the driver's side of the car, opens the back door, and reaches in for me.

"I'm good," I say, swinging my feet out the door.

He grabs my arm and pulls me the rest of the way out. I know what he's doing. He's trying to intimidate me. It's something I already know, so this pisses me off. I really want to take a swing at the sonuvabitch, even though I know it will only make things worse. This is a fight I can't possibly win. On the other hand, I know I'll feel a lot better if I show some kind of resistance and, against my better judgment, I'm ready to put up a fight. But before I can, Teardrop, as if sensing there might be trouble, puts down his newspaper and gets out of the car. He's even bigger than Ponytail and although the size of a man never seems to stop me from throwing a punch, the size of two men almost twice my size is a great inhibitor.

Ponytail points me toward the front door of the building, which looks like one of those mob social clubs in the East Village or Brooklyn. But I don't connect these guys with the Mafia. For one thing, they're not dressed well enough. My best guess is they're Russians or Albanians, neither of which is a good thing. I'm no expert on the Albanians or the Russians, but what I do know is they're both ruthless and violent, not a good combination. The Russians are bad, but the Albanians are worse. Much worse. Years ago, while looking for a missing young woman, I brushed up against the Albanians. They're a nasty bunch. They traffic in drugs, arms, humans, and human organs. Everything you need to know about them is summed up in a comment once made by a member of the Kielbasa Posse, a Polish mob out of Philly. "We Poles are willing to do business with just about anybody. Dominicans, blacks, Italians, Asian street gangs, Russians, but we don't go near the Albanian mob. They're much too violent and unpredictable."

I eventually found the woman, half dead in a secluded area of Central Park, beaten so bad even her own family couldn't recognize her. If that's how they treat a woman you can imagine what they'll do to a man. If I'm right about these guys being Albanians, depending on what they want from me, the chances are better than even that I will arrive but I won't necessarily depart—at least not in the same condition I'm in now.

Still grasping my left arm so hard that I'm afraid the circulation will be cut off, Ponytail leads me through a large room with maybe a dozen tough-looking dudes of varying ages trying to look busy. It reminds me of an enormous kids' playroom. At one end there's a round table covered with green felt, where four burly guys in shirtsleeves are playing cards. At another end of the room there's a pool table where a couple of young guys in black T-shirts are playing what looks to me like a game of 8-ball. Against the back wall there are two idle pinball machines side by side. Running alongside that wall is a six-foot bar with four empty stools in front. Behind the bar there's a shelf with bottles of liquor. To my right, there are a couple tough-looking kids, just out of their teens, passing around a joint while they sit in upholstered chairs and stare bleary-eyed up at a large flat-screen TV attached to the wall that's tuned to a soccer game. One of the kids has an open girlie magazine in his lap, the other is polishing what looks like an AK-15 cradled in his lap. At the far end of the bar there's a juke box.

No one pays me the slightest bit of attention. Is it because they know they'll never see me, I think, as a chill shoots up my back.

Ponytail steers me in the direction of a long hallway on the right side of the room. When I try to slow down, he gives me a hard shove forward, so hard I almost stumble over my own feet.

"Easy, big fella," I say.

From the look on his face, I can see he's not happy with me. I know he'd like to beat the crap out of me. I know this because it's the way I feel. Both of us are far too familiar with the world of violence and for guys like us it's a first response rather than a last resort. I've learned to control that part of me, at least most of the time. Guys like him would be out of a job if they learned to control their violent side. His whole life has been about violence. His fists are nothing more than another instrument of expression. Where words fail, actions rarely do. I've seen plenty of these guys like these at those anger management classes. At times, I've been one of them. Those who have been court-ordered last as long as they have to, then leave when they've put in their time, probably having even less control over their anger despite the handy tips on how to disguise or temporarily suppress it. Me? I'm there not only because going keeps my record clean, but also because, in truth, I don't like being angry all the time. I don't like to be on the edge of committing a violent act any time someone, even slightly and unknowingly, trips my switch, accidentally or on purpose. Sure, I'm there because my lawyer thinks that'll keep me out of the clink, but I'm also there because taking these classes is a form of self-preservation. Still, there's a big part of me that thinks ultimately, when push comes to shove, I will be who I am.

And why should it be any different for Ponytail?

By himself, even though he outweighs me by the weight of a Siberian husky, I think can take this asshole. If I'm quick enough, he won't see it coming. And I know just where to strike. The neck and the groin. Playing the fight out in my head, I know that with all these other guys around, I have no chance. Nevertheless, I imagine where, when, how I'd throw the first punches and where they'd land, as I choreograph this imaginary fight in my head. Evidently, the mere planning of a beatdown is enough to calm me down. I wonder if I should mention this at my next class and suggest others try it instead of counting, which has never worked for me anyway.

As we walk down a corridor that's maybe ten, fifteen feet long, we pass a bathroom on the left which stinks of a combination of urine, bleach, beer, and cigarette smoke. My stomach starts to jump and without realizing it I begin counting steps. I don't know why, but I do it anyway. For some reason, it helps anchor me in the here and now.

We stop when we reach the end of the corridor, where Ponytail hesitates a moment before giving two hard raps to the door.

A heavily accented voice says, "Yes?"

"I got your package here, boss."

"Bring it in."

Suddenly, I'm not a *he* anymore. I'm an *it*. An unwrapped package.

Ponytail opens the door and pushes me forward into the dimly lit room. I turn back to see him standing in front of the door, arms folded across his chest. His message is clear: *You want out of here, you're gonna have to get through me first.*

The room, maybe twelve by twenty, looks like someone else's idea of a cozy den. The walls are paneled in fake dark wood. There's a couch, a small round table surrounded by three chairs, and a large mahogany desk, behind which there's large upholstered chair where my host sits. The desk is clear except for a couple of glasses, a bottle of whisky, and a foreign newspaper. My host is anywhere from his late forties to mid-fifties. He's wearing a tie and powder blue button-down shirt. His hair is slicked back and he's clean-shaven. Standing to his left there's another guy in the room. He looks to be in his mid-twenties. He's wearing a neon-colored Hawaiian shirt and black, neatly pressed jeans.

I can see a resemblance to the man behind the desk. Father and son? Brothers? Uncle and nephew? Not unexpected, since criminal enterprises like these are usually clannish, only putting trust in their own.

The man at the desk motions me forward, then points to the couch. "Have a seat," he orders in an accent similar to that of Ponytail and Teardrop. I can't swear to it, but it sounds Eastern European enough to be Albanian.

"Allow me to introduce myself. I'm Sergio," he says.

"Normally, I'd probably say 'pleased to meet you, Sergio,' but we both know that'd be a lie."

He nods. His face is frozen in a scowl. When I was on the mound I called it my "game face," the one that was supposed to let the batter know that "I don't give a fuck whether I hit you or not, all I know is you're not gonna get close to me."

"Yes. It would."

I'm familiar with the structure of the Albanian mob because of that earlier brush with them. They work very much like any mid-size corporation, with a strict hierarchy resembling a pyramid. The various families are organized into as many as five or six levels, which allows them to make sure the organization can function even if some of its members are eliminated or arrested.

Each family clan is referred to as a *fis*. Every *fis* has an executive committee called a *Bajrak*. The *Bajrak* selects a high-ranking member for each unit which is led by a *Krye* who selects a *Kryetar* or underboss who is second in command. The *Kryetar* chooses a *Mik*, or "friend," who acts as a liaison to the other members of the family and is responsible for coordinating the family's activities.

The Albanians adhere to a strong code of honor, called *besa*, which is very much like a contract between members. Breaking that contract is not an option, at least it's not if you want to continue to exist in this world. This, of course, makes it very difficult for law enforcement to go after them. Breaking someone in the mob and getting them to flip is almost impossible.

Albanian gangs showed up in this country in the mid-1980s. At first, they affiliated themselves with Cosa Nostra crime families, but eventually they got strong enough to go out on their own. And that's when the real trouble began. They began to spread their wings and had no compunction about going up against their former partners.

Most likely, he's a *Kryetar*, since very few outsiders are introduced to the head of the family. But I think it's in my best interests to play dumb, keep my mouth shut, and see where this is going. I don't have a good feeling about this, but I'm hoping whatever this is about, I can talk my way out of it. At least that's what I keep telling myself.

Sergio stares me down for what seems like several minutes but is probably far less. I recognize what he's doing. It's a power play. The quieter he is, the more I'm supposed to sweat. He'd love it if I spoke first, but I'm not going to give him the satisfaction. At least not yet. It's in situations like this that my competitive streak kicks in. But like they say, you gotta know when to hold 'em and know when to fold 'em, and in this case I know I'm gonna be the one to blink first. And so I do.

"You gonna tell me why I'm here, Sergio?"

He's scored the first point and his expression begins to soften. I wouldn't call it a smile, but it's probably as close as I'm gonna get to one.

He leans back in his chair. "Under other circumstances, I would offer you something to drink, Mr. Fortunato. But I'm afraid that would send the wrong message."

"What message would that be?"

"That you are a guest. If you were a guest, I would have to treat you with respect and honor your visit." His expression changes. He stares at me with the coldest, hardest, so-brown-they're-almost-black eyes I've ever seen. One beat. Two beats. Three beats. Damn, he's good. "I'm afraid, under these circumstances that is not in the cards."

"So, I'm not a guest. What am I? And what are these circumstances you're referring to?"

"You're here because whether you know it or not, you're in the middle of a situation where you do not belong. And because you are, I believe you have certain information that we are in need of. Important information that can get you in a lot of trouble if you don't cooperate."

"I don't have any idea what you're talking about."

"All right. Have it your way. We need to find a man named Travis Chapman."

"Travis Chapman?"

He smiles, though it's definitely not the kind of smile that communicates amusement.

"You're not going to waste my time and yours by trying to make me believe you have no idea who he is."

"No. That wouldn't be wise, would it?"

"Certainly not."

"Why are you looking for Chapman?"

He closes his eyes and moves his head back and forth very slowly. I'm trying his patience. He does not like having his patience tried. And besides, I've broken protocol. I'm not here to get answers, I'm here to give them. Period.

"Okay. Fine. I get it. It's none of my business. But what makes you think I know where he is?"

"I think, Mr. Fortunato, that before I answer your question, perhaps it might help if you understand who I am and what I'm capable of doing."

"That's really not necessary," I say.

"Oh, but it is. The last thing I want is for you to misunderstand the situation, to think that your visit here has any other purpose than to give me what I want. Let me make this as clear as I can. I represent an organization, a very dangerous organization. This means I am responsible for everything that happens under my leadership. If someone or something is not right, it's my job to make it right. And there are no rules or restrictions on how far I can go to make it right. Do I make myself clear?"

"Crystal. And you've also made it clear this is not a get-to-know-you visit. If it was a visit that would make me a visitor, which means I can get up and leave any time I want. But I can't do that, can I?"

He shrugs. "There's the door behind you, Mr. Fortunato. Would you like to find out?"

I look back and see Ponytail still standing there, arms crossed just below his massive chest. I see the bulge in his jeans pocket where he's put my Glock and I see another bulge under his leather jacket where he's carrying his own weapon. I'm not going anywhere. At least not yet.

I know my only value lies in information they think I have or can get. If I give it up now, information I honestly don't have, or convince them I know nothing and never will, I'm of absolutely no value to them. That's a very risky position to be in. I suppose they could let me go, but life is cheap to these guys and so if Sergio doesn't get what he wants, it's much more like that he'd simply dispose of me. No life is cheaper than mine at this moment. It's a thin line I'm walking here and I've got to play it very carefully. I have no idea where Travis is, but I have to convince Sergio that either I know where he is or I know how to find him. That's my only chance of walking out of here instead of being carried out in their version of a body bag.

"I've only met him once, you know."

"It's of absolutely no consequence to me how many times you've met him."

"He tried to get me to work for him, but I refused."

Silence.

I'm starting to sweat and it's not from the room being overheated. I'm trapped. I know it. Sergio knows it. The only way I'm getting out of here alive is to give Sergio what he wants. Or at least convince him I can find what he wants and give it to him.

"I have no skin in this game," I say, giving it one last shot at talking my way out.

"Yes. You do," he says. "I want Travis Chapman and I believe you can give him to me. It's as simple as that."

"Don't you think I would if I could?"

Silence.

"Do you really think I give a shit about what happens to Travis Chapman? Whatever trouble he's gotten himself into is his business, not mine. I honestly don't know where he is. But how about I try to find him for you."

Sergio reaches into his desk drawer and removes a pack of cigarettes. He taps the pack and one pops out halfway. He pulls it out with his teeth, then reaches into the drawer again and takes out a book of matches and strikes one. He lights the cigarette, holding the match in between his fingers. He lets it burn all the way down close to his fingertips before he waves it out. He inhales deep, then exhales a cloud of smoke in my direction.

"This is an offer to find him and bring him to me?"

"I guess. Sure. But it might help to know why you're looking for him."

"It would not help. All you need to know is that at one time we were in business together and some of that business remains unfinished. You are to bring him to me so we can finish that business."

"He owes you money?"

His face turns to stone, which is my answer. Of course, it's about money. It's always about money. If I help him find Travis and the money, then I'm putting myself in business with some very dangerous people. I learned this several years ago from a friend who was FBI who told me this story.

In the late '90s, after the Albanians had struck out on their own, they began to battle with the Lucchese and Gambino families for territory in Queens, the Bronx, and Westchester Country. We're not talking a sit-down here. The Albanians don't work like that. For them, talk comes out of the barrel of a gun. And so, they did the unthinkable. They stormed a Gambino hangout, much like the one I'm in now, in Astoria, Queens, to send a message to the "families." The club was called Soccer Fever—how can I forget a name like that? And it's now in the hands of the Albanians, so you know how that turned out. Seven members of the gang invaded the basement club, tore the joint apart, shot off handguns, and beat the club manager bloody. It was a bold move, one that had no precedent, but it worked. It forced the Gambino leader, Arnold Squitieri, to call for a talk with the rogue gangsters. The sit-down took place at a gas station rest area near the Jersey turnpike. Squitieri showed up with twenty armed Gambino mobsters. The leader of the Albanians, Alex Rudaj, only brought along six members of his crew. Unknown to both sides was that the FBI had an undercover agent, my friend, who had infiltrated the Gambino family. So, they had the inside scoop on what happened. Squitieri informed Rudaj they'd gone too far and should stop expanding their operations. That didn't go over well with Rudaj and his crew. Both sides pulled out their weapons. Knowing they were outnumbered, the Albanians, instead o-f backing off, threatened to blow up the gas station with all of them in it. The threat worked, but only because the Italians knew the Albanians well enough to know that they'd do what they threatened to do, even if it meant they'd all die. Evidently, so far as the Albanians are concerned, life is cheaper than pride. At an obvious impasse, both groups holstered their weapons and walked away.

"It is no concern of yours why I'm looking for Travis Chapman. It's enough to know that I am. And since I know you've seen him in the last few days, I expect you will be able to find him for me."

"I'm telling you the truth when I say I have no idea where Travis is..."

"Then you've not seen him recently?"

Have I been followed? Watched? Suddenly, the game changes and I realize I have to stick as close to the truth as possible.

"I have seen him. He came to my office the other day and tried to hire me."

"For what purpose?"

"To keep him safe from..." I stop for a moment. "...someone like you."

Sergio crushes the cigarette out on his desk and smiles. "Do you think you could do that? Keep him safe from me? From us?"

"I told him I'm not a bodyguard and sent him packing."

"Then you know how to get in touch with him."

"Why are you so interested in a nobody like Travis Chapman?"

"He has something that doesn't belong to him."

I'm curious to know more but probing further would be stupid. I realize the less I know, the better.

"Like I said, I don't know where he is, but given enough time, I might be able to track him down."

"And why would you do that?"

"Not often, but on occasion I've been known to do favors for people."

"Why would you do a favor for me?"

I look behind me at Ponytail who is still standing, arms folded, blocking the door. Then to the young guy standing silently behind Sergio.

"I think it's probably good business."

Sergio smiles as he leans back in his chair again.

"I don't like the idea of favors, Mr. Fortunato. Favors lead to indebtedness. I don't like owing anyone anything. On the other hand, if I employ someone I have control over them. If I pay you it becomes a business proposition. Then we would become partners. I don't need partners. I don't want you in my business. I just want to find Travis Chapman."

"If all you want is for me to find Travis Chapman, that's all I'll do."

"But I do believe in incentives."

"What do you have in mind?"

"If you find him and bring him back to me, I will reward you, Mr. Fortunato. And to show you good faith, I will pay you one dollar as a retainer. Just to remind you that you are working for me. I think in this situation that's enough to buy your loyalty, don't you?"

He reaches into his back pocket, takes out his wallet, opens it up and tosses a dollar bill on the desk.

Under other circumstances I might laugh. But this is not funny. I'm dealing with a very ruthless, very cunning man. Of this I'm sure: He can and will unleash violence without the slightest provocation. If taking a buck from him will get me back out on the streets in one piece, it is more than enough. It will buy me time. Time, I hope I can use to figure a way out of this. And that does not include saving Travis's ass. As far as I'm concerned, he's on his own. He got himself into this, he can get himself out of it.

"Sounds like a deal to me," I say. I get up and approach his desk. I reach down and pick up the buck. I snap it a couple times, then stuff it in my shirt pocket.

Sergio stands and reaches his hand across the desk toward me. I see he's got silver rings on four fingers of his right hand. It occurs to me this is not a style choice but rather it has a far more practical use. Brass knuckles are illegal in this town. Rings aren't.

"Then we have a deal. And perhaps, if you deliver the goods in a timely fashion, there will be an even larger bonus. But remember this, Mr. Fortunato, I have very high standards. I expect my employees to do their job and do it without any bringing any trouble on me. If, for instance, you involve the police, well, that would break our contract and..."

He doesn't have to go any further. I'm already waist deep in the Big Muddy and it's far too late to turn around.

11
Counting Sheep

On my way out of the club, escorted by Ponytail, I ask for the return of my Glock. He cracks a smile and says, "Now, why would I wanna do that?"

So, I can cap your fucking ass, you oversized jerk-off.

This is not what I want to hear. The gun is registered. Now, I have to report it missing. If I don't and it winds up being used to commit a crime—and seeing who I'm dealing with that's not much of a stretch—I'm in deep shit. This is not something I want to do, make out a police report. Chances are good Divicek and Murphy will be notified and I certainly don't want to give those two an excuse to crawl up my ass again. The less I have to do with the cops, the better. But I have no choice. So, I'll report it missing—stolen, not lost because that would make me seem irresponsible and make it more difficult to replace it—and make sure I spin a believable yarn. Truth is, I'm not sure I'll replace it so quick. I'm playing with the big boys now and a pistol is not going to do me much good. In fact, there's probably more chance of getting shot at if they know I'm carrying. Besides, these things don't come cheap and that buck burning a hole in my pocket won't even pay for a single bullet. A buck buys almost nothing today, except making me look for a guy I don't want to find. I'll probably just tack Serge's buck retainer up on the bulletin board behind my desk at Philly's as a reminder that maybe one of these days I ought to give some serious thought to looking for another line of work.

"How about my phone?" I ask, as we exit the building.

He gives me a long, hard look. He's enjoying fucking with me. Like I'm some kind of animal in the zoo. I really want to deck this sonuvabitch. Right then. Right there. He doesn't scare me. I know I can take him, no matter what his size is because I know where to land the first blows. But we're colleagues now, in a way, and how would that look to the boss?

I reach out my hand. He gives me one of those shit-eating grins, then digs into his jacket pocket and pulls out my phone. He looks at it closely.

"Piece of shit. Not even a fucking iPhone."

He drops it.

"Oops."

Before I can bend down to pick it up, his booted foot finds it, steps on it, and grinds it into the ground.

"What the fuck..." I say, as my fists automatically ball up at my sides.

"Sorry about that, man. I don't know. Sometimes I drop things."

"And then step on them?"

"I guess I should be more careful, huh?"

I bend over and pick up what was my phone. The glass is a spiderweb of cracks. I power it up and, miraculously, it turns on. As for what condition my information is in, and whether or not it works, I have no idea.

"Asshole," I hiss. I'm actually hoping he takes a swing at me, because I know I'm quick enough to avoid it and get in a couple of my own. But he doesn't. He just laughs, turns, and goes back into the social club.

Just what I need. Another damn expense.

Hopefully, it still works well enough so I can avoid having to replace it. Which I can't afford to do.

The rain has stopped, but the streets are still damp. The air is so heavy, so oppressive, I can practically taste it. In the country, the rain cleanses. Here in the city, it just brings out the smell of all the garbage. Maybe I should give some serious thought to leaving the city for someplace where a good rainfall gives the illusion of a new beginning.

Ponytail doesn't offer to drive me back to the city, so I pull out my cracked phone and hope it still works. Miraculously, it does, and I use it to find the nearest subway stop that'll take me back into Manhattan and as far away from Sergio as possible.

Working for the Albanian mob is definitely not something I want on my resume. But I'm stuck. I guess I could try to disappear, creating my own witness protection program, but somehow this doesn't seem like a doable solution. Starting over, on my own, doesn't seem doable either. Besides, I'm guessing that whatever this is all about, it's got lots of $$$ signs in the answer. People will go through a lot of shit and do a lot of crazy things for money. I should know. I'm one of them. Besides, thinking the Albanians wouldn't send a search party after me is naïve. In fact, I'm going forward with the belief that I'm being watched. Sergio has a piece of me now and I don't see him letting me walk away. This is not the way to run a successful organization. I know it. He knows it. And he knows I know it.

The way I see it, I've got two options. Option one, try to find Travis Chapman and once I do, hand him over to the Albanians. Option two, go through the motions of trying to find him, report that I can't, and hope they believe me and look for another way to find him.

As of now, I'm being squeezed between the Albanians who want Travis and the cops who are looking for Donald Alston's killer. If it was the Albanians who iced him, and now that I'm working for them, I will find it very difficult to explain to the cops my being in Chapman's apartment alone with the deceased Mr. Alston.

As I wait for my train, my mind works overtime, trying to

piece together how all these things fit together. This is one scenario I come up with.

The Albanians get involved with Alston. Perhaps he's laundering money for them. Alston double-crosses them. Either steals the dough or mismanages it and loses it all. Alston, looking for someone to take the fall, hooks up with Chapman, letting it be known that now they're in this together. The Albanians only know one way to solve a problem: violence. They want their money back. They think Alston has it. They knock off Alston and make it look like Chapman is involved. But they can't find the money and now they think Chapman is the one who has it or knows how to get his hands on it. So, naturally, they go after him to get their money.

This is all conjecture, of course, but it makes sense. There's no way of knowing whether this has any relationship to what's really going on, but the pieces appear to fit. I used to have a friend who liked doing crossword puzzles. He also liked to finish them, whether he had the right answers or not. And so, when he was stumped on let's say a five-letter word and could think of only a six-letter word that fit the clue, he'd simply write it in, adding the dangling letter to now filled final box. As far as he was concerned, he'd successfully completed the puzzle.

I don't like to lose either and right now, I'm one of those extra letters. It's just a matter of which box I'm going to try to fit it into. At the same time, my priority is to figure a way to get out alive, which the way things look now, won't be easy.

By the time I'm back in Manhattan it's almost eleven. I'm not hungry anymore. I consider dropping in for a drink or two, but the mood I'm in I'm afraid I wouldn't stop there. So, I head back to my apartment.

My body feels like two hundred pounds of dead weight, and my brain is fried, so maybe I'll be able to fall asleep perchance to dream my way out of this mess I've got myself into.

No such luck.

Tonight, I have several good reasons for my insomnia to kick in. And, so it does. My mind is racing all over the damn place. All I can think about is how I'm going to get the Albanians off my back, while making sure the cops don't pop me for Alston's murder. When I finally realize, no matter how tired I am, that sleep will not be coming any time soon, I swallow a couple melatonin tablets. But that doesn't work. I've still got half dozen Ambien in my bathroom cabinet. I don't like to take them unless I really have to because they make me feel like shit in the morning. This might be one of those times when it's worth it, but my body is so beat the idea of getting up, going to the bathroom to get one is beyond my capability.

Finally, I give up trying to sleep and spend the rest of the night stretched out on my couch watching old movies on AMC, hoping one of them will put me to sleep.

Instead, they do just the opposite. By six a.m., when the sun starts peeking through the blinds, I'm so wired I don't even need that lovely jolt of caffeine from that first cup of coffee.

12
Back in the Saddle Again

The hope is once daylight breaks and all our sins from yesterday have been magically washed away by sleep (more likely forgotten) an answer will miraculously come to us. The world will become clearer. The rain from the day before will have washed away the dirt and grime and detritus which cluttered our life, distorting our ability to see the truth. All my cares and woes will be packed up and mailed off to someone else who can handle them far better than me.

Alas, this is a pipe dream propelled by drugs or alcohol or endorphins or just plain misguided beliefs. It does not happen like that. In truth, it never happens. Because, in order for this to work, you'd have to actually sleep. And even after popping one of those Ambien in my bathroom cabinet, I manage maybe a couple hours of fitful sleep.

I've always lived by this admittedly cynical credo: just when you think things can't get worse, they do. And yet every time I close my eyes, and on those rare occasions when sleep finally comes, this fairytale version of life, that every day is a new day and not just an ugly continuation of the last, is what I look forward to.

On a night like the one I've just lived through, a night filled with threats both real and imagined, when no matter what I do sleep never comes, all bets are off.

In the light of day on this particular morning, after showering and shaving, hoping this ritual will take my mind off what I see in the mirror, I realize things have gotten no better. In fact, they are worse. I am still buried in a deep mound of shit up to my waist. Waiting for some divine answer of how to extricate myself from the mess I'm in, to come to me in a dream, just doesn't happen. Especially since dreaming only comes after sleep that puts a period to the day you've just lived through. For me, it's not a period but more a comma or, at best, a semicolon.

As surreal as last night's encounter with Sergio, Teardrop, and Ponytail seems, I know it's all true. I also know my only option, if I'm to remain on this earth, is to find Travis Chapman. What happens to him after I do find him is no concern of mine. If he was stupid enough to rip off the Albanians, he deserves what he gets. And if he didn't, well then, it's his job to convince them of that, not mine.

I don't really know where to start so I decide to go back to who got me in this jam in the first place. Lila Alston, the woman who started the whole thing by offering me a bite of that poison apple.

I know where she lives, so that's my first stop. I haven't quite settled on the ruse that will get me in to see her, but I figure something will come to me. It usually does. Just my luck, I find the same doorman from the previous time I showed up at her apartment house. He recognizes me and refuses me entry. There's a good chance he got reamed out by Mrs. Alston that last time I caught up to her at the bank across the street and he isn't going to let that happen again. Not on his watch. Not when his yearly tip depends on it.

"She's not in, sir," he says. But the way he says "sir," as if he's mocking me, makes me want to slap him around a little.

"I don't think you're telling me the truth, Jeeves."

He looks at me like I'm speaking another language.

"I'll say it again. Mrs. Alston is not at home."

"How can you be so sure?"

For the moment, he's stumped.

"I saw her leave," he stutters.

"When?"

"Um...earlier this morning."

"Look, Jeeves, it's not even nine o'clock yet. The chances of me winning the lottery are better than the chances Mrs. Alston left this early in the morning. Why not do what you're paid to do. Go over to that intercom thing, buzz her apartment, and tell her Pete Fortunato is here to see her."

"She gave strict instructions that you were not to be allowed in the building," he says.

"I thought she wasn't home."

"I didn't say she was..."

"You didn't have to, Jeeves."

"Would you please stop calling me that. And if you don't leave the premises, I'm going to call the police."

"I'm not on the premises. I'm on the sidewalk. A public sidewalk, I might add. And go right ahead and call the cops. I'll just stick around till they show up and I'd be very happy to provide them with some information about Mrs. Alston she might not appreciate being made public. Why don't you call her up and see what she says? I could be wrong,"

He's not going to take the chance. I know it and he knows it. He's just looking for a way to get out of this with the least amount of damage to his ego.

He stands there dumbfounded. I'm starting to feel sorry for him. After all, he's only doing his job and I know those Christmas tips are what makes his job worthwhile. Jeopardizing that by insubordination is not the wisest move on his part. So, he's between a rock and a hard place. But as the rock, I'm not about to back down.

"I have her phone number. Would you like me to give her a call and see what she says?"

I'm bluffing, of course. Once she sees it's me on caller ID, I doubt she'll take the call. But Jeeves doesn't know this.

I'm tired of the back and forth. I'm not out to bust anyone's balls, so I pull out my wallet, extract a twenty and dangle it in front of him.

"Blame it on me. Tell her I won't leave until I see her. Tell her I slipped by your replacement while you were on your break. Tell her anything you want. Meanwhile, just turn your back and I'll do what I do."

He stares at the bill for a moment, then snatches it from my hand, stuffs it in his pocket, turns, and goes inside the building to the intercom.

When he returns he says, "She'll see you but she'd like you to wait ten minutes before you come up.

Something seems off Why would Lila want to stall? She needs time to put on her makeup? To dry off from a shower. I don't think so. She's doing something up there. Maybe calling someone? Getting rid of someone who's up there with her?

"I'll wait in the lobby," I say.

The doorman nods, but as I start to walk into the lobby, knowing the kind of woman I'm dealing with—the kind of woman who'll issue a bad check, just because she can—I change my mind.

"You know what," I say, "I think I'll take the time to run across the street and grab a coffee. I'll be back in ten, fifteen minutes."

"Suit yourself," he shrugs.

I walk to the corner and head north on Madison, toward 89th Street. About a third of the way up the block, I find what I'm looking for. A service entrance to the building. *Look, sister, I may have been born on a Tuesday but it wasn't yesterday.*

I go back to the corner and take a spot where I can keep my eye out on both the service entrance and the front entrance. Just in case Lila tries to split before I get upstairs.

I let twelve minutes pass and when I don't see her come out the service entrance, I go back to the front door. Part of me is glad she isn't trying to run. I want to trust her. I want to believe that maybe that rubber check was really a mistake. Another part of me is sorry she doesn't try to run. At least then I'd know exactly who I was dealing with. And me catching her would let her know that I don't believe a word of what she tells me.

"What's her apartment number?"

"Three-A. Make a left off the elevator. It's at the end of the hall."

Lila answers the door in a pair of skin-tight black leotards with red stripes down the side and a blue, low-cut sweater. Her red hair, shorter than I remember it, is still damp, as if she's recently come out of the shower.

"To be honest with you, I never expected to see you again, Fortunato."

"I'm a bad penny, Lila. I just seem to pop up at the most unexpected times."

"I suppose you'd like to come in."

"I promise I've been deloused recently."

"Well, that's a relief."

She leads me into the apartment, through a large foyer that's almost the size of my entire apartment, into a sunken living room which has two exposures, east and south, so at this hour of the morning the room is flooded with sunlight. The furniture is modern and expensive, a cacophony of metal and glass. In the corner, there's a baby grand piano. The window ledges are lined with flowerpots. There's a tan leather couch and two Eames chairs to match. There's a large breakfront filled with books.

"Nice place you got here."

"We've been here two years and it's still not completely finished."

"Looks finished to me."

"Tell that to our decorator."

She points to the couch. "Have a seat, why don't you?"

"I'm good."

"You didn't expect me to be hospitable, did you?"

I throw up my hands. "Not really."

"I'm full of surprises. I was just making some coffee. Would you like a cup?"

"Sure, why not?"

"Cream? Sugar?"

"Black."

"You're so predictable," she laughs, as she climbs up the two steps and makes a left into the kitchen.

A few moments later she returns with a tray with a silver pitcher, two cups and a plate of scones. She puts it on the coffee table in front of the couch then sits down next to me. She pours a cup for me then one for her. She rips open a couple of packs of Sweet'N Low, pours them into her coffee, then stirs it gently.

"I must admit I'm curious as to why you're here. I assume it's not because the cash I gave you turned out to be counterfeit."

"So far, so good."

"I hope you don't take this the wrong way, but you look like shit."

"There's a right way to take it?"

"Well..."

"You're right. I look the way I feel."

"Bad night?"

"Every night's a bad night, though last night was worse than most."

"You look like you haven't slept in days."

"That would be an accurate statement. Let's just say sleep doesn't always come easy to me."

"Guilty conscience?"

"I'm flattered you think I have one."

"I'm just guessing. And being polite."

"Insomnia. Had it since my teens. I wouldn't wish it on my worst enemy."

"In that case, maybe you don't look quite that bad."

She takes a sip of her coffee and I mirror her.

"So, how about we get down to why you're here."

"I'm here about Travis."

She laughs, that throaty laugh that travels the speed of light from my ears to my groin, and puts down her cup.

"Oh, honey, that can't possibly be why you're here. Are you secretly in love with me, by any chance? Oh. Wait. Even worse. Travis!"

"I'm sure both of you are lovely people, but no. Besides, if I were I wouldn't keep it a secret."

"Oh shit. I love the idea of a secret admirer."

"I'm sure you've had plenty."

"It's the ones who aren't so secret that are the problem. I'll tell you a little secret, Fortunato, I don't always have the best taste when it comes to men."

"How many times you been married?"

"My, my, you really don't believe in proper etiquette, do you?"

"There's actually very little I believe in, Lila. But I'll tell you this, I've never met a beautiful woman yet who didn't know how much power she can wield. And who isn't shy about wielding it, either."

"Honey, I do believe you've just handed me a compliment," she says in a very convincing Blanche DuBois-like honey-sweet Southern drawl.

"Take it any way you like."

"That's the way I shall take it. Thank you very much, Fortunato."

"I never liked that name but coming from you it's beginning to sound a little better."

"Why not? I think it's a rather nice name."

"Because it gives people the wrong impression."

"What kind of impression would that be?"

"That I was born under a lucky star when in fact, I'm pretty sure I was born on a starless night and that I've been out of step with the world ever since."

"You poor, poor man."

She puts down her coffee, rips open another packet of Sweet'N Low, pours it in, then slowly stirs it with her spoon.

"As you've probably noticed, I like things on the sweet side," she says.

"I can see," I say, even though I've never actually seen her drink from her artificially sweetened drinks.

She looks up at a clock on the wall.

"I don't want to rush you, but I'm running a little late for my yoga class. Why don't you tell me why you think I can help you with Travis. I haven't seen the man for, oh, I don't know, weeks probably."

I don't believe that, but I let it slide.

"I need to find him."

"Why in the world would you need to find Travis? I mean, let's face it, he's no one's idea of a prize package. Wait. He didn't stiff you on some deal, did he?"

I shake my head.

"Then I can't imagine…"

"What difference does it make, Lila? I need to find him and I think you can make that easier for me."

She picks up a scone, breaks it in half, but puts both halves back down on the tray. This woman has some very odd eating habits. Her intentions don't quite fit her actions, which should tell me all I need to know about her.

"Tell me, why would I want to do that?"

"Because you've got a soft spot in your heart for me?"

"Oh, darling, and I thought I've hidden that so well. I don't suppose you'd consider running away with me. After all, I am a free woman now. A very vulnerable widow. Think about it," she says, waving her hands, "half of all this could be yours."

"I can't afford the maintenance," I say, as I pick up my coffee. I get it halfway to my mouth when I realize the last thing I want is more caffeine in my system.

"So, got any ideas on how I can find him?"

"You know how to whistle, don't you?"

"Is that how you think of him? As a dog? A family pet?"

"Now that you mention it, he does have a puppy-dog quality about him."

"I'm serious, Lila."

"Are you telling me it's a matter of life and death?"

"Could be."

"Oh, darling, you do have a flair for the dramatic, don't you?"

"I'm dead serious."

"Now, you've got my attention. Yours or his?"

"Both. And I'm not sure you're out of the woods on this either."

"What's that supposed to mean?" she snaps.

"Your late husband and Travis seem to have gotten themselves into a little trouble. They've been doing business with the wrong people."

"What kind of business?"

"I don't know and I don't care. I just need to find him."

"Well," she says, giving me one those eye rolls probably left over from her teen years. "I haven't the foggiest idea where he is. And if you ask me if I care…"

"I have no intention of asking you that. But you could get to him if you needed to, couldn't you?"

"Darling, we were over a long time ago. And we were never that much of a 'thing' in the first place. We didn't exchange friendship rings at the end, and we didn't promise to keep in touch after the summer was over."

"This is not a joke, Lila. We could all be in some serious shit if I don't get to Travis, and soon."

"You really are serious, aren't you?"

"Like a heart attack, honey."

She's silent for a moment. I can see her weighing her options. She might not know exactly where Travis is, but I believe she can find him if she needs to. Or at the very least can point me in the right direction. But even if she doesn't help me, I'm pretty sure that as soon as I leave, she'll get in touch with him.

"Have you tried his cell?" she asks.

"I don't have the number."

"Well, I probably have it somewhere."

Probably?

"Give it to me. I'll call, though I'll be surprised if he answers."

"Why's that?"

"He split for a reason, Lila. He knows where your husband was found. He knows a call from me isn't likely to be good news."

I can't quite decide if Lila knows more than she admits or if she really doesn't know what her lover and husband were into. For now, it doesn't matter. Maybe it never will. I'm not solving puzzles. I'm not looking for answers. I just want to get myself out from being in the middle of something that could explode in my face.

"You found him once without my help. I'm sure you can do it again," she says, in a harsh tone that surprises me.

"Different time. Different circumstance."

"You know where he works, right? Maybe someone there can help you."

"He quit that job."

"You've been to his apartment. Maybe there's something there that'll tell you where he is."

"First off, I doubt he'd go back there after having a stiff in his bed. And second, that's the last place I want to go because I'm sure the cops have an eye on it. Next?"

"I haven't the foggiest idea what's next. It's your job, Fortunato. It's what you're supposed to be good at. You're an investigator, right? So, why don't you just get out there and investigate?"

Suddenly, I have a very un-PC thought. No, it's more than a thought. It's an almost uncontrollable urge to pop Lila Alston in her beautiful face, a face so beautiful she can get away with all kinds of crap. Of course, I'd never hit a woman. I haven't hit one yet. I doubt I ever will. But that doesn't mean I don't have the urge. And that doesn't mean that someday the urge might morph into action. It just won't be today.

Lila knows exactly what she can get away with. How far she can go. She's probably gotten away with things all her life. I know it. And everyone she's ever been in contact probably knows it. But what I also know is that behind that smile she knows way more than she's willing to say. She's good. Real good. So good I'm guessing I could spend the rest of the day with her and I still wouldn't get anything out of her that she doesn't want to tell me. Which if the past ten minutes is any indication, is nothing.

I'm frustrated. I want out of there. In the worst way. I don't believe for a minute that Lila couldn't reach him if she needed to. I wouldn't be surprised if as soon as I leave she's on the phone with him. Before I split, I give it one last shot.

"If Travis gets in touch, I want you to tell him to contact me immediately. Tell him he's in a shitload of trouble. He'll know what I'm talking about."

I start to get up.

"You're leaving?"

"Any reason I should stay?"

"Not really. Though I am beginning to develop a fondness for you."

"That'll pass. Just tell him, okay?"

"He won't get in touch with me..."

"But if he does..."

"Then I shall give him your message and urge him to contact you. Is that what you want to hear?"

I nod. "Exactly what I want to hear."

"You don't have to rush out, you know."

"What about that yoga class?"

"I've missed classes before..."

She winks at me. I can't remember the last time anyone winked at me. In fact, I'm not even sure there was a last time.

She walks me to the door and, as she opens it for me, she puts a hand on my shoulder. It's warm. Her hand, not my shoulder. It's a touch that promises so much more than it'll ever deliver.

I turn back to her.

"By the way, I don't think you're quite out of the woods yet in terms of your husband's death."

She looks startled. "What do you mean?"

"I was a cop, Lila. I know how they work. I know how they think. Nine out of ten times, it's the spouse."

"You just made that up, didn't you?"

"You think?"

"They've already interviewed me—with my attorney present, of course—and I don't think I'm a suspect. And neither does my attorney."

"Cops are sneaky like that, Lila. They lie all the time. Just because they don't slap the cuffs on after the interview doesn't mean you're in the clear."

"I'm not worried," she says, like she's not worried. But I can see in her eyes that she is. That's what I want. To make her think she's not off the hook yet, even if she's not guilty. But if she is, I know she'll do everything she can to throw suspicion elsewhere. That's what I want. Because if she does that, she's bound to make a mistake. And if Travis is involved, she'll drag him down with herself.

"Suit yourself," say.

Before I can turn to leave, she leans forward and gives me a glancing kiss on the cheek.

It's the kind of kiss that means nothing and everything at the same time. I can't help but remember a line from a Robert Frost. *It was only a small commitment anyway, like a kiss.*

And they don't get any smaller than a Lila Alston kiss.

13
Checking the Grid

I leave Lila Alston's apartment not knowing exactly what I'm going to do next.

If Travis has an instinct for survival, and I think he does, he skips town, getting as far away as possible. But even after the little time I've spent with him, I know he's not a deep thinker and the fact that he got himself in this mess in the first place tells me he doesn't always make good choices. Maybe never. I figure he's one of two places. Either he's hiding out somewhere in the city, with friends maybe, if he has any; or, he's retreated to someplace familiar, like his hometown or somewhere he's lived before moving here to become a star. There's always that chance that he's following his dream to have a star on Hollywood Boulevard by going west, but from what he's told me he either doesn't have the money yet or if he's stolen anything from Sergio and the Albanians, he's smart enough not to throw it around, which would lead a trail of greenbacks a child could follow.

The best way to track someone today is electronically. Everyone, and I mean everyone, has an electronic or digital footprint. This includes Travis. I'd be surprised if he doesn't have a strong social media presence. That's the best way for him to network and get word out about any appearance he's making on stage.

First thing I do is put out the word to certain people I know.

It's that Kevin Bacon Six Degrees of...thing. You don't have to be Kevin Bacon to prove the genius of that game. If you know enough people and let them know who or what you're looking for then inevitably you'll find someone who's got a connection that can lead you to your prey. And that's exactly what Travis is to me now: prey.

After leaving Lila, I head straight for the closest library, where I can log onto one of their computers and check all the social media sites, Facebook, Google, LinkedIn, Twitter, Instagram, and Craig's List. I have a computer at the office, but I don't want to go back there in case the Albanians have it staked out. I'm not naïve nor stupid enough to think that they just set me loose with no oversight. I'm pretty sure they've got someone keeping an eye on me. Maybe more than one. My aim is to make this as difficult as possible.

Over the years, I've become somewhat proficient at web surfing—the result of too much time on my hands, perhaps—but I've got "a guy" I can rely on who knows a lot more than I do. His name's Freddie. I don't even know his last name because, as he was quick to inform me, "I like to be as off the grid as possible." Why's that, I asked. "Big Brother, man. He's watching us all the time. Don't you know there are cameras everywhere except up your butt, and I wouldn't be surprised if they aren't working on butt cameras already, so I'm not sure even that's gonna be safe in a couple years."

I'm tempted to call Freddie paranoid, but I realize he probably knows what he's talking about.

The last time I used him he delivered a half hour lecture on how drones were gonna take over. That we'd all be followed by our personal "eyes in the sky drone" he insisted. "Look up in the sky sometime, Pete. Now, you'll probably see the occasional plane or maybe helicopter. A couple years from now, the skies will turn black from all those drones. You ever see those old movies with the locusts, how they turn day into night? Well, that's the way it's gonna be. Everyone's gonna have their own personal watchdog drone. Mark my words, Pete. It won't be long before the word 'privacy' ain't even in the dictionary. It'll be like one of those archaic languages, you know, like Latin or Pygmy, that are dead as doornails."

An hour on the library computer is enough to come away with a treasure trove of information about Travis. He's all over Facebook. I see many of his friends are from a town called Booth, Texas, not far outside Houston. They appear to be pretty much the same age as Travis, so it's a good bet that's where he grew up. Also, he's a big Dallas Cowboy fan and U.T. fan—I have my fill of "Hook 'em, horns" photos—cinches it for me. He's a big movie fan, of course. His favorite actors are Brad Pitt, Jake Gyllenhaal and the other guy I always confuse with Gyllenhaal, Ryan Gosling, or maybe it's Ryan Reynolds. In fact, he's posted one photo of Gosling next to a headshot photo of himself with the caption, "Separated at birth?" And they actually do bear a slight resemblance, though probably not as much as Travis would like to believe. He's also a bowler. Several shots of him at various bowling alleys in New York, and there's even a photo of a scoresheet with his name and 265 circled. Making it no surprise that one of his favorite films is *The Big Lebowski*. There's even one photo where he's super-imposed his face on the body of John Turturro—Jesus Quintana, in the movie—and next to that, he's super-imposed his face onto Jeff Bridges' body, with the caption, "The Dude abides."

There are also a host of photos of him with various women, all of them on a scale of ten, seven or above. Obviously, Lila Alston is not his first conquest, though I'm pretty certain the only one he's been paid to romance.

From LinkedIn, I get more information. I get who represents him now and then for acting work. And it's there that I'm able to verify that he did grow up in Texas and it gives both his high school and University of Texas as the college he attended—no graduation date, so I assume he quit after a couple years.

And so, I'm able to put together a pretty good file on him.

Plenty of places to begin to look for him.

Of course, the easiest way to find him is let him find me. So, I leave messages for him both on LinkedIn and Facebook. I simply write, "Call me, Travis, ASAP. Important!" I don't bother leaving my phone number because I know he already has it.

Next, I surf the net looking for any information I can get on the Albanians, hoping to add to what I already know. And there's plenty there. In one article, I learn how widespread they are. A report from Interpol says that they're active in trafficking drugs, arms, human, and human organs and that the Kosovo chapter alone directs heroin markets in Switzerland, Austria, Germany, Belgium, Hungary, the Czech Republic, Sweden, and Norway. One FI expert describes the Albanians as a sixth crime family, comparing them to the Italian Mafia in its wilder, less organized, more violent early days. At one point, the Gambino family hired Albanians to do their killing for them, just like Murder Incorporated back in the '30s. Many of the Albanians are Muslims, and some are even thought to be Al Qaeda sympathizers and have links to that terrorist organization. Another recent article reports that the gang is in the midst of getting a strong foothold in the Bronx, which explains why they dragged me up there, especially targeting the vending machine or "Joker Poker" industry. There's plenty more, but I have my fill. The more I read, the worse it gets and the more I know I have to figure a way out of this.

By this time, it's almost one. I can't decide if I'm hungrier or more sleep-deprived, but seeing as hope often springs eternal, I decide the possibility of sleep takes precedence—how long can I possibly go on a grand total of maybe two hours sleep for the past forty-eight hours?

I go back to my apartment. Pull down all the blinds so that it's pitch dark. I strip off my clothes, down to my underwear, flick on my white sound machine, and stretch out on the couch.

Miraculously, within minutes I'm in what for me passes as deep sleep.

14

The Prodigal Asshole Reappears

It doesn't take much to wake me. The slightest sound, like a neighbor's door closing, can jolt me awake. This time, it's the vibration my cellphone makes on the coffee table in front of the couch. It's attached to the cord attached to a wall socket to recharge the battery, and I watch as the vibration causes it to move closer to me and the edge of the table, like a snake on a leash.

I catch it only inches from the edge, just before it's about to take a nose-dive off the table. Before I pick up the call, I check the time. It's a little after four p.m., which means I've managed to log a couple hours sleep. I can't say I feel refreshed, but there is a certain joy knowing that occasionally I actually can fall asleep. When I can't, when I'm in the middle of a sleepless streak, I feel like I'll never sleep again. Even those couple hours give me hope of someday getting a regular night's sleep. But my next thought is back in the real world. *Dammit, who the fuck is bothering me?*

The number that pops up is unfamiliar.

I drag my finger across the screen and, my voice still husky from sleep, manages, "Yeah."

There's a moment of silence. I'm ready to hang up on another fucking annoying robo-call.

Then.

"Pete? Is this you?"

I swing my legs over the side of the couch and sit up straight. I recognize the voice. It's Travis.

"Where the hell are you, Travis?"

"Huh?"

"Where are you?"

"Why do you need to know?"

"All right. Skip it. You got my messages, right?"

"Yeah. Sure. Why do you think I'm calling you? What's up?" he asks, as if he's talking to a friend who's just making an average *how the hell are you?* phone call.

"Do you have any idea how much shit you've got me into?" I say, raising my voice in hopes he'll take this more seriously.

"Huh? I don't know what you're talking about."

Is this guy for real? Is he playing with a full deck? I swear, if he was in the room with me, counting or no counting, I'd be taking a swing at him.

"The guys you're playing footsie with, you asshole. The fucking mob. And not just any fucking mob, the fucking Albanians. Do you have any idea what they do to guys like you? What the hell were you thinking?"

"Hey! I don't like the way you're talking to me. Maybe I should hang up."

If I could punch this asshole through the phone, I would. If we weren't miles apart, I'd be taking him apart piece by piece.

Just as I'm about to scream something into the phone, I realize if I'm going to get anywhere with this guy, I have to moderate my tone and try to eliminate any hint of anger from my voice. I keep reminding myself that this guy is a wannabe actor. He lives in a fantasy world. He probably *doesn't* have any idea how serious this is, despite the fact that a stiff was found in his bed.

"No. No. I don't want you to hang up. I want you to tell me what's going on. Why are the Albanians are looking for you?"

"They're looking for me?"

Oh, Jesus Christ. What kind of moron am I dealing with?

Can he really be this stupid?

"Of course, they're looking for you, asshole. But they found me instead. I'm lucky I got out of there alive," I exaggerate. "What I want to know is why are they looking for you? And how the hell do I get myself out of this? Whatever the fuck it is."

"I don't understand. How'd you get in the middle of this?"

Oh, Jeez...

"Because you put me there, asshole. You're the one who came to my office and tried to hire me. You're the one that let yourself get hooked up to Lila Alston and then to Donald Alston. You don't think these guys have got eyes and ears everywhere? You don't think they've been keeping tabs on you?"

There's a moment of silence.

"You think they were following me?" he asks in this surprised tone that's just making things worse.

"How the hell do I know? And what the fuck does it matter? They know. We don't have to know how they know. They just know."

"I guess I didn't count on this," he says, and I can practically see him scratching his head like some country yokel.

"I guess you didn't. You know, Travis, this is no video game. This is real life, man."

"How am I going to get out of this?"

Maybe it's finally sinking in. I sure hope so, because I'm very close to hanging up and really doing everything I can to help Sergio find this asshole and then hand him over. If he winds up in a woodchipper, well, that's not my problem.

"You mean how are *we* going to get out of this. I'm in this now, Travis. I want to know where you are and what they're so pissed about."

"I don't think it's in my best interest to tell you where I am."

"Do I give a fuck about your best interests? Let me answer that. I. Do. Not. Fucking. Care. One. Iota. About. You. I only care about me. But unfortunately, we're now in this together and I don't even know what *this* is."

"I thought it would end once Alston was gone."

"No. It didn't end. It only got worse. And are you saying they're the ones who killed him?"

"I don't know. Maybe. I mean, from what you're telling me it sounds like they'd be capable of it..."

"Oh, yeah. You can go to the bank with that one, Travis. Now, where are you?"

"I don't think I should say. I mean, if it's as bad as you say they'd be following you, right? And maybe they're listening to this conversation."

"They aren't the FBI or CIA, Travis. They haven't tapped my cellphone and they haven't bugged my apartment."

"How can you be so sure?"

This is pointless. I have to meet with him face to face.

"If you don't tell me where you are, Travis, I'll find you. That's what I do for a living, you know? I will fucking find you and I won't be responsible for what happens next."

Dead air.

"I think maybe I should get off this line," he sighs.

"Do what you want, Travis. But right now, I'm your only hope. I'm the only one who can pull you out of this shithole you're in. Hang up. Go ahead. But I promise you within two days I'll be at your doorstep."

"I don't think so," he says.

And he hangs up.

15
A Friend in Need

Now that I have a phone number for Travis, I call Freddie and ask him if there's any way I can track him through his cell.

"If you get the records from the phone company they can tell you which cell towers he pinged. But that ain't gonna happen. Not without a court order. And you're not getting any kind of court order, are you?"

"Could you do it?"

"Of course, I can do it. They don't call me The Miracle Man for nothing."

"How?"

"That's privileged information, my friend. But in this age of the computer, there are no secrets. You just need to know where to look and how to look...and maybe a friend or two in strategic places."

"Are you talking about hacking, Freddie? Which you know is against the law."

"Me? Hack? Pete, you know I wouldn't do anything to break the law."

I can hear him smile through the phone.

"Okay, how much is it going to cost me and how long will it take you?"

"Well, I'll have to..."

"I don't want any of the details. I'm on thin enough ice as is, and my license is up for renewal. I gotta toe the line here. I just want results, Freddie. I don't care how you get them. I don't even want to know how you get them. And I need them fast."

"You in some kind of trouble?"

"What do you think?"

"Stupid question, right?"

"Right."

"I'll have it for you first thing in the morning."

"Not sooner?"

"Man, it's almost five o'clock. I've got a dinner appointment. Besides, what can you possibly do with the information in the middle of the night when everyone's asleep?"

"Not everyone, my friend."

"Who are you? The guy who makes the donuts?"

"No. But I could be. I may need to find another line of work after this. Just let me know as soon as you get the information, okay?"

I give him Travis's full name and number.

"If it's a burner, I probably won't be able to help you."

"He's not smart enough to use one of those, Freddie. Trust me. It's his line. Now about the cost?"

"Rush jobs cost a little more."

"I get that."

"Five hundred?"

"I'm on a strict budget. Two-fifty."

Silence.

"Okay. I guess you qualify for the friends and relatives' discount. Besides, I have a feeling from the tone of your voice, this really is important."

"It is."

"Okay, consider it done. I'll text you the information as soon as I get it. That way, I won't wake you up."

"Not much chance of that happening," I say.

16
The Art of the Steal

Less than an hour later I get Freddie's text.
Call me.
"You get it?" I ask when he picks up after the third ring.
"I really am hot shit, aren't I?"
"Enough patting yourself on your back. You'll break your friggin' arm."
"Hey, if I don't do it, who will? The call came from some little town outside Houston..."
"Booth, right?"
"How'd you know?"
"Because I'm also very good at what I do, Freddie."
"Then what the hell did you need me for?"
"Corroboration."
"Expensive corroboration. Now, about that three hundred dollars—"
"It was two-fifty and I'll mail you a check."
"Oh, man, if I had a dime for every time I've heard that one...It's not that I don't trust you, Pete, but you wouldn't happen to have PayPal or Venmo?"
"Nope." I'm lying. I have no idea what Venmo is but I certainly have PayPal. I also have an almost nonexistent checking account.

"Do you bank at Chase?"

"Nope," I lie. I know exactly what he's getting at. He wants the money right away. He knows me far too well.

"How 'bout we do it the old-fashioned way. You give me your address and I send you a check?"

"It's not that I don't trust you, Pete, but I'd rather have cash. Why don't we meet today?"

"Unfortunately, I'm headed out of town very early tomorrow morning—you can guess where I'm headed. But I promise, first thing when I get back, we meet and I give you the cash."

"Really?"

"Have you ever known me to lie?"

His laughter almost bursts my eardrum. "Okay, okay. I'm gonna trust you. This time. But only because I know you're gonna need me again somewhere down the line and you know there's no way I'm gonna work for you if you stiff me this time. You know that, right?"

"You're a prince, Freddie," I say, and then I add a few more empty promises and words of praise before I hang up.

First things first.

I am almost positive I've got eyes on me. It would be naïve to think the Albanians would "hire" me to do a job and not keep tabs on me. I don't like the idea of being watched. That's not the way I like to work. When I work. I don't like people knowing my business. My comings and goings. That didn't sit well with my ex-wife. It wasn't the reason we split up, but it might have made the top ten. Even as a kid I rebelled against my parents knowing where I was and what I was doing. I had an unexplained need to be unencumbered. Meaning, I wanted to do what I wanted to do when I wanted to do it.

This did not go unnoticed by my parents, especially my mother. Truth is, my father couldn't give a damn where I was or what I was doing. This became official when, at the age of twelve, he went out for the proverbial "pack of smokes," and never came back. When I was working that deputy job upstate, giving me access to all kinds of tracking tools, I had a momentary urge to track down the son of a bitch, but it passed. After all, what did I think I'd do with him or to him if I found him? When I finally figure that out, I tell myself, then maybe I'll actually go to the trouble of finding him. But let's face it, I know that's never going to happen. What would I do? What would I say? What would he do? What would he say? Knowing me, the meeting would probably turn into a free for all. No one would benefit from that, unless, of course, punching him in the face could erase years of anger and sadness.

The crazy thing is, things got better once he left. Much better. And after a few weeks I prayed every night that he wouldn't come back. I prayed to his Catholic god and I prayed to my mother's Jewish god. I figured I'd be covering most of the bases and what did I have to lose? Only when I wandered into a philosophy class in college (I only lasted three weeks—even then I realized it was pretty much a waste of time even having a philosophy much less studying it) was I able to put a name to the way I felt: Pascal's Wager.

Like with my father, I'm not quite sure what I'm going to do once I find Travis. Am I going to turn him into Sergio? Am I going to try to get him out of a mess that has nothing to do with me? Am I going to beat the crap out of him for risking my life by getting me involved in this in the first place?

Whatever choice I make, I'm pretty sure it'll be spur of the moment and chances are pretty good it'll be the wrong choice. But over the years I've learned to live with all my bad choices. And believe me, there have been plenty of them.

For now, everything is on my dime. Unless, of course, I can somehow convince Lila Alston that fronting me a few bucks is in her best interest. If nothing else, it's worth a try. It won't be easy. Somehow, I'll have to convince her it's in her best interests that I find Travis and clean up this mess he and Donald Alston have left for us.

The next morning, I give her a call. Oddly enough, she seems happy to hear from me. I can't quite figure out why, but rather than obsess on it I decide to consider it a good sign. A sign that I'm making progress, that she's come to realize my success is her success.

"To what do I owe the honor?" she asks, after I identify myself.

"I've got a lead on where Travis is."

"Well, good for you."

"He's out of state."

"Even better. I have to give you a lot of credit, Peter." It's the first time she's called me that. "I was right to hire you in the first place. You seem to know what you're doing."

I'm not going to argue with her. Especially since the next part of this conversation is going to be very delicate.

"I've been at this a while, Lila. I'm not perfect, but I get the job done. After all, I did find your husband, didn't I?"

"That you did. Well, thanks for keeping me in the loop about Travis. But from now on, you'll find out I'm totally disinterested in Mr. Chapman."

"Well, I'm not so sure about that. To be honest, this call is about more than just keeping you in the loop."

"Ah, I should have known..."

"Nothing bad. It's just that I need your help."

"Do you need me to take care of your cat or dog?"

"No. I'm pet-less. I have enough trouble taking care of myself, much less a dog or a cat or even a goldfish. The thing of it is, I need you to advance me a little traveling money. I'm kind of tapped out."

"And why would I do that?"

"Because it's in your best interest."

"How do you figure?"

"A couple ways, actually. I'm pretty sure Travis holds the key to who murdered your husband."

"You assume, that at this point, it matters to me who killed him."

"It should. Until it's nailed down, you're going to be a prime suspect."

"Really? How's that work?"

"The spouse is always the first go-to suspect. Especially when there's money involved. I'm assuming your husband leaves an estate."

"You would be correct."

"Cops love that as a possible motive."

"Is that so?"

"Yup. But there's another reason you might want to help me, or rather us, out."

"And that would be?"

"I think your husband was involved in some business dealings that involved a good deal of money. I think Travis is the key to finding out where it is, how much it is, and how you can get your hands on it. I think your husband was a smart cookie, especially when it came to money."

Here's where I take the leap off the ledge, without a parachute or a net to catch me.

"So, unless he left you a pretty hefty insurance policy, I'm guessing he made sure you didn't get his entire estate. In fact, I'm guessing he didn't leave you much more than ca fare..."

Silence. I've hit the bullseye.

"Lila?"

"I'm here. Keep talking."

"Seems to me, putting up with your husband's antics over the years, well, you've pretty much earned everything you can get. And I think there's a lot more out there that's rightfully yours."

"Really?"

"I think you know what I'm talking about. He was into something shady, so it's not like he kept the money in the bank, or in a safe in his office or at home. No safe there, correct?"

"No safe."

"I don't need much, Lila. Enough for a round-trip ticket, a few nights at a hotel, and meals. I'm not looking to make a killing on this." In fact, I was hoping to avoid a killing—my own.

"How much are we talking about?"

"Couple grand should do it. Anything left over, I return to you. I'll provide you with receipts, of course," I say knowing, of course, there's not a chance in hell I do that. But it sounds like the professional thing to say, so I say it.

Silence.

"And what, may I ask, is in this for you? I don't mean to be insulting, but I don't picture you as the charitable type. There's something going on here and I'm not quite sure what it is."

"You're right, Lila. There is something going on. Thanks to you, I'm in the middle of some deep shit. I need to find Travis to get out of it."

"So, it's really all about you."

"Not *all.* You're in there somewhere."

"So, you don't want anything from me except to finance this expedition to find Travis?"

"Exactly. Unless, of course, I uncover some hidden assets, or cash, which would rightfully be yours, as the surviving spouse."

"Why do you think there's money involved?"

"There's always money involved, Lila."

"How much?"

"I haven't the foggiest idea. But I'm guessing it's a substantial amount. No one's going to bother chasing after a few thousand. And by the way, if there is a chunk of money out there, I think I should get a finder's fee."

"What kind of finder's fee did you have in mind?"

"I'm not a greedy man, Lila. I live simply. No wife. No kids. No mortgage. I'd just like to cover my nut and maybe have a little something in the bank. How does twenty-percent sound?"

"Ten percent sounds a lot better."

"Fifteen."

Silence.

"All right. I think I can live with that."

Mission accomplished. There's no way I can hold her to that bonus. But her offer to pay me a finder's fee means we're in business together. It also means she'll advance me the two grand.

The rest of our conversation has to do with details. I impress upon her how important it is for me to act fast, before Travis has too much time to get lost. There's no way I'll take a check from her and she doesn't have the cash lying around. She asks me to drop by after two p.m. and pick up an envelope with the cash that she'll leave with her doorman.

17

Deep in the Heart of Texas

With Lila's dough, I go straight to the bank and pay off my credit card so I can use it if I need to. I book a flight on Southwest, where I don't have to worry about being tied down to a no-refund return flight. If Booth, Texas is where Travis is, I'm pretty sure I won't have much trouble finding him there. In small towns like that everyone knows everyone else's business and, unlike New Yorkers, they tend to be less suspicious and more likely to help a stranger. And in Texas, there's no one stranger than a half Italian half Jewish New York private dick.

I don't have time to waste, so I am to fly out early the next morning. Now, all I'm worrying about is getting to sleep and, if I do manage the impossible, waking up in time to make my flight.

Before I leave though, there's something I have to take care of. I'd bet my last dollar that Sergio is having me watched. He'd be stupid if he wasn't, and you don't get to the position Sergio's in by being stupid.

The last thing I want is having him up in my business. The only way to fix that is find the guy or guys watching me and make sure I get rid of them.

A little before eight p.m., I leave my apartment and take a leisurely walk through my East Village neighborhood. I'm hoping it looks as if I'm just taking an early evening stroll, but what I'm really doing is trying to flush out my tail. Once I do, then I'll figure out a way to get rid of him.

It doesn't take long to spot him. Half a block from my apartment I glance over my shoulder and see someone open the driver's side of a small black Toyota. It's not Ponytail and it's not Teardrop, but he stinks of mob. By this time, I can spot them a mile away. They don't all look or dress the same, but there's something about them that always gives them away. It could be the way they walk, really more of a strut, with their hands jammed into their pockets. They're almost always wearing some kind of head covering—a baseball cap, a watch cap, even a beret; and they dress inappropriately for the job they're doing and where they're doing it. Sometimes, they look as if they're going to a wedding or a funeral—think about that scene in *The Pope of Greenwich Village* when the wise guys are playing stickball in a school yard, all of them dressed in suits and ties. Other times, they're dressed like a bouncer from one of those after-hours clubs. Whatever it is, so long as you know what you're looking for, it's not hard to make them.

Years ago, I was sitting in on a mob court case—I was doing some investigating for one of the defendants in a RICO case. It was a big deal. Six or seven defendants, all members of one crime family, which meant there were at least as many attorneys. They were all crammed together, sitting at one long table. Much as I tried, I couldn't tell the crooks from the attorneys until the judge called the lawyers up to consult with him one some technicality. Only then could I tell them apart: the mob defendants wore well-tailored suits, while the lawyers' suits looked like they'd been picked up at the Salvation Army Thrift Shop.

I walk a few blocks north, then turn the corner and head toward Avenue A. Sure enough, my tail is following about half a block behind me. I smile to myself. This guy could use some serious schooling on how to tail someone without being made.

I make it to Avenue A, then I hang a left then walk back uptown. When I get to my street, I turn left and walk half a block, then disappear into my building. Making sure I can't be seen, I peek through the flimsy white curtain and watch as my tail walks over to a black Chevy parked directly across from my building, smack in front of a fire hydrant. I know he, or someone else who relieves him, is likely to be babysitting me here all night. They'll be there in the morning, I'm sure, so I need to figure out how I'm going to lose him before I take off for the airport early the next day.

I try falling asleep but the fear of missing my flight and the excitement tied to getting out to the airport without being followed is too much on my mind. I go over all the possibilities of how I'm going to lose this guy.

A little before one a.m., I finally give up. It's a close to four-hour flight. I'll take one of those Ambien in my bathroom cabinet and pop it just before takeoff. Maybe that'll be good for at least a couple hours' sleep. Even that much will be welcome.

I get on my computer and book a car service for seven a.m., but I give an address a block away. There's no back entrance in my building, so there's no way I can get out of the building without coming out the front door. But if what I'm planning works, I should be able to get to the airport without anyone knowing it.

When alarm goes off at five a.m., I hop off the couch, take a quick shower, and I'm ready to go.

18
It's All in the Wrist

It's five thirty, still dark, when I grab my backpack, sling it over my shoulder, and head downstairs.

I have a plan, but even as I reach the bottom of the last flight of stairs, it's still nebulous and negotiable, which means I'm pretty much going to play it by ear. I'm hoping my watchdog has left for the night—deciding that after tucking me in there's no way I'd be up and out this early.

No such luck. I peer out the front door window, protected by a flimsy, diaphanous curtain that's supposed to provide privacy to the tenants. The car from last night is still there. In it, I can make out a figure sitting in the front seat. My hope is he's fallen asleep. I've been on plenty of night stakeouts and unless there's someone with me, I've only managed to stay awake half the time.

I open the front door slowly and step outside. There's a nip in the air and I immediately feel the chill. Dressed for Texas weather not New York, I'm wearing a light-weight windbreaker. I check my watch. I'm ten minutes early for the car service. I check my phone and see a text from Sanjay, my driver. He's early, around the corner waiting at the appointed stop. I step back, as close as I can to the building, and text him that I'll be there in ten minutes.

I step out on the sidewalk and see that the guy in the car

across the street is looking right at me, which means there's no chance of sneaking by without him seeing me. I have no choice but to deal with this head-on.

I cross the street and come around to the driver's side of the car. He picks up a newspaper and is pretending to read it. I tap on the window and twirl my finger in a motion asking him to roll down the window.

At first, he just sits there, unsure what he should do. Me?

I twirl my finger again.

This time, he can't ignore me so he rolls down the window about half way. I need more.

"Hey," I say, "mind rolling it down a little more so we can talk?"

"What's to talk about?" he says.

I make the motion again.

He rolls the window down all the way. He's clean-shaven, maybe in his mid to late twenties. I know right away he's nothing more than an errand boy, low man on the totem pole, earning his stripes and hoping to move up. If he messes this up, it's not going to be good for him. But that's his problem, not mine. Maybe he'll have to find himself another line of work. And maybe that'll be a good thing. So, I figure what I'm going to do is do him a favor.

"What's your problem, man?" he asks.

"Funny, that's just what I was going to ask you. Why don't you step out of the car and we can talk about it?"

"Ain't nothing to talk about. I don't know what your problem is, man, but why don't you just toddle off." He makes a waving, dismissive motion with his hand, like he's telling some punk-ass kid to get lost.

"I want to know why you're parked out here at," I check my watch, "five thirty in the morning."

"How's that any of your business?"

"Neighborhood watch, pal."

"What?"

"You heard me."

I can see he's getting steamed, which is exactly what I want. I want him pissed off enough so that he'll get out of his car in an effort to intimidate me. The thing about these guys is they're easy to anger. I know the type. I've dealt with them all my life. Let's face it, I am one of them. We have that anger in common. Only difference is I know enough about the subject, and myself, to know this anger can easily be used against guys like him. When you're angry, you don't think straight. The id takes over. You do stupid things—believe me, I know. I've done plenty of them myself. That's exactly what's happening now. I see him reach for the door handle and I know it's game on. He starts to open the door and bingo! I'm in business.

Before the door is even halfway open, I grab him by the shirt and start to pull him out of the car. I've got the element of surprise—I can see that on his face. It wouldn't matter if he's bigger and stronger than me, though as he's halfway out I see he's just a short, skinny punk. I'm doing something unexpected and I can see a look of confusion on his face. He's startled enough so that he isn't resisting. When I've got him halfway out of the car, I haul off and smash him in the face with my right fist, making sure I connect with the bridge of his nose, the most sensitive part of the face. I can hear a crack. He cries out like a wounded animal. My adrenaline starts pumping. I'm back on the ballfield, clocking someone, anyone, the nearest one in a brawl that's started at the pitcher's mound. I smash him again in the face. This time catching him on the chin. I pound him twice more. Man, it feels good. Quick, short punches, but they do the job. Blood is spurting out his nose making it look a lot worse than it is. I twist my body away, so I don't get any on me. That's the last thing I need, getting on a plane wearing bloody clothes.

He's gagging for air. When I finally feel him go limp, I deliver the coup de grace, banging his head against the side of the door.

He's still conscious, but he's dazed enough that I'm free to

159

leave. He won't be in any condition to follow me.

I look around to make sure no one's watching.

At first, I feel kind of bad, blindsiding him like that. But that feeling doesn't last long. Instead, there's something oddly exhilarating happening. With every move, which seems to be choreographed by some unseen hand guiding me, I feel better. Calmer. Not hepped up, like on drugs or alcohol. It's something else. The release of violence seems to get into my heartbeat, slowing it down. In turn, it travels to my brain, and suddenly it's like I'm on a potent drug that's making me one with the world.

This is not the way it should be. But it is. I can't help it. It's a part of me. I'm sure the urge comes from somewhere hidden deep in my childhood. The anger I couldn't express at adults mistreating me, real or imagined.

But this is not the time for self-reflection. This is a time for action. Maybe I'll deal with these emotions later. Maybe not.

I stuff him back into the car and close the door. I look around to make sure no one's seen what's just happened. Except for the muffled sound of the guy still moaning, it's totally quiet and the streets are empty. I look up and see there are no lights on in any of the buildings on the block.

I guess I should feel sorry for him. Not only for the beating, but because whatever Sergio is going to do to him will probably be worse. I wonder what he's going to say. I wonder saying anything will do any good. He fucked up the only job he had. And now I'm getting away and Sergio will have no idea where I'm going. I hope it worries him. I hope he realizes he's not dealing with a chimp.

I leave the guy slumped over the steering wheel and start to jog away, headed a block south where Sanjay is waiting for me.

When I arrive, Sanjay seems to be catching a quick nap, his head leaning against the side window. I tap gently on the window and he stirs. I make that same twirling motion with my finger for him to roll down his window.

"Mr. Fortune?" he asks.

"That's me. Listen, I prepaid for this ride but," I reach into my back pocket, pull out my wallet and take out a ten. "But it turns out I don't need you, Sanjay. Change of plans. So, here's a little something extra for your trouble."

"You don't want I should drive you to the airport?"

"No. Take a nap. Take another call. Do anything you like. Early Christmas gift. Okay?"

He takes the bill from me and looks at it, as if to make sure it's real."

"You sure, Mr. Fortune?"

"I'm sure. This is good news, Sanjay. A gift from heaven. You believe in heaven, don't you?"

He looks at me like I'm crazy. I can't blame him. I roll my index finger the opposite way, motioning that he should roll up his window. He shrugs then rolls it up.

I jump out onto First Avenue and hail the first cab I see. He stops. I get in. As we head up First Avenue, I look back to see Sanjay still sitting there, probably wondering what the hell is going on.

Part Two
Texas

"That's a trail nothing but a nose can follow."
—James Fenimore Cooper, *The Last of the Mohicans*

1
Soft Landing

After more than three hours in the air, we touch down at George Bush Airport. I'm disappointed none of the Bushes are there to greet my arrival, but I'm guessing they have other things on their minds, what with their dynasty crumbling.

With the one-hour time difference, it's not yet noon. I've given myself plenty of time to get to Booth and maybe finish this thing off by the end of the day. I'm not quite sure how I want things to go, but I know that the only way I'm going to see my way clear of this mess is to confront Travis face to face. Whether he likes it or not. At this point I'm fighting for my survival, not his.

I rent a car from Alamo, trying to get into the Texas spirit, and pick up a map of Houston and environs. I know the car has GPS and I have my smart phone to dial up Google Maps, but there's just something about a map spread out on my lap that makes everything more real. I chart my course first with my finger and then with a pen I've appropriated from the rental car desk. As soon as I know the route, I head out on I-69 in the direction of Booth which according to Google is only about forty minutes southwest of Houston.

I've never been to Houston before but I'm immediately impressed by two things: the humidity and the flatness of the terrain. From the airport I can see the city rising from the ground, with no hills or mountains to challenge the height of the buildings. Houston, from what friends tell me is a more liberal city than its rival, Dallas, but politics matter little to me at this point. I want to be in and out, the quicker the better.

I've stuffed myself with snack food on the plane—I'm surprised how generous the flight attendants are when it comes to pretzels, peanuts, and various kinds of chips—so I don't have to waste time finding a place to eat. I promise myself that if I'm successful in finding Travis, I'll treat myself to a steak dinner before I get back on the plane.

As I get closer to Booth, there's something familiar about the houses. If I close my eyes I can see similar houses on Long Island, where I grew up after my mother's divorce. We moved out there from Queens because she insisted the schools were better. The houses are in what's known as the colonial style, a popular style of houses throughout much of New England. But this is Texas, not Long Island and certainly not New England.

It's approaching midafternoon and the car air-conditioning creates a safe cocoon shielding me from the hot Texas sun. That changes when I stop at a roadside barbeque joint a couple miles outside of town. It's not so much that I'm hungry as it is that I need to stretch my legs. I've been in seated position for close to six hours now and I'm starting to get cranky.

The midday heat is oppressive and since I've arrived from late fall in the city, I'm just not prepared. Even the short walk from the car has me perspiring.

Seeing as it's a little after two o'clock, I'm just about the only one in the place. The working folk have eaten and are probably back at work. Only in New York City do people eat at any hour of the day. Outside New York, lunch is twelve to two. Before and after that, people are doing what they're supposed to be doing. And it isn't eating.

The roadhouse, that's probably what they call it down here, gives off the pungent, familiar odor of barbeque sauce. It reminds me of when I was working in upstate New York. I'd travel almost an hour to the Dinosaur BBQ joint, just outside Syracuse. I stumbled across it accidentally one day as I was driving aimlessly through the area. I was drawn to it by a line of motorcycles parked out front. Only when I went inside did I find that it was legendary in those parts. A hangout for cyclists and blues aficionados because of the performances they offered almost every evening. Turns out, upstate New York, for some unknown reason, was on the "blues circuit," and the Dinosaur was one of the big stops for blues performers.

I sit down at a table near the back and order a plate of ribs, with a side of coleslaw and a Dos Equis. I'm served by a middle-aged woman dressed in an apron, her bleached blonde hair piled atop her head. Suddenly, maybe it's the aroma of the ribs, I'm hungry, hungrier than I thought.

I take out my phone and punch in Google, then I type in Booth, Texas white pages. I scroll down until I reach the Chapmans. Sure enough, there are a few of them in the greater Booth area.

"Anything else, hon," the waitress asks, as I'm finishing off my last rib and fourth napkin. "Another beer, maybe?"

I love being called *hon*. It gives me the obviously false but still satisfying feeling that someone cares.

"No, thanks," I say. I nod toward the rental parked outside. "I'm driving."

She smiles. "Never stopped anyone else around these parts," she says.

"Yeah, well, I'm not from around these parts. How about you?"

"All my life, hon. I jest can't seem to get away. Where you from? Wait! Let me guess."

"Have at it."

She looks me over, eyes the seat across from me, then pulls out the chair and sits down.

"Feels good to get off these dogs every once in a while. You don't mind, do ya?"

"Absolutely not."

She leans forward and rests her chin on two fists. I see the tat on her forearm, a blue and red Lonestar.

"Name's Ruby. Yours?"

"Pete."

"I'm guessing you're a Yankee, Pete. But not one of those obnoxious ones."

"We're all obnoxious, Ruthie."

She smiles. "New York City, right?" She claps her hands together triumphantly. "I'm right, ain't I?"

"You are. How'd you do that?"

"You got that New York City *I don't give a damn* attitude. I knew it right off when you said you're as obnoxious as the next guy. By the way, hon, you say that to a born and bred Texan and you'd be staring down the barrel of one of them shotguns they keep behind the seat of their pickup."

"I'll try to watch what I say down here."

"What business you got down here, hon?"

"I'm looking for someone. You wouldn't happen to know anything about the Chapman family who lives around here, would you?"

"We got us a whole lot of Chapmans down this way, hon. You got one in particular in mind?"

"I do. Name's Travis."

Her face breaks into a wide grin.

"You know him?"

"I sure as hell do. Quite a hell-raiser that one was. When he was a kid, a' course. Real handsome, but woo-whee. He was some kinda heart-breaker, that one was. But once you open the package you better be prepared for what comes outta the box."

"Trouble, huh?"

"You can say that again. Nothin' real bad, y'understan'. Just a typical good-looking kid who gets away with almost anything 'cause a the way he looks. Why you lookin' for him, hon?"

"He's in a little trouble and I want to warn him."

"Trouble? What kind of trouble?"

"I really can't say. It would be breaking a confidence."

"As I recall, ole Travis wanted to be one of them movie stars."

"That's how we met," I lie. "Saw him do his thing up on stage."

"That boy have any real talent?"

"I'm no expert, but he was pretty convincing."

"You're shittin' me! Travis made it on Broadway, huh? Well, I guess he looks the part, but I never thought he'd be one to make somethin' of hisself."

"Well, we're not talking Broadway here. More like off-off…"

"Still. I'm kinda proud that little shit made somethin' of hisself. But you think he's back down here? What? Visiting, maybe?"

"Exactly. I'm not positive, but I think there's a good chance he's around. Do you know where his family lives?"

"His people have a spread a few miles south of town."

"You wouldn't happen to have the address, would you?"

She smiles. "Address? No. But I can tell you how to get there."

"That'd be much appreciated."

She leans back. The grin disappears. "How do I know you ain't the trouble he's trying to get away from?"

"Do I look like someone who could make trouble for anyone?"

The smile returns. "Nah. You look pretty harmless to me. And you know what? I'm a pretty good judge of character. I mean, waitressing all these years you get kind of a sixth sense about folks. You can tell the good from the bad, pretty easy. Let me tell you something, hon. You got a minute?"

"I do."

"You sure you don't want another beer? On me."

I don't, but I also don't want to insult her. "You know what? As a matter of fact, I am getting a little thirsty."

She pops up and pats me on the shoulder as she passes by, heading back to the bar area.

After Ruby returns with my beer, I sit through a couple of stories about the characters she's met, and a little about her life—three husbands, "one worser than the other," and four kids. "Not one of 'em takes after me."

Finally, I see a spot where I can make my getaway, but only after she jots down directions to the Chapman place. I leave a hefty tip, hop back into my rental, and head off to find good ole Travis.

2
How to Make Friends and Influence People

Ruby's directions are on the money. The house she's described is set back from the road, behind a wooden fence. Immediately, I'm transported back in time to the neighborhood I spent several years growing up in back in Manhasset, Long Island. Only here neighbors aren't on top of each other, but sometimes as far as half a mile apart. How far, I ask myself, do I have to travel to get right back to where I came from?

I drive past the house once, just to get the lay of the land, and then park about a hundred yards down the road. Before I pull into the gravel driveway, I'm thinking I ought to have some kind of plan, but for the life of me I can't quite figure out what it is or should be.

If someone answers the door who isn't Travis how do I explain why I'm looking for him? Do I tell the truth? Or a version of the truth? Or do I make up a semi-plausible tale that will get this unknown person to open up about where I can find Travis?

And what if Travis is the one who opens the door? Do I grab onto him, pull him outside and read him the riot act? And what is the riot act? Do I tell him the truth, that Sergio and his people are after him? Will that spook him enough so that he makes like a rabbit and runs into an even deeper hole? Or do I lie to him with some kind of fantastical story that lures him back to New

York, to what is almost certainly a death sentence for him? Do I to help him figure a way out of the mess he's got himself into?

These are the questions running through my mind as I flip on the radio and cruise until I can find a classic rock station. The Beach Boys are singing about Daddy taking the T-Bird away. And then there's the Beatles singing "Blackbird." I sit there absently humming along to the music, tapping rhythmically on the steering wheel. What I'm doing is just wasting time, putting off the inevitable.

Finally, as the Rolling Stones begin singing about tumbling dice, I switch off the radio, then the engine. The air-conditioning goes off. I sit in silence for another moment or two and then, finally, I switch the engine back on, turn the car around and slowly head back toward the Chapman's driveway.

Showtime.

The crunching of the wheels meeting the gravel is somehow reassuring. In what seems like a surreal situation, the sound grounds me, reminding me I really am in Texas, about to confront someone who has put my life in jeopardy.

I stop halfway up the long driveway and get out of the car. I slam the door, as a signal to anyone who might be watching that I have nothing to hide. No need to get out the shotgun and threaten to blow me off the property if I don't leave. I'm not the one who's dangerous. I'm lying. Of course, I'm dangerous. I hold Travis's fate in my hands. Everything depends on what I tell him and how I tell it. Once Travis and I connect, his life will be altered forever. Even I'm not sure how. But it will be.

There's a two-car garage next to the house, but the door is closed so I can't tell if anyone's home. The house is in disrepair, desperately in need of a paint job. The lawn in front has patches of brown, burned-out grass, and it looks like it hasn't been cut in a while. There are two large trees hovering above the house, offering much needed shade, I'm sure. There are two floors. The windows on both floors are open, probably to let in the slight, erratic breeze.

I walk up the three steps leading to the screened in porch on which there's one of those swinging benches and two beat-up lawn chairs. There are a couple of abandoned toys on the floor. Travis must have a sibling who has a kid or two. I listen for sounds of kids playing, but there's nothing. I knock on the door. No answer. I knock again. Still nothing.

I'm about to get back in the car and wait there until someone shows up, when I hear something coming from behind the house. Children's screams, not from terror but from delight. Where there are children there are most likely adults, so I turn around and head toward the back of the house, where I find a small, aboveground pool, with two small children frolicking in it. One boy. One girl. Six, seven, eight years old. It's hard to tell for sure. The girl is older and her younger brother screeches gleefully whenever she flicks water in his direction. Behind the pool is a rusted double-swing set. Next to it, a trampoline.

About thirty feet away, there's a guy, too old to be Travis, lying in one of those self-contained hammocks, a newspaper lying open across his chest, his arm hanging over the side. Two women are sitting in folding chairs under a large tree, a small table with two drinks on it between them. One's older, maybe in her late fifties, early sixties. The other is younger, in her late twenties or early thirties. As I move closer, I can see they resemble each other enough to know they're mother and daughter.

"Hey, there," I call out, as I approach. The figure in the hammock doesn't react—he's fast asleep—but the two women look up.

"I'm awfully sorry to bother you," I say.

The older woman gets up and walks toward me. She's wearing a yellow, summery dress and her gray hair is tied up in a bun. "Not a bother yet," she says. "Least not till you explain why you're in my backyard."

"I'm real sorry about that, ma'am, but I knocked and no one answered."

"That's cause we're all back here," she says. "How can I

help you? You lost or something?"

If I'm to answer truthfully, I would say yes, because I'm always feeling a little lost. But that doesn't seem appropriate. At least not if I'm going to make this as quick as possible.

I take a chance.

"I'm looking for your son. Travis."

She looks at me a moment before answering. "You a friend of his?"

"You might say."

"From New York?"

"That's right."

"You one of those actors, too?"

I shake my head and smile. "Not a chance."

The younger woman joins us, carrying her now empty glass.

"Who's this, Mama?" she asks, ignoring me, as if I'm not there.

"Says he's a friend of Travis. From up there in New York."

"How do you know him?" the younger woman asks.

"We had some business dealings."

She smiles. "My brother has a business? I thought he was an actor. You some kind of producer or director or something?"

I shake my head no.

"Then what kind of business?" asks the younger one.

"Hold on, Sissy," says the older one. "Maybe his business is none of our business."

"It's not that, ma'am," I say. "It's just that I don't know what Travis's told you and I don't want to get in the middle of anything."

"Seems to me," says the younger one, "you're already there."

"All right, Sissy. I think we're making a bad impression on this young man. We're forgetting our manners. We ought to offer the gentleman something to drink." She turns to me. "Would you like something cold to drink? Lemonade? Sun tea? A beer, maybe?"

Saying yes buys me more time. Saying yes makes me more of

a guest than an interloper.

"That would be nice," I say. "It's a pretty hot day."

"This here's Texas," says Sissy. "It's supposed to be hot."

I can see the older one is starting to lose patience with her daughter.

"Sissy, why don't you go inside and bring the gentleman a glass of...?"

She looks back at me.

"Iced tea would be fine, thank you."

Sissy disappears into the white clapboard house through the screen door and I'm left alone with this woman who I assume is Travis's mother—and the two kids still splashing around in the pool.

"What'd you say your name was?" she asks.

"It's Pete. Or Peter." I stick out my hand.

"Well, it's nice to meet you, Peter. Or do you prefer Pete?"

"Either one's fine, ma'am."

"My name's Esther Chapman. And that there's..." she gestures with her head in the direction of the house, "Danielle, though she prefers to be called Dana. God knows why. And them's her two kids over there. Jesse and Amanda."

"Nice family..."

"When they're behaving themselves. You'll excuse me a second and I'll find you something to sit on."

Esther grabs a folding chair that's leaning against the house next to a cellar door on the ground and drags it back toward the tree, beckoning me to follow her.

As I sit down, she calls over to the kids the pool. "Now, you children behave yourselves or else your momma and me are gonna call a time out."

At the sound of her voice, the kids stop splashing around and are frozen in space, looking back at their grandmother like two little angels.

She smiles.

"They're really good kids, but they sometimes get a little

rambunctious. Sit," she says, gesturing toward the new chair.

The two little angels, who've been silent for a few seconds, are now back to screeching and splashing around in the pool. Sissy returns with a tray of an empty glass filled with ice and a pitcher of tea and a bottle of Rolling Rock. She sets the tray down on the table. She begins to pour tea into my glass, then hands it to me.

"Mama?"

Esther puts her hand up in a stop position.

"No, thanks, honey."

Sissy twists open the beer and takes a slug.

"Now," Sissy says, turning to me. "What is it that brings you all the way down here? I can't imagine it's just to see my brother."

"Well, ma'am, it is. Do you know where he is?"

"Approximately," Sissy says, a slight smile curling up the edges of her mouth. "Why'd you say you were looking for him?"

"I didn't."

"He ain't in any trouble, is he?" asks Esther.

"Like Travis would go anywhere near trouble," says Sissy.

"Sissy, you oughtn't talk about your brother that way."

"Well, Mama, it's not like Travis is any stranger to trouble."

"Hush. You're gonna give Mr.? Well, you know, I never did get last your name, Mr.?"

"Fortunato."

"That's an Italian name, ain't it?"

"I'm half Italian."

"What's the other half?" asks Sissy.

"Something else," I say.

Her mother smiles. "He got you there, Mary Margaret."

Sissy's face collapses into a pout.

"I'm sorry, Mama. I didn't mean to be nosy."

"Sure, you did."

"It's okay, Mrs. Chapman."

"It's Esther, honey. Mrs. Chapman would be my mother-in-law, may she not rest in peace."

"Is Mr. Chapman around? Maybe he knows where Travis is."

"I surely doubt that since Mr. Chapman ain't been around for quite some time."

"I'm sorry..."

"Don't be sorry, honey. First of all, he ain't dead. Second of all, that would be an improvement for everyone. He jest took up one day and we ain't heard from him since."

"Not like he's missed," says Sissy, taking another slug of her Rolling Rock.

"You know we don't like to speak ill of the departed, Sissy. Even if they ain't actually dead. Truth is," she turns to me, "it would be better if he were. That way, I wouldn't have to worry 'bout him jest showin' up one day out of the blue."

"We're better off pretending he is..."

I've never seen anyone smile and give a disapproving look at the same time, but somehow Travis's mother carries it off.

"I'd really appreciate it if you could tell me where to find Travis, Esther. Or at least get word to him that I'm here looking for him."

She runs two fingers over her lips. "I'm guessing you ain't about to tell me what kind of trouble he's in."

"I didn't say he's in trouble."

"Sure, you did. You just didn't put it in words. What kind of business did you say you were in?"

I could make something up, but at this point I don't see any reason to lie.

"I'm a private investigator."

"I don't know as if I like the sound of that."

"I know exactly what you mean. It's not something I brag about."

"You know, Pete, there's something about you that makes me want to help you out even if you are one of those private eyes from New York City."

"I'm flattered, Esther. Most people don't look at me kindly."

"You seem like an okay enough fella. Far as I know, Travis is off riding somewheres." She checks her watch. "I reckon he'll be back within an hour or so. But it could be later if he stops off at Slater's."

"Slater's?"

"A bar," says Sissy.

"It's a roadhouse, Sissy. Don't you go making it sound worse than it is."

"Instead of waiting for him here and getting in your way, what if you just give me directions to Slater's and I hop over there and see if I can find Travis. If he's not there, I'll just come back here and wait for him, if you don't mind. But if I miss him, I sure hope you hold onto him until I get back. This really is serious, Esther."

"When isn't it serious with Travis," says Sissy.

I stare at his mother, trying to figure if I've got her on my side or not. It's not like if I keep talking I'm going to convince her. It's obvious she knows what she wants and I have a strong feeling she's not someone who changes her mind very often.

"Tell you what. You finish your tea and I'll go inside and write down the directions to Slater's. How's that sound?"

"Sounds perfect, Esther."

3

Mama Don't Let Your Babies Grow Up to Be Cowboys

Slater's is, as Esther explains, only about fifteen minutes or so down the road, southwest of town.

I click on the radio and find a country-western station that doesn't sound too corny. It's soothing to listen to someone else's troubles about runaway dogs, love affairs gone bad, and mamas who don't let their babies become cowboys. It doesn't actually matter what kind of music it is, so long as I can crank up the volume to the point where it takes my mind off what's coming up: confronting Travis.

There's a small parking area in the back. A couple cars, two or three motorcycles. I'm hoping one of the vehicles belongs to Travis because I don't relish chasing him all over Texas. After Houston and Booth, I've pretty much had my fill.

After parking the car, I sit there several minutes, thinking about what I'm going to do if Travis is inside. To be honest, I'm hoping if I sit here long enough Travis will walk out the door and I can grab hold of him in neutral territory.

This is homefield advantage for Travis and I'm afraid he has plenty of good old boy drinking buddies in Slater's. The last thing I want is to get into a ruckus where I'm outnumbered from the get-go. Look, I don't mind a good tussle—it keeps me sharp and I know I won't have to work up much of a sweat to take Travis down. Sure, he's bigger than me. And younger than me. But I'm well-schooled in the art of brawling, and I'd bet pretty *boy* has managed to avoid physical confrontations.

I work best when confronted with a challenge but I'm always better when I have the element of surprise and when I've isolated my target so I'm not taking on the world. I've done that enough times to know I never come out on top when I'm outnumbered. But I was younger then. Stupider. Less inhibited. Back when I was playing ball, I was the catalyst for more than my share of free-for-alls on the diamond. When you're the instigator and you find yourself in the middle of the scrum, it's more than likely that you're going to get the worst of it. Unless you choose your targets well. Always go for the little guy. For the guy who isn't looking. Sure, I got my share of bruises, but no matter how bad I looked at the end of the melee, the other guy or guys looked worse. I never took formal boxing lessons. With me, it was a matter of trial and error. But I'm a fast learner and it wasn't long before I learned where to hit and how hard.

I'm older now—I'd say wiser, too, except that wouldn't be true—and do my best to avoid physical confrontations. That doesn't mean I'm any easier to get along with. I've still got that temper, though I'd like to think I've got a longer fuse. And there are alternatives. For instance, if the other guy sees that look in your eyes that says, *I'm one bad-ass, crazy motherfucker and there is nothing I won't do*, he'll most likely back off without so much as a punch being thrown.

The older I get, the harder it gets to summon up that look. That attitude. That persona. What scares me is that one day, when I least expect it and when I most need it, I won't be able to find it. It's like losing your fastball. Or your bat is just a wee bit slower. And when that day comes, and it comes when you never expect it, you're never gonna get it back. It's over, baby, and when it is you might as well find another line of work.

That's one of the things that frightens me about this anger management business. What if I don't want to manage it? What if it's so much a part of me that if I don't have it, I'll shrink into nothingness? What if I need that anger to prove to myself I'm alive?

It's these times when I begin to doubt whether I'm *real*. And I'm afraid it's during these times that, even if it's unconsciously, I find myself looking for a good fight. A fight that will prove to me I'm still alive. You're supposed to mellow with age, but if I lose that fire in my gut? What am I then? Who am I?

Still, I try to avoid physical altercations when I can. Mostly it because these days I'm more likely to hurt myself throwing a punch more than hurt my target. And let's face it, learning how to control my temper, how to channel it into something less dangerous, getting rid of my crazy streak, has probably saved me from more than one good old-fashioned beatdown.

I check my watch. It's close to five thirty. If I wait any longer I'm afraid the joint will fill up with the after-work crowd which will only make it more difficult to isolate Travis. If he gives me trouble, I'm not about to challenge him against those odds.

It's time. I step out of the car. Out of habit, I lock the door, even though the chances of anyone jacking this rental are practically nil.

Slater's reminds me of that dive bar on 9th Avenue where Travis used to work. Some guys have a type of woman they're attracted to. With Travis, it appears to be bars.

The joint is dark and smells of beer. There are a dozen or so tables. Sawdust on the floor. A long bar, with all kinds of neon signs flashing behind it, advertising various brands of beer. There's a pool table in the back, but no one's using it. There's a juke box and a stage big enough for a small country-western combo. It's bare now, except for a drum set and two microphone stands. There's an open area in the middle of the room which I'm guessing is in use later in the evening when inhibitions have long since disappeared and patrons are dancing the Texas Two-Step. In the back, there are two separate restrooms. A blue neon light flashes *Hombres*. A red neon light flashes *Las Mujeres*.

There are maybe a dozen or so patrons, most of them men in jeans and T-shirts. The bartender is a sexy blonde wearing a denim shirt with rolled up sleeves. There are three seats taken at the bar and one of them is occupied by none other than Travis Chapman.

Travis doesn't see me as I slide onto the stool next to him. He's talking to two middle-aged men wearing cowboy hats with their big beer bellies hanging out in front of them.

Only when the bartender asks, "What can I get you, stranger?" does he turn around.

For a split second, there's a confused look on his face because he doesn't recognize me. I'm not surprised. I'm probably the last person he'd expect to see sitting next to him at his local hangout. Slowly, his expression changes from confusion to shock, as it sinks in who I am and why I'm there.

"What the fuck…?" he says.

I put my hand on his shoulder in part to keep him from bolting and to show him I'm not a figment of his imagination.

"Your second worst nightmare is here, Travis."

For a moment he's too stunned to say anything but finally he manages, "Second worst?"

I smile. "Sergio sends his regards."

I've hit a nerve. The color drains from Travis's face. All I can do is smile.

"I…um…"

"Why don't we find somewhere we can talk, Travis?"

His eyes, which look like they're going to leap out of his head, dart left, then right. I can practically see the wheels turning in his head. He's wondering what to do. Should he run? Should he talk to me? I've had my fun. I give him a little push in the right direction.

"You're in a shitload of trouble, my friend. You know it and I know it. Unfortunately, you've dragged me into the muck with you, so I'm here to see if I can help *us* out of it."

He's in shock. He's having trouble processing the situation.

Fine by me. The more he thinks I'm his only way out of this, the more likely it is I can figure out something that works for both of us. If not both of us, certainly me.

"Come on," I say, patting him on the shoulder. "Let's take a walk, okay?"

I don't have to ask again. Like a little puppy dog, he starts to get up and follow me. He doesn't take more than a step when the middle-aged cowboy sitting next to him, wearing a fancy white cowboy shirt and faded blue jeans, his face deeply lined from the sun, turns his head.

"Hey, Travis, everything okay, man?"

Travis nods.

He gets up, tapping the shoulder of the guy next to him. "You sure about that?"

"It's okay," says Travis.

"Who is this guy?" the cowboy asks, jerking a thumb my way. "He ain't giving you no trouble, is he?"

This is the do or die moment. If Travis hesitates or says something derogatory about me, I'm gonna have to fight my way out of there. I start planning my getaway. Maybe shove Travis into the other guy and then throw a couple punches? Or pick up the half-empty beer bottle sitting on the bar in front of Travis? I try calculating how long it'll take me to make it out the front door. Past the bar, I see daylight. There's a back entrance. Maybe I should head for that? I'm glad I don't have my Glock because I'd be tempted to pull it out and that would be a bad idea, seeing as there's a good chance every one of these dudes is packing.

Travis does his best to soothe the situation. "Everything's fine," he says as he puts a hand on my shoulder. "Unexpected visit from a pal from New York. Good to see you, Pete."

He's a better actor than I thought.

"You sure?" says the cowboy, taking a step toward us. One more step and he's officially in my space. My hands, at my sides, become fists. I don't want to hit him. But I know I will if he takes one step closer.

"Sure as shit. Pete, meet Jordan. Jordan, this here is Pete Fortunato. I can't believe he came all the way down here from the city."

Somehow, between here and New York City, Travis has reconnected with his Texas drawl which he probably spent good money trying to get rid of in acting school.

Jordan eyes me warily. His face is tight. A moment or two passes then slowly his face turns soft. He smiles. I can see from the expression on his face he believes Travis is not in any danger. At least not from me. He extends his hand.

"Sorry, pardner. Just looking out for my friend here." He claps Travis twice on the back, as I take his hand and shake it.

"No harm, no foul," I say. I turn to Travis. "Maybe we ought to move along. There's that deadline…"

"Sure. Sure," he says. "Hey, Jordan, see you boys tomorrow, right? And don't forget about that boar hunting thing we're gonna put together."

"You bet," says Jordan, who slides back onto his stool.

The other guy, who till this point was just an interested bystander, gives a little wave.

Once we get outside, I point to my rental parked off to the side.

"Boar hunting?" I say.

"Yeah. It's a big deal down here. Plenty of wild boar. They're mean sons of bitches. That's what they do down here to mean sons of bitches. They hunt them and when they fine 'em, they bring 'em down. Maybe they know what they're doing." He stops and fixes me with a grin. "And that's what they do to people, too."

"Why don't we take a little ride, Travis? When we're finished, I'll bring you back here and you can pick up your car."

"You mean my bike," he says, nodding toward the Harley parked under a tree.

"Whatever."

"Why don't I just follow you? It'll make things a whole lot easier."

"Because I want to make sure you don't turn rabbit on me."

He doesn't say anything. Those wheels again. I'm sure he doesn't like the idea of me being in charge, but he realizes I'm not about to do it any other way. And I'm hoping he's smart enough to know I'm his only way out.

"Okay," he says, reluctantly. "Let's get this fucking thing over with."

4
The Reading of the Riot Act

We drive a few miles further out of town until we reach a small complex of buildings which, from the look of it, is a school. I can see from the look on his face that this place means something to Travis. But I don't ask because I don't want to know. I want to get this over with as soon as possible. Something I certainly don't want is to relive Travis's life story All I want is my own life back.

Travis instructs me to pull into the empty parking lot.

"Park over there," he orders, pointing to a spot near the back, under a tree. "I went to high school here," he explains. Damn! Just what I didn't want to hear. But now he's off and running.

"When I was a senior I finally saved up enough to buy a car. It was such a piece of shit. I was embarrassed, so this is where I used to park." He shrugs. "My folks wouldn't give me a dime, not that they had one to spare, so I had to use everything I saved up pumping gas at the station. I'd come home smelling like a fucking refinery. My mom could never seem to get that smell out of my clothes. When I left for college, I burned them in the backyard. I can still smell that damn smell though."

I try to act disinterested. I don't want to encourage him to stroll me down memory lane with him. What I want is to get out of Texas as quick as I can. Besides, I can't think of anything I want less than to hear Travis's gut-wrenching life story. If I start feeling sorry for him, I might wind up doing something that's good for me. I don't want to do anything like that.

I turn off the engine. I figure we can just sit here and get it over with. But Travis has other ideas.

"Let's go over there," he says, pointing to a large athletic field behind and to the left of the school building. "We'll sit in the bleachers."

"What's wrong with right here?"

"I want to be out in the open. Where I can breathe real air..."

"Okay, so long as I don't have to hear any of your damn coming of age stories, Travis. Like how you scored the winning touchdown and became the goddamn school hero. Because then I'd feel compelled to tell you mine and trust me, no one wants to go down that road, least of all me."

"Second string, my man, and I was lucky to make that. I was a scrawny-ass kid. I only went out for the team to satisfy my dad. He was a real hotshot in school, played for the Longhorns," he makes the hook 'em horns sign with the fingers of his right hand. "Used to say that he coulda been All-Conference, 'cept he hurt his knee. So, you don't have to worry about school hero stories from me."

I could tell him my sad athletic tales, but even I'm tired of hearing about them. And that's not what I'm here for. Bonding with Travis is way down on my to-do list.

"Me? All's I wanted to do was get on that stage. My pop thought that was sissy shit. That's what he used to call it," he tells me as we make our way to the bleachers.

Once we're there, I let him lead me up to the top row and we sit down at what turns out to be the fifty-yard line.

He looks down. "Man, could I tell you stories about what went on under these bleachers late at night."

"Another time, Travis. We've got more important things to talk about now."

"Yeah. Another time. So, what's so important you had to come all the way down here. And how the fuck did you find me, anyway?"

"I'm a fucking PI, Travis. It's what I do. That's my superpower. But it doesn't matter how I did it, I found you and now we've got a lot to talk about. And I don't have to tell you how important it is…to you."

"How do you know about Sergio?"

"He arranged for me to meet him. Or, more to the point, he kidnapped me."

"Oh, shit, man. I'm sorry about that."

"So am I."

Travis stares out into space. I can't be sure if he's tripping down memory lane, recalling his high school days, or he's thinking about the trouble he's in. Finally, he breaks the silence.

"So, why are you here? What do you want from me?"

I can lie, make up some cock and bull story I'm sure Travis will buy. He's not the brightest bulb on the circuit. But for some reason I figure the best way to deal with this situation is to be straight with him.

"You know what kind of trouble you're in, Travis, so it shouldn't come as a surprise that Sergio wants to get his hands on you. I'm not going to lie to you. He sent me to bring you back."

"Oh, man…" he moans, his head sinking into his hands.

"You're not surprised, are you?"

He shakes his head no.

Finally, he looks up. "I'm a fucking dead man, aren't I?"

"That's not my job, Travis. My job is to find you."

"You could make believe you didn't. You could do that, right?"

"You think he's going to buy that? He's no moron, Travis. He knows eventually I'll track you down."

"You haven't said anything yet, have you?"

I shake my head no.

"So, you could just say you weren't able to track me down

and then I could just disappear. That would work, wouldn't it?"

I shake my head. "He's not the type who'll give up. He'll just hire someone else. Maybe he already has. That's not the way you're getting out of this. And the thing of it is, Travis, you've managed to pull me into the shit with you. You really think he's going to just let me walk away? You do know the reputation the Albanians have, don't you?"

He's practically in tears. "Yeah. I know."

"I don't know why the hell you got involved with them in the first place, man."

"It wasn't me! It was Alston. He's the one who got me into this mess."

"What mess are we talking about? Maybe, if you come clean and tell me all about it, I can figure some way out of this. What was this business you guys were in?"

"The thing is, I don't exactly know. All I can tell you is that it had to do with money laundering. They had all this cash— god knows where it came from…"

"It doesn't take much imagination to figure out where. They're into all kinds of shit. But it doesn't matter how they got it, it's where you guys put it. How much are we talking about?"

"I'm not sure. But it was a lot."

"What's a lot, Travis?"

"A million. Maybe two?"

I whistle through my teeth.

"So, let me guess. Some of that money stuck to Alston's fingers, right?"

"I guess." He hesitates for a moment. "Maybe more than just some."

"Don't guess, Travis. Tell me everything you know."

"It's not much. I swear. I was just his errand boy most of the time. He needed someone to do the legwork. To bounce ideas off."

"Do you know what he did with the dough?"

"He probably invested it in all kinds of things. He was big

on diversifying. It didn't matter to them what he did with it just so long as the money came back scrubbed clean. Alston used to talk about precious metals all the time, so part of it might have been in that."

"You mean he bought silver or gold? And, if so, where the hell would he keep it?"

"Nah. It wasn't like that. He set up a company that bought and sold gold and silver and maybe even diamonds. But it's not like he ever had the stuff in his hands. It was all on paper. He'd buy the stocks or bonds or whatever and then he'd sell them off and the cash from those sales would be clean. It didn't even matter if he lost a little money on the sale. He just called that the cost of doing business. I think his end of the deal was that he got two percent, or something like that. At least that's what he told me. But you know, he could have been conning me…"

"Or the Albanians."

"I guess. I mean, if Sergio is after money, Alston must have ripped him off."

"Who's to say he ever actually bought anything? He could have just kept the cash himself, told Sergio he invested it and lost a little, then returned the clean cash to Sergio minus his percentage and the money he skimmed off the top."

"I never thought of that."

"You just haven't developed your criminal mind yet, Travis. You think Sergio could have had Alston killed?"

He shrugs. "I guess it's possible."

"You're gonna have to do better than that, Travis."

"How should I know? All's I know is it wasn't me. Besides, what difference does it make who killed him? The only thing that's important now is to get Sergio off my ass. And," he grins, "now yours, too."

Unfortunately, he's right. We're in the same fix, which is the only reason I'm sitting here talking to this asshole.

"The only way that's going to happen is for him to get back whatever he thinks is his. And even then, I gotta be honest with you, Travis, I wouldn't be surprised if he wants to make a lesson out of you."

"A lesson?"

"A warning to anyone else who might want to rip him off."

"But I didn't rip him off. I swear. It was all Alston."

"That doesn't matter. Now, it's all about the dough. Who's got it, Travis?"

"I honestly don't know."

"If you don't have it, who does?"

He repeats that he doesn't know. I stare at him square in the eyes.

He throws his hands in the air. "I swear, man. On my fucking mother's grave."

"You're mother's alive and well, Travis."

"I mean figuratively on her grave."

"You know something, Travis. I know you do."

He shakes his head. "All I know is that before he died, Alston gave me twenty-five grand, which was supposed to be my cut. I mean, how do you think I paid for this trip down here? And the bike?"

"I thought you were saving up to go to Hollywood and become a star?"

"Yeah, yeah. I was gonna do that. That's why I got the bike. It was cheaper than a car. I was..."

"Enough, Travis!"

His head sinks into his hands again. "Oh, man, I am in deep, deep shit here, aren't I? What the hell am I going to do? If you found me, someone else can. Or maybe," I can hear the panic in his voice, "maybe they followed you."

"Give me some credit, Travis. Don't you think I covered my tracks?"

He looks up at me. His pupils are dilated but I know it's fear not beer.

He shakes his head back and forth, like one of those bobble-head dolls.

"That doesn't make me feel any better. These guys probably have eyes everywhere. And even if I get out of here, my family. They could come after my family…"

I see tears starting to form at the corners of his eyes.

I want him scared. I want him scared to death.

"And they would, Travis. They would."

"How am I going to get out of this? How?"

I look him straight in the eyes. "First off, did you kill Alston?"

"No. I swear it. No way," he says, shaking his head back and forth.

"Who did?"

"How should I know?"

"The Albanians?"

"Maybe…" He's silent for a moment. "They could have, right?"

"Sure. But why would they kill him before they got their money back, if that's what it's all about? They couldn't be certain you'd know where the dough is. They wouldn't kill him unless, one," I hold up a finger, "he told them you had it. Or two," I hold up another finger, "they didn't care about the dough and just wanted to make a statement."

"What kind of statement?"

"That you don't fuck around with the mob. But if you ask me, I don't think they were behind it."

"Why not?"

"Because they would have tortured him first to get him to give back their money, or at least tell them where they could find it."

"But if he told them I had it…?"

I shake my head. "Then they'd keep him on ice until they found you and determined if he was lying or not."

"Hell, then why should I give a damn who killed him, so long as it wasn't the Albanians? I mean, I don't really give a shit about him. He got me into all this. Fuck him. He deserved what he got."

"Yeah, but the question is do we deserve what we're going to get if we don't think of some way out of this?"

"I just gotta get lost…"

"No. What we've got to do is find out what they're looking for and then find it. If it's money, we have to track it down and give it back."

"How are we going to do that?" he says, and the truth is, I don't have an answer.

5
On the Road Again

I drive back to Slater's, drop Travis off so he can get his motorcycle, then follow him back to his mother's place.

Travis has me spooked, so every so often I check my rearview mirror to see if anyone's following us. I'm pretty sure there's no way anyone could have followed me down from the city, but he's right. If I found Travis I see no reason why they couldn't. I don't even want to think about what's waiting for me back in the city even if we do find and give back what they're looking for. It's not like they're going to greet me with open arms after the good beating I gave that dude outside my building. These Albanians, with their blood feuds, have very long memories. It's that eye for an eye thing that worries me. The Albanians are known for their obsession with revenge. You kill one of theirs, they'll hunt you down and kill you and your family. The only way those feuds end is if everyone's in the ground.

Fact is, I'm in almost as much trouble as Travis unless there's some way I can talk or bargain my way out of this mess. I don't think it's simply a matter of handing Travis over to them. I've considered it, and if I thought that would do the trick, I might hand him over.

Travis would be collateral damage. He's the one who got himself involved in shady business. I'm the innocent bystander.

Okay, he is growing on me and so I'd like to help him out if I can. But my number one priority is me, and if it means sacrificing Travis, well, I can't even say I'll lose much sleep over it since I hardly ever get much sleep anyway. Besides, I have no idea whether Travis is telling the truth. About anything. My gut tells me there's stuff he's holding back, but there's nothing I can do about it.

Before we get back to the Chapmans' we agree that we won't say anything to his mother or sister. "Do not, under any circumstances, get them involved," I say as firmly as I can. "The less they know about this shit the better. Unless, of course, you want them in the middle of this?"

"No. No. I don't want them anywhere near this."

"Then stick to the story. I'm a friend who just happens to be passing through and thought I'd visit you and you've invited me to spend the night. Tomorrow, we'll both be gone. Or at least I will."

He nods.

"Say it, Travis. I want to hear the words come out of your mouth."

"You're a fucking pain in the ass, you know that?"

"What else is new? The words..."

"I won't tell my mom or Sissy anything about all this. You happy?"

"I haven't been happy my whole life, Travis, so I doubt that's gonna do the trick."

Because I trust Travis about as far as I can throw him, I insist on sleeping in the same room with him.

"My mom's gonna think we're a coupla fags."

"She'll get over it. It's a good test as to how much she loves you."

"I'll tell her we've got some reminiscing to do and I'll make sure she sees me bring in a sleeping bag for you."

"You mean for you."

"What the fuck, man? It's my fucking bed. Since I was eight

years old."

"You earned the floor, my friend."

"How's that?"

"You're the one who decided to hook up with Alston, not me."

Reluctantly, he sleeps on the floor, in the sleeping bag. I make sure it's on the side of the bed furthest from the door. I doubt I'll fall asleep, and even if I do, the slightest sound will wake me up, but I don't want to take any chances. Besides, it's better for both of us if Travis thinks getting out of the room without me knowing it is likely to happen.

"What if I have to take a piss?" he asks, as he puts on a pair of striped pajamas.

"If I'm asleep, you wake me up and I escort you."

"Jesus H. Christ. My mom sees that she's gonna know I'm queer."

"She's a good woman. She'll love you no less."

I'm right, of course. Within minutes Travis is snoring away, but my eyes are wide open. I'm staring at the ceiling. It doesn't help that the traffic sounds I've lived with all my life aren't there. The silence is killing me.

Just as dawn is breaking, I formulate a plan. I don't know if it's a good one, but it's the only plan I have. I stand up and nudge Travis with my foot.

"Huh?"

"Get up, man."

"It's still dark out. What the fuck time is it?"

"Five thirty."

He rolls over. "Wake me in an hour, man."

I nudge him again with my foot.

"Now!"

"What the fuck is wrong with you?"

"Nothing. And that's the way I want to keep it. I've got some ideas and I want to talk them over with you."

"Can't it wait for an hour or two? I mean even the fucking

chickens aren't up yet."

"If I want to talk to chickens I'll go outside. Come on, get up. And if you need coffee we'll go downstairs and brew some."

"Fucking A, I need coffee."

I make Travis change out of his PJs. I also make him pack up all his belongings in a backpack he has hanging behind his closet door.

"Why?" he asks.

"Because we're getting the hell out of here."

"Why? You said you weren't followed. I don't see the point. We're probably safer here than anywhere else."

"First off, I don't care if you see the point. I'm calling the shots now and if you want any chance of winning that Oscar or Emmy or Tony or Golden Globe, or whatever the fuck your dream is, you'll do what I say and you will not waste my time asking questions."

If you say something with authority, even if you don't have any, people tend to listen. And Travis is listening. Without saying another word, he changes into his jeans and a denim work shirt, then packs up a few items while I check my phone for emails and messages. There's the usual junk, but there's also a text from an unfamiliar number. It reads:

You've pissed me off, Fortunato. This, you will find, is a big mistake. And even worse, you've pissed off Andrei. You've made me discipline him for not doing his job but I hope you're doing yours. You've got forty-eight hours. Let's hope you're using them well.

Sergio

This is good news and bad. The good news is, I'm pretty sure Sergio has no idea where I am. If he did, someone would already be knocking at our door. Or surrounding the house. The bad news is, he's pissed and I've only got forty-eight hours to get him off my back. The other good news is now I've got a phone number and a way to communicate with him at arm's length and on my terms.

"Finished packing?"

"How much am I taking?"

"Anything you're gonna need to go back to the city."

He looks around the room, as if he's making a mental list of what he wants to take back with him.

After a little more prodding, he finishes stuffing his belongings in his green duffle bag. Finally, under my watchful eye, he's packed, dressed, and ready to go. I open the door and as quietly as I can, we head toward the stairway.

Travis moves like a slug. I want to give him a shove, but I don't want to make a fuss and risk waking anyone. Part of my plan is to get out with as few complications as possible. The last thing I need is Mrs. Chapman or Sissy asking questions and saying long goodbyes.

While I make coffee, I have Travis write a note to his family. I tell him what to write but let him use his own words. When he's finished, I check it.

Mom, Sissy, sorry I had to run out without saying goodbye. I've got some business back up in the city—got a call from an agent and he's booked me a terrific gig. Promise I'll be better about calling. And thanks for taking such good care of me. Oh, and please don't let anyone use my bike!

Love, T

I hand the note back to him. "Good enough," I tell him.

Before we take off, I have one hanging thread I need to pull.

"Listen, Travis, you got a firearm we can take with us?"

"Huh?"

"You heard me. A pistol. A rifle. A shotgun."

"You expecting trouble?"

"I want to be ready for it in case it comes. All you Texans have firearms, right?"

"Yeah."

"So, get something for us."

"Don't you have one?"

"Not anymore."

"Why?"

"No more questions. Just do it."

He doesn't say anything for a moment or two. Finally, he turns to leave the kitchen, but before he does, a thought occurs to me.

"Hey, you know that baseball bat you've got up there. Bring it down with you."

He stops and turns. "My old baseball bat?"

"Yeah."

"Why?"

"It might come in handy."

"You planning to stop for a pickup game?" he mutters, shaking his as he heads back upstairs.

By the time I finish my coffee, Travis is back carrying a shotgun, a handgun that looks like something out of the old west, like something Wyatt Earp might use, and the aluminum baseball bat.

"This one's mine," he says, holding out the shotgun. "Got it for my twelfth birthday. This one was my dad's. It's the only thing he left when he took off."

"Looks like something out of the 1890s."

"It works, man. That's all that's important."

"You're sure about that?"

"It did last time I took it out back and smashed some Coke bottles."

"How long ago was that?"

"Oh, I guess it was back in the 1880s, when Pa was teaching me how to shoot."

"Very funny."

He puts his hand in his pocket and it comes out with a handful of bullets. From the other pocket he flashes a handful of shotgun shells.

"I think this ought to do the trick," he says. "Want me to load 'em up now?"

"No need yet. You got a permit for the pistol?"

"This is Texas, man. No one's gonna hassle me over a six-shooter or a shotgun."

"What about when we cross state lines?"

"Long as we don't get stopped, I don't see a problem. Besides, the shotgun's legal and we can just say the pistol is a collector's item that don't work anymore."

I give him a look.

"They won't know that it does…"

He puts the weapons down on the kitchen table and takes a couple swings with the silver bat.

"You know, I used to be pretty good," he says. "Varsity. Okay, mostly on the bench, but if I wasn't wasting all that time chasing skirts. How 'bout you? Ever play?"

"Yeah, a little," I lie, because it's a subject I don't really want to get into.

"What position?"

"A little pitching. A little infield."

"You're kinda small for a ballplayer," he says, taking another couple swings through the air. I can see all his weaknesses. He doesn't put his weight on his back foot. He doesn't swivel his hips enough. He doesn't lead with his hips. His stance is too open. In my prime, I could've struck him out with four, maybe five pitches. Even now, after all these years and with my bum shoulder, I still doubt he could get much more than a foul tip off me.

But that was then and this is now and my never-got-off-the-ground baseball career isn't something I want to talk about. Or think about. So, I change the subject.

"And you're sure these things still work?" I ask, pointing to the weapons on the table.

"Yeah. They work. You want we should go out back and fire them off?"

I let it go. After all, I feel a lot better now that we've got some firepower in case we need it. And even if that pistol doesn't work, it might still scare the hell out of someone. It sure scares the shit out of me.

It's almost seven o'clock before we're finally on the road. At the last minute, Travis wants to say goodbye to his family in person, but I put my foot down.

"I don't want any questions, Travis, about where we're going and what we're going to do."

"You think I'm stupid enough to..."

I put my hand up. "Enough. Let's get the fuck out of here."

We throw our stuff in the trunk and pile into my rental. I ask Travis if he wants to sit in the back, where he can stretch out and catch up on some sleep, but he says no. He prefers to sit up front with me. I'm not crazy about that, because I might have to engage in conversation with him. And, to be honest, I'd just as soon have quiet, giving me time to think.

As we get on the road, heading back up toward Houston, I get lucky and Travis remains silent.

Unfortunately, his silence doesn't last long.

"So, where are we going?"

"Back to the city."

"Are you crazy? You know I'm a dead man once we get back there."

"Not if we play this right."

"What's that supposed to mean? And who's paying for my plane ticket back?"

"No one."

"Huh?"

"No plane. We're driving."

"Get out. You're kidding."

I look over at him, stare him right in the eyes. "No, Travis, I'm not kidding. You and me. In this car. For however many hours it takes to get back to New York."

"Are you fucking serious? We're something like two thousand miles away."

"A little over sixteen hundred, to be precise."

"That's a fucking full day's drive, if we don't stop."

"We'll see about stopping."

Travis shakes his head back and forth and mutters, "I don't like this. I just don't like this."

Neither do I, but I don't feel like getting into a conversation with him. But he's not quite finished.

"So, what are we going to do when we get there?"

"I'm not sure yet."

"You're shitting me, right? I mean, we're headed back up to that hornet's nest and you don't know what we're going to do."

"I'll figure out something...if you shut up for a while, so I can think."

Before he can answer, I turn on the radio. It's Sunday and all I can find is one holy-roller religious station after another, and so, because I'm in no mood for a sermon, I shut it down and we drive in silence for the next few miles.

Every so often, I look over at Travis and can see he's stewing. Finally, he breaks the silence.

"So, I assume by now you've got some kind of plan."

"Plans never work out, Travis. Like my Italian grandmother used to say, 'Man proposes, God disposes.'"

"What's that supposed to mean?"

"It means plans never go the way you think they're gonna go. It's that Mice and Men thing."

"You probably don't think I know what you're talking about."

I look over at him and smile. "You're an actor. I'm pretty sure you've run across that particular story."

"You'd be right," he says, with a self-satisfied look plastered over his face. I smile because I'm happy I've given him the opportunity to appear smart. He's really not a bad guy, just a little naïve. And I don't think he's stupid, either.

"Oh, great. So, we're headed back to the city, where someone's gonna probably finish me off, and you don't have a plan."

"I've got ideas, Travis..."

"Oh, yeah? What kind of ideas?"

"You'll see."

"You expect me to trust you? Man, this is my life we're talking about."

"Unfortunately, mine, too." I look over at him. "And I didn't do a fucking thing other than try to do my job and find Lila's husband. And look where I am now."

"No one told you to take the job. No one forced you to keep it."

I don't answer him. Because he's right. But did I really have a choice? After all, this is the life I chose for myself and in that choice comes responsibility.

He's silent for a few moments, but then he picks up again. "You know, don't you, I could make you stop this car any time and get out..."

"Really?"

"Yeah. I mean, strictly speaking this is kidnapping."

I turn the wheel to the right and pull off the highway onto the gravel. I put the gear in park and turn to him.

"Okay, hotshot. Get out."

"What?"

"You heard me. Get out. You're right. I can't make you come back with me. So, get out and you can take your chances. You know fucking well I'm better off as far away from you as possible."

"You're throwing me out?"

"No. You asked to get out."

"Hey, calm down, man. I wasn't asking to get out. I just...I just want to know what I'm in for."

"Okay, let's have a little talk. First, let me lay this out so you understand exactly where we're at—and yes, Travis, we're a *we* now, thanks to you and your former boss. You tell me if I don't have this right."

He nods.

"You and Alston went into business with the Albanians. You either ripped them off or they think you ripped them off. They want what's theirs. They think you have what's theirs. They send me to find you and bring you back so they can get what's theirs. Have I got that right?"

He shrugs. "Not exactly."

"I don't give a fuck about exactly, Travis. I just want to get myself out of this jam so they don't find pieces of me in dumpsters all over the damn city. Now, I want you to tell me everything you know. Because if you don't, if you lie to me, I really am going to throw you out of this car and then I'll make a call to Sergio and tell him exactly where you are...if he doesn't already know."

"Wait a minute! You think he knows where I am?"

"I found you, I don't see why he couldn't."

He's silent for a moment.

"I guess that changes everything."

I smile. Maybe I'm finally getting it through his thick skull how much trouble he's in.

"What do you want me to do?"

"First off, if I'm going to help you, I need to know exactly what went down with you and Alston."

"Yeah. Okay. But not here, man. I mean, we're right out in the open. I'm hungry. Haven't had breakfast. Let's find something off the highway where we can get something to eat and then I'll tell you everything."

6
The Horns of a Dilemma

I'm never hungry in the morning, although with my sleep habits it's sometimes hard to tell what morning is. Part of that might be because I sleep so poorly, if at all. As a result, I never know what meal I'm eating or when I'm eating it. But watching Travis chow down gives me a sudden appetite.

He's ordered a stack of pancakes, bacon, wheat toast, two sunny-side-up eggs, orange juice, and coffee.

"My grammy used to tell me breakfast is the most important meal of the day," he explains, as he slaps two pats of butter and then pours a steady stream of syrup onto the pancake stack. "You ought to order something," he adds.

I didn't order anything because I thought I wasn't hungry when I first sat down, but now Travis has changed this. I signal to the waitress and when she comes over, I say, "I'm sorry, but I've changed my mind. I think I will order something."

"No problem, sweetheart," she says, whipping out her order pad. "What can I get you?"

"Those flapjacks look pretty good."

"Chef's specialty. I suggest the blueberry. But if you're not a blueberry fan, I might be able to persuade him to add banana. Depends what kinda mood he's in this morning. Or, you can jes' have 'em plain."

"Surprise me," I say. "And I'll have a coffee, too. And you got any cold cereal?"

"We got whatever your little heart desires, sweetheart."

I haven't had cold cereal since I was a kid, but now I have a sudden urge. The first thing that comes out of my mouth is, "Rice Krispies?"

Travis laughs. "You like your cereal to talk to you, huh?"

"What?"

"Snap. Crackle. Pop." He laughs again.

I'm a little embarrassed, but I try not to show it.

"That it, sweetheart?" asks the waitress.

"He's eating enough for both of us, don't you think?" I say, gesturing to Travis who's back into shoveling food into his mouth.

After the waitress has left and when he finally comes up for air, I restart the conversation.

"All right, Travis, let's hear it."

"What exactly do you want to hear? Because there are certain things, whether you believe me or not, I'm in the dark about."

"It's simple. I want to know everything you know about Alston and your dealings with Sergio and the Albanians."

"I'll give you what I can, man, but I don't think you're gonna be happy with it because it's kinda sketchy."

"Let's just try to cut through all the bullshit, okay?"

He takes a swig of orange juice. "It has to do with money laundering, okay? Alston was hired by the Albanians to scrub some money."

"How much?"

"I don't know for sure, but we're not talking small change here."

"How was he gonna clean it?"

"Well, here's where it gets a little sketchy. Because remember, I'm only a hired hand."

"I remember," I say, though something tells me he was a lot more than that.

"I think it had something to do with precious metals. Alston was supposed to take the dough and invest it in gold, silver, platinum, whatever. After a while he was supposed to sell it all and hand the dough back over to the Albanians, minus his cut."

"What kind of cut are we talking about?"

He shrugs. "I don't honestly know. He didn't tell me. I'd guess a few percentage points."

"He was supposed to give it back, but he didn't, right?"

"Well, that's what they say."

"Why would they say it if it wasn't true?"

Travis shrugs, then digs into the last remnants of what's on his plate. He takes a section of wheat toast, folds it up, and sweeps it across the plate until it practically sparkles.

"Let's go back a little, Travis. What was Alston doing in your apartment?"

"I honestly don't know."

I look him in the eye with the most serious look I can muster.

"I swear, man. I mean, it's not like I invited him over."

"How'd he get in?"

"A key, probably."

"You gave him a key?"

He shakes his head. "No, I didn't give him a key."

"Then how did he get one?"

"He probably knew I kept a spare key on that little ridge above the door. I got tired of going to my super every time I locked myself out. Sometimes, I can be a little spacy, you know"

I ignore an opening. I want to keep him on track.

"How'd he *probably* know about it?"

He shrugs. "I don't know. I think maybe he mighta seen me reach up there one time when we were there together. I probably told him the same thing I just told you."

"What exactly was your relationship with him?"

"Hey, hey, get your mind out of the gutter, man. It wasn't anything sexual, if that's what you're insinuating."

"I'm not insinuating anything. I'm asking."

"Business. Purely business. First it was the Lila thing, but then I guess when he saw he could trust me, he brought me into the other thing."

"Why did he need you for this 'other thing'? What did he want you to do?"

"Look. Here's the truth. I was nothing more than a glorified errand boy. Delivering papers to be signed, shit like that."

I shoot him my "death ray" stare.

"Really. It's the truth, man."

"You were just a delivery boy? You expect me to believe that?"

"Okay, it was a little more than that. I was supposed to have his back, too."

I can't help but laugh. "You were his goon?"

"I guess you could call me that. Look at me, man. I'm in pretty good shape. I work out all the time. I take my shirt off, you'd see what I mean."

"No thanks."

"It's not like I was going to actually get physical with anybody. I was just there as 'muscle.' It was an acting job, man. I wasn't going to actually do anything. Acting. That's what acting is, you know. Altered perception."

"I know this is going to surprise you, Travis, but I don't give a fuck about acting. We're not here for you to give me a fucking acting lesson. Or a thumbnail sketch of Method. How much did he tell you about what he was doing?"

"Practically nothing. And even if he had, you think I would have understood it?"

"Where's the money, Travis?"

He shrugs. "I have no idea."

"Sergio seems to think you do."

"He's wrong, man. Do you really think Alston would have trusted me with information like that? Anything I know I just picked up from conversations I overheard. Or maybe papers I had to deliver. I thought it was an honest business operation,

Pete. I really did."

The thing with these actors is you never know when they're telling the truth or when they're lying. Even a dipshit like Travis can memorize a script and give a convincing reading. Especially if he has enough rehearsal time. But what he's telling me makes sense. Why would Alston trust him with inside information as to what he was doing? But what he might need is a fall guy and if anyone qualifies for that position, it's Travis Chapman. Maybe he was there to be set up. If money was missing or unaccounted for, Travis could have been the one Alston blamed. He could easily have told Sergio that Travis ripped him off. That Travis had the dough. And maybe Alston died because he actually convinced Sergio of that scenario. Only it backfires on him because if Sergio believes it, he doesn't need Alston anymore. He just gets in the way. Now, Travis is the target and I'm the one in the way.

The long silence while I try to figure this out bothers Travis. He's like one of those volcanoes that's been dormant for so long but then, without anyone seeing it, starts to bubble up right before it finally blows. He starts to fidget and then, finally, the volcano blows.

"So, what are we going to do? What's your brilliant idea?"

"I'm gonna let Sergio know I'm bringing you back."

"What? What the fuck, man! He'll fucking kill me, but first he'll torture me. When he finishes with me my own mother won't recognize my corpse. You think I'm going back with you, you're crazy!"

"Relax, Travis. Me telling him I'm bringing you back is only to buy us some time."

"Time? What the fuck we gonna do with more time?"

"The only way out of his is to find that money and return it to Sergio. Or..."

"Or what?"

"I'm working on another angle."

"What's to stop me from getting up and walking out of here?"

"Because I think you're smarter than that."

"What's that supposed to mean?"

"You think Sergio's not going to hunt you down? You think he needs me to find you? And Travis, when it comes down to it, if it's between you and me, who do you think I'm going to choose? You walk out of here, in just the time it takes me to dial my phone, Sergio finds out where you are. And to be honest, I'm not so sure he doesn't already know."

"What do you mean?"

"I found you, didn't I? I wouldn't be surprised if he's got guys on their way down here already. And if you really care about your family—your mom, you sister and your niece and nephew—you'll do anything you can to keep him away from them. If I call and say I'm bringing you back, he has no reason to bother with them. You understand?"

I don't necessarily believe any of this, but I need Travis to believe it. The more frightened he is the more likely I am to get the truth out of him.

He's quiet for a moment, digesting all this information. Finally, in a half whisper, he relents. "Yeah. Okay. I understand. I don't like it but I guess I gotta trust you."

There's a hint of a bad taste in my mouth that warns me Travis still isn't telling me the truth, the whole truth and nothing but the truth. I think he knows more about Alston's death than he admits. I's inconsequential to me. It's the cops' problem, not mine. So long as I'm out of it, I'm out of it.

While Travis is waiting for a coffee refill, I excuse myself.

"Where you going?" he asks. "The can?"

"I'm going to make that call."

"To Sergio?"

"Yeah."

I can see the fear pop up in his eyes. One minute it wasn't there, a flick of the eyelash later it is. It's like I can control him just by what I say. Just by manipulating his emotions. A little scary having this power, and yet it makes me feel almost as good as when I was beating the hell out of that guy who was going to try to tail me.

Travis still isn't onboard with this thing. But he must realize there's nothing he can do about it, because he gives up the fight.

"Okay," he says in an almost child-like voice.

"Be right back," I say, as I head toward the door. I don't know exactly what I'll say to Sergio but whatever it is, I don't want Travis to hear me.

On my way out, I look back over my shoulder. Travis is staring straight ahead, as if in a trance. I notice a back door. He could take off like a rabbit, out the back door, and there'd be nothing I could do to stop him. But I've got the keys to the car, so I don't know how far he'd get. He'd probably try hitching back to Booth. He doesn't necessarily know it, but he's better off throwing in with me, hitching his wagon to my star. I can't guarantee I can pull his bacon out of the fire, but one thing I do know: he certainly can't. So, let him try.

But I don't think he'll run. He's too scared to death. He's much better off sticking with me. At least there's the possibility I can come up with something to get us out of this mess.

7

You Trust Your Mother, But You Still Cut the Cards

Leaning against the car, one eye fixed on the front entrance of the roadhouse, I punch in Sergio's number. It rings four times before I connect. At first, I think it's voicemail, but it's not. It's the big man himself.

"Yeah," says the gruff, slightly accented voice.

"It's me."

I don't bother identifying myself. He doesn't have to recognize my voice to know who I am. I'm sure my name or number appears on his screen.

"So?" he asks in a bored, I-couldn't-care-less-who-this-is voice.

"I've got the package you're waiting for."

This sounds like some cheap pulp novel or magazine line, referring to Travis as a "package," but chances are pretty good Sergio's phone is tapped. The feds. The New York City cops. The CIA. The FBI. Maybe all of them. Does it matter? I'm in enough trouble as is. The last thing I want is to be tied to the Albanians.

"Where are you?" he asks in an almost matter-of-fact tone.

"Not important."

"It is to me," he says, his voice turning harsh travels through the phone and straight to my gut. This is one scary dude. Even with fifteen hundred miles between us.

"Too fucking bad," I say, taking a chance Sergio thrives on weakness and respects and maybe even fears strength. Not that it's a slam dunk he fears anything. Guys like Sergio, guys with experience at the top, know how to play the game. They know when to push and when to pull. They know when to charge ahead and when to retreat. In other words, they know how to use power after they've gotten it. And how to hold on to it. It's not hard for me to act tough because although I respect all the damage he can do to me and anyone else who gets in his way, I'm too pissed and too far down along the road to care.

There is a moment or two of silence. I don't want to make the first move because I'd rather have him commit himself to what he wants and when he wants it. And yet I don't want to give him too much time to think. He's undoubtedly a clever man and the biggest mistake I could make is underestimating him. Too much time for him to think is definitely not in my best interest.

"I assume you're on your way back to deliver this 'package,'" he says, finally breaking the silence.

"That's a pretty fair assumption. But not without some assurances."

"Assurances? I don't give assurances."

"You do if you want your package."

"Continue."

"I'm assuming all you want is what's yours. Correct?"

He hesitates. He's trying to figure out where I'm coming from before he commits. That's okay. In his shoes I'd do the same.

"Correct."

"So, you don't really care about Travis, right?"

"I fucking want what's mine."

"I get that. It's a perfectly fair request. So, before making any promises about returning this package to you, I want to make sure we're on the same page."

"What page is that?"

"My battery's low," I lie, "so I'm going to make this short and sweet. In three days, we're going to meet and you're going to get what's yours. We'll meet in a public place. In two days, I'll text you the location. But I need your word on two things, Sergio. One, you'll stop looking for us. Two, once you get what you want, it's over. No one else gets hurt. I go my way, you go yours. Understood?"

"You think you are in a position to make demands?"

"I do."

He laughs. It's not an *You amuse me* kind of laugh. It's the *If you believe me you're a bigger fool than I thought* kind of laugh.

"I don't know why, Peter Fortunato, but I am fond of you. And I'm inclined to trust you. So, I will accept your ridiculous demands."

He's fucking lying. I know it and if he's as smart as I think he is, he knows I know he's lying. We both know what the game is and how to play it. But that's okay. I'm just buying us time. And it's important for him to at least consider the possibility I trust him even though he knows I'd be a fool to do that.

"Okay. I'm hanging up now. You'll hear from me in a couple days."

He starts to say something else, but I've disconnected us before he can get the words out.

I feel very good about that.

I shove my cell phone back in my pocket and wipe the perspiration from my forehead and neck. I stand there a minute or two, taking deep breaths. I wish I knew what I was doing. Not that that would make it any easier.

Travis is in the same place I left him, sitting at the table, which means he's trusting me to take care of him. I suppose he is my responsibility now. It's lucky for him he doesn't know I'd probably sell him out in a heartbeat if it meant saving my own hide.

"So, we good?" he asks.

"So far," I say, even though I'm far from sure we are. There's a wildcard in this. I've got that bad taste in my mouth again. I can't shake this feeling that we're not alone. I don't know if it's Sergio's people or someone else, but I just have this sense we're being followed. Sergio does not strike me as a man who sits back and lets things happen. My telling him we're headed back to the city and that we'll meet in three days will not satisfy him. I'm pretty sure he's working another angle. I'd be shocked if he didn't have his people out looking for us. I don't want to tell this to Travis, but I'm less afraid of him bolting than I am of having unwanted company. I'll have to keep my guard up. And maybe I should take that baseball bat out of the trunk and put it in the back seat.

8
Now You See Us, Now You Don't

We're on the road again. I find a radio station playing outlaw country guys like Willie Nelson, Waylon Jennings, Merle Haggard, and Johnny Cash, interspersed with the likes of Dolly Parton, Patsy Cline, June Carter, and Emmylou Harris. It makes me feel dangerous. Pumps me up. Gets me out of my own head, at least for a while.

It makes me feel almost as if I'm on top of this thing which, of course, couldn't be further from the truth. But that's what music's supposed to do, right? Inspire. Make you think you can vanquish any foe.

Just outside New Orleans I start to get a little jumpy. The scene from *Easy Rider* where Dennis Hopper and Peter Fonda get blown off their bikes by rednecks keeps replaying in my head as if it's on a loop that I can't seem to stop. Maybe that's why I'm getting nervous. Or maybe it's something else. Like maybe I start to see, or imagine I see, a car that appears to be following us. It's a black Suburban with tinted side windows. Two people in the front seat. Can't see if there's anyone in the back. I see it in my rearview mirror. I speed up. It speeds up. I slow down. It slows down. You know what they say. It's not paranoia when the little green men really are following you.

Travis, his head leaning against the window, is napping. I

could wake him, but then I'd have to talk to him and that would only make my life more miserable than it already is. Besides, the one thing I don't need is Travis panicking.

If, in fact, we are being followed, it's got to be Sergio's people. Are they just keeping an eye on us, providing us with a safety convoy? Or is it something else? Something more dangerous? Are they just looking for the right time and place to intercept us? Will they try to run us off the road? Will they grab us out of the car and bring us, bound and gagged, to some out of the way spot and then put the screws to us?

I have a pretty high tolerance for pain, but Travis here, the one sitting next to me snoring away lightly, well, I figure he'd break as soon as he catches a glimpse of the rubber hose.

I've either got to lose these guys or confront them. I think about the weapons half hidden on the floor under the back seat. Not very much fire power there. I'm not even sure the pistol works, even though earlier a bored Travis loaded it. The shotgun is a much better option—he loaded that, too. But blowing them away, even if I were able to get the drop on them, is messy. And we can be sure they're armed to the teeth. The only thing stopping them from taking us down is that they need one of us to lead them to whatever Sergio is looking for. And that someone isn't me.

My fingers thump the steering wheel as I try to come up with a plan. I've rejected the direct confrontation option—you know, pull over to the side of the road and let them stop behind us. No one wins when it comes to war, and I'm pretty sure they're much better armed and prepared than we are. And I'm also sure they're programmed for violence. I don't think I can stand up to that kind of thing. And I know Travis won't be able to.

That leaves evasion. I decide the best thing to do is do nothing until we hit New Orleans. Let them stick behind us as we pile into town like a parade. There, it should be much easier to lose them.

As we make it to the outskirts of the city, I nudge Travis

with my elbow.

"Huh," he says groggily. How he's able to sleep at a time like this amazes me. But then, anyone who can sleep at any time amazes me. I can't remember the last time I got a good night's sleep, and I certainly can't remember ever falling asleep in a car, train, bus or plane.

"We're gonna make a stop."

He checks his watch.

"Lunch?" he asks, as if we're on some kind of travel meal plan.

"Sure," I say, figuring the less he knows about why we're really getting off the road, the better.

"You ever been to the Big Easy before?" I ask.

"Plenty times. I even thought about moving here once. I wasn't getting nowhere up there in New York, didn't have the dough to make the move to Hollywood, but I heard there was a pretty good movie industry down here. Tax breaks. That's what brought production down here. But then the hurricane hit, I always get 'em mixed up...Sandy, right?"

"Katrina."

"Yeah. That's right. Sandy was the one hit us back home. Anyway, I figured it wasn't a good time. Maybe I was wrong. Maybe it was the best time. You know, cheap housing and all. It's all about timing, isn't it? How's about you?"

"Once. Overnight. Skip-trace thing."

"Then you don't know what you're missing, Pete. It's a music town, man. You come during Mardi Gras and they're actually playing incredible music in street. It's not even a paying thing. You just stop, look, and listen. And it's a great town for food, if you like that Cajun stuff. I love it. Spicier the better. I know a bunch of places. Real good clams and oysters. And pretty cheap. At least compared to prices back home. Want me to look 'em up on my phone?"

"That's okay. Let's just play it by ear," I say." "But as long as you've got it out, what you can do is look for a hotel in the

Quarter."

"Hotel? We stopping here for the night?"

"Nope."

"Then why you need a hotel?"

"Stop asking so many damn questions, Travis. Just do what the fuck I ask you to do."

"Jeez," he says. "You're pretty touchy today. You get up on the wrong side of the bed?"

"There is no right side for me." I nod toward the phone now in his hand. "Let me know what you come up with."

He plays with his phone and a moment or two later he says, "I got a few here."

"Any got underground parking?"

He laughs.

"What's so funny?"

"New Orleans is built on a swamp, man. There are no basements which means no underground parking. That's why everyone's buried above ground."

"Okay. Make it a parking lot. But I want it in the Quarter."

"I don't get—"

"Just do what I say, Travis. All right? Stop questioning every fucking thing I say."

I'm edgy. I'm close to losing my temper. I know that's not a good thing. First off, it's counterproductive. Second, it's off-putting because it immediately puts the other guy, in this case Travis, on the defensive. I need his help, his cooperation, and if Travis has to deal with my temper, he won't be focusing on what I ask him to do. I have to keep reminding myself we're in this together, whether I like it or not. I'm under a lot of pressure, but I gotta calm down. I'm making myself crazy but I'm making Travis even crazier.

He's looking down at his phone, but I can see he's 's got this pouty expression on his face, like he's either angry or thinking I don't take him seriously. Either way, I've got to get him back on track.

"Listen," I say. "I'm sorry. I didn't mean to snap at you. I didn't get much sleep last night."

He looks up and there's a smile on his face. I can see I've done the right thing. My apology is something Travis needs. It's something I should probably do more of. I keep forgetting he's an actor and most actors have oversize egos. They take everything personally. It's not like I have to get up and applaud every damn thing he does, but I do have to stroke him every once in a while. I tuck that information away for the future. It's not so much that I did the right thing as it is that I did something that works, something that mollifies Travis and keeps him an ally not an enemy. This is something that can, in the future, help me control him. Get him to do what I need him to do. *Be contrite,* I repeat to myself. *Don't be afraid to apologize.* Like I don't have enough problems with that anger management thing. Fuck! Now I actually be aware of how I treat other people.

Travis comes up with a hotel with a good-size parking area, as well as directions to get us there.

We're about ten miles outside the heart of the city and I see I'm not imagining things. Whether I speed up or slow down, black Suburban stubbornly remains on our tail.

When we get to the hotel, I pull up and a porter quickly appears.

"Park your car, sir?"

"No thanks. Just point me in the direction of the parking, and I'll do it myself."

I can see from his expression he isn't taking self-help well. It's no mystery why. I park my own car, he loses his tip. I dig out my wallet, hand him a five-spot, and his smile returns. "Go straight ahead, hang a right at the corner and you'll see it right there. You'll get a ticket and they'll validate it at the front desk when you check in. Parking's free for guests," he drawls.

I pull in, take a ticket from the attendant, then find a space as far away from the entrance/exit as I can.

"Wanna take a walk through the Quarter? I can show you

around," says Travis, as we unload from the vehicle.

"Not right now," I say working overtime to maintain a friendly tone. It's not easy because what I really want to do is punch someone or something. That black Suburban is haunting me. We've got to get rid of it.

I walk to the back of the car, pop open the trunk, and take out my backpack and Travis's duffle bag. I throw my backpack over my shoulder and hand Travis his duffle.

"What's going on?" he asks. "I thought you said we weren't gonna stay?"

"We're not," I answer, as I look around to see if the Suburban has followed us onto the lot. It hasn't, which doesn't surprise me. If I'm guessing right, they'll park it out front of the hotel and then one or both of them will look for us in the lobby. Or, maybe they'll let one guy out of the car to watch the front entrance and the other to drive around the block a few times. I'm gonna have to guess which one is more likely because I can't plan around both.

"Then...?"

I open up the back door of the car, making sure no one's watching us, I pull out the shotgun and the baseball bat and hand them to Travis. "Stow this in your duffle, okay?"

"Pete...?"

"Just do what I say, okay? I'll explain everything later." That last line is all about making Travis feel included. As if I give a damn.

Like me, hiding the weapons with his body, he looks around to see if anyone's watching. They're not, so he quickly shoves the shotgun and the bat into the bag.

"It's probably not the best time to be walking into a hotel looking like we're getting ready to hit a bank," he says.

"Don't worry. No one's gonna know what's in there. Where's the pistol?"

"It's right here," he says, patting his duffle.

"Give it to me."

"Huh?"

"You heard me. Give me the pistol."

He unzips the bag, takes out the pistol and hands it to me. I unzip my backpack and shove it deep down inside.

"I really don't know what's going on here, Pete."

"Stop asking so many damn questions, Travis. Just do what I say. I promise I'll explain everything later. Right now, you're gonna have to trust me. Now, come on," I say, as we head out of the lot.

I remove the key from the ignition and bury it under the front seat mat.

"Hey, what are you doing?"

"Never mind."

"But the keys—"

"I know what I'm doing, Travis."

"I hope so, man."

I slam the door shut and look around. I see we can leave the lot from a different entrance from the one we drove in. If the Suburban is idling on the entrance where we came in, they might not be able to see us leaving from this other one.

"Mind telling me where we're going?" Travis asks, as he falls in step behind me.

"To the hotel."

"Man, this is some crazy shit," he says, shaking his head back and forth like a bobble-head doll.

When we get to the lobby it's filled with people. Tourists checking and out. People who like hanging out in hotel lobbies. Just what I'm hoping for.

"Go sit over there," I say, pointing to a big easy chair facing the front desk. "I'll be right back."

"Where you going?"

"I gotta get some information and make a couple calls. I won't be long. But Travis, don't talk to anyone, you hear?"

"Who'm I gonna talk to?"

"No one, got it?"

"Are you losing it, Pete? I mean all this secret fucking agent shit."

I pull him close to me. "All right, Travis. You want to know what's going on?"

"Yeah. Sure."

"We're being followed."

"Followed?"

"That's right."

"By who?"

"Two guys. I noticed them a while back. They're in a black Suburban."

"Who are they?"

"I don't know. But making a wild guess, I'd say they work for Sergio."

He visibly tenses.

"This is exactly why I didn't want to tell you. I don't want you freaking out. Just do what I say and we'll be fine. And don't fucking talk to anyone. Someone approaches you, I don't care who it is, fucking Kate Beckinsale, you make like you're deaf and dumb. Got it?"

He nods, yes. But with a confused look on his face.

"Okay. Now just go sit over there and keep your eye on our stuff." I hand him my backpack.

"Jesus, Pete. This is not a good thing. This is not a good thing, at all."

"You're telling me. But just let me handle it and we'll be fine."

"You don't want me to do anything else?"

"I just want you to sit over there till I need you. Think you can do that?"

He nods, yes.

As soon as he's seated, I scan the large lobby. I don't know what either guy looks like but I'm pretty sure if either of them are here in the lobby, they'll stick out like a sore thumb. The scenario I'm going with, and I sure as hell hope I'm right, is that one of them will come inside while the other remains outside, either on the sidewalk or in the car, if they've found a spot to park.

I walk over to the concierge's desk, where a pretty blonde is in the middle of giving directions to a middle-aged couple. Her nametag identifies her as Jane. As I wait my turn, I keep my eye on Travis and an eye out for whoever's following us. Travis is nervously drumming his fingers on the small round wooden table next to him.

Finished with the couple, the cute little concierge, a dead ringer for Reese Witherspoon, turns to me. Just as I'm about to ask my question I see a burly guy in a leather jacket come in through the main door. Bingo! This has to be one of the guys in the Suburban. It's not Teardrop and it's not Ponytail, but he's definitely drawn from the same tough-guy gene pool.

"May I help you?" she asks in a soft, sweet voice that's meant to reassure any guest that they're welcome and help is on the way. I wonder if she can help me out of this mess Travis has got me into.

"I sure hope so, Jane. Could you tell me where the nearest Budget Car Rental office is?"

"I believe the airport is their only site, sir. I'm awfully sorry, but if it has to be Budget, I'm afraid you'll have to go all the way out to the airport. But there are other car rental...I've got a list..." she reaches into a drawer.

"I'm afraid it has to be Budget. You see, I've got a credit with them and..."

She smiles. "Of course. No need to explain, sir. Is there anything else I can help you with?"

"If you happen to have their phone number, that would save me a lot of trouble."

"No problem, sir" she says, as she pulls out a large black binder with the name of the hotel on the cover. She searches it a moment, then scribbles something down on a hotel pad, rips the page off and hands it to me. "Will there be anything else? Perhaps you'd like some suggestion as to where to..."

"No, I'm good, sweetheart. But if I think of anything, I know where to come. You've really been terrific. Thanks so much."

"My pleasure," she says, flashing an almost irresistible smile.

I start to turn away but spin back on my heels. "Oh, there is one more thing. I was wondering if there's another exit from the hotel."

"You mean other than the front?"

"Yes." I lean forward and lower my voice. "You see, my wife's having me followed and I'm afraid if she's followed me here, she might be waiting outside to ambush me. She's a little," I twirl my finger beside my right temple. "She's got a perfect right to be pissed at me. Fact is, I cheated on her. It was a long time ago, but she just found out about it. I've apologized all over the place, told her it was only that once and that I'll never do it again. That I love her. But she's really hurt and I can't blame her. We're separated now and I just want her to calm down a little before we can have a civil conversation and I try to patch things up. A hotel lobby is really not the right place to have that discussion."

She winks at me. "I totally understand, sir. There *is* another exit. Just follow the signs to the bathrooms and if you take a right you'll see a door that exits onto the street in back."

"Thanks so much, Jane. I really appreciate it."

I look over at Travis, who's engrossed in some brochure he's picked up. I smile. He's like an obedient dog. I say "stay" and that's what he does.

I take a seat next a few feet away from him and grab a newspaper on the table that sits between us, so that it's not obvious that we're together.

"You done?" he asks.

"Not quite. I need you to do something."

"What?"

"I want you to go outside and see if you can find a black Suburban."

"The car that was following us?"

"Right. And when you find it, I want you to let the air out of at least two of the tires."

"Huh?"

"Let the air out of the damn tires, Travis."

He shakes his head. "I don't get it. What if the guys are in the car?"

"One of them's over there," I gesture with a slight movement of my head. "Don't look, man. Just trust me."

"What about the other?"

"I'm betting that unless they found a spot right in front of the hotel, he's standing outside waiting for his partner."

"What if he's not? What if he's in the car?"

"Why can't you do it?"

"First off, they're going to be watching me. I'm guessing you never actually met Sergio…"

"That's true."

"But Sergio has met me, which means he's told his men what I look like."

"That's an awful lot of maybes, Pete."

"Look, Travis, we can sit here all afternoon debating, but it's not going to get either of us out here in one piece. Just do what I say, okay?"

"Let the air out of their tires?"

"That's right."

"But what if you're wrong and the other guy is in the car?"

"Look, Travis, maybe I'm giving you more credit than you deserve, but I think you can figure out a way to do this without him seeing you. Walk across the street, come back over on his blindside. You'll figure it out. All I want you to do is either let the air out of a couple tires or slash them."

"How'm I gonna do that?"

I open up a side pouch on my backpack and pull out a small Swiss Army knife and, making certain no one's watching me, I slip it to him.

"Use this."

He thinks for a moment, then breaks into a smile. "Yeah. I guess I can do that."

"Now, get going. And if you have any problem, just give me a call." I pull out my small notebook and a pen and hand both to him. "Write down your phone number. I'll text you and then you'll have mine."

"Okay. How'm I gonna get out of here without the other guy seeing me?"

"There's a back exit." I gesture in the direction with my upper body.

"This is real spy, undercover shit, isn't it?" he says with a hint of glee in his voice. This, I realize, is right up Travis's alley. It's play-acting. I've got him playing the part of a hard-ass. And he's loving every minute of it.

Because of this, I want to slap some sense into him, so he realizes how serious this is. But then I realize this attitude will probably make it easier for him to do what I need him to do.

"You got it, my friend. Let's see how good you are."

He nods. "No problemo."

"Sit here a couple minutes before you leave. I'm gonna go make a couple calls. Meet me back here in fifteen minutes. If you run into any problems, use the phone. Text me, okay?"

"Got it, chief. What about all this stuff?" he asks, indicating his duffle bag and my backpack.

"I'll take care of it. Good luck," I say, patting him on the shoulder. Suddenly, I realize Travis and I have become unlikely partners. Our fate is tied together. If he goes down, I go down. And if I go down, we both go down. This is not the way it is supposed to turn out.

I get up and walk toward a corner of the hotel lobby, as far away from Travis as I can manage.

My first call is to the rental car agency. I tell them there's been a change of plans—a death in the family—and I want to return the car early. Because of the emergency, I have to leave the car in the hotel lot, with the keys under the front seat mat.

They don't take kindly to this unconventional way of returning one of their vehicles, but I'm persuasive enough—playing up a nonexistent family tragedy seems to do the trick—that they agree to pick up the car.

When I look up, I see Travis has disappeared from the chair he was sitting in. I check my phone. There's no text from him. I'm starting to get a little nervous but then I realize he needs time to find the Suburban and then, when he does, he has to make sure it's unoccupied. If it's not, he's going to have to do the deed while making sure he isn't seen. All that takes time.

My second call is to Sergio who this time answers before the phone has a chance to ring twice.

"Yeah."

"Tsk. Tsk. Tsk. You're not playing fair, Sergio."

"What the hell's that supposed to mean?"

"You don't trust me to do what you've hired me to do so you send your own guys down."

"What makes you think I've sent anyone?"

"Let's not play games."

"What's that supposed to mean?"

"Never mind. I've got something you want. I can make it so you never see him again, and with it whatever you think he has of yours. Or, I can deliver him and you can do whatever it is you have to do to get what you're looking for."

"What makes you think I need you? What makes you think I can't do it myself?"

"Go ahead. See how far you get."

"So, what the hell do you want from me, motherfucker?"

"I want you to back the fuck off. I want you to call your guys off, so I can get on with my job."

Silence.

"Don't fuck with me, Sergio. If you do, you're gonna be sorry."

I disconnect the call.

I don't know why he won't own up to having us followed.

But it doesn't matter. He's on notice now that I know.

It's been almost ten minutes since Travis left, and I'm getting a little jittery. Finally, after checking my texts three or four times, I hear from him.

The Eagle has landed!!!! Back in five.

I respond, *Look for me in the bar area.*

A few minutes later, Travis appears in the doorway. He's got a big, fat grin on his face.

He takes a seat next to me.

"Mission accomplished," he announces.

"You got the tires?"

"Yup."

"Was there anyone in the car?"

"Nope. You were right. I saw this guy leaning against a store window across the street. I'm guessing he's our man."

"What's he look like?"

"I don't know..."

"Dammit, Travis..."

"He looks like...a thug. He's wearing a gray sport jacket. Jeans. He's got that three or four days' growth thing. Nothing distinguishable. What's next?"

He doesn't quite match the image of the other Albanians I've had the pleasure of meeting, but that doesn't necessarily mean anything. I pull out my phone. Search for the Uber app, then click on it.

Looking over my shoulder, Travis asks, "What are you doing? Aren't we gonna get back in the car and take off?"

"No."

"Why not?"

"Because they know what the car looks like."

"So, what are we gonna do now?"

"We're gonna slip out of here without them seeing us and we're gonna rent ourselves another car and get back on track."

He thinks for a moment and then breaks out into a gigantic smile.

He pats me hard on my shoulder. Twice. "You know something, Pete, you are the fuckin' man. That's who you are."

I'm not so sure about that but so long as Travis thinks I am, he'll do what I say. And the way I see it, that's the only way out of this mess.

Before I book the Uber, I take the extra precaution to book a room in the hotel. I'm not one to throw money around, even if it's not mine, but I think it's worth the hundred and fifty bucks to throw a little more sand in the faces of Sergio's flunkies. If they check, and I'm sure they will, they'll see we're staying the night and either that will buy us an extra day's head start, or if they try to confront us in a room we're not in, that'll just confuse them that much more.

Once that's taken care of, I summon an Uber and have it pick us up a couple blocks away.

I guide Travis out the back door and ten minutes later we're sitting in the back seat of our Uber, headed for the closest rent-a-car office.

9

The Truth, the Whole Truth, and Everything but the Truth

I can see the excitement in Travis's eyes. He can hardly contain himself. Suddenly, he is not in a life and death struggle with the forces of evil. Now he sees himself as having a starring role in his own personal thriller. Once we switch out our Uber for a new rental car, Travis simply cannot contain himself.

"I don't believe how fucking easy it was," he says, his eyes practically popping out of his skull. It's like he's on something, but it's not artificial. "I mean, I spotted the guy as soon as I came around the front of the hotel. I figured they'd park the car as close as they could get to the front entrance and sure enough, less than a block away, there it was..."

He keeps babbling on. I make no move to stop him. Not because I'm interested in the least in his tale of derring-do, but because regaling me with his experience is keeping him busy. The more he talks the less I have to engage with him, the fewer questions I have to answer. The fewer answers I have to have.

Every so often, I tune back in long enough to catch the gist of what he did, which is exactly what I told him to do: find the car, slash the tires, or find some way to take the air out of them, and then report back to me.

"What do you figure they're going to do next?" he asks, bobbing up and down in his seat like a four-year-old.

"You mean after they get reamed out by Sergio? Or maybe worse."

"Oh, man, I never thought about that. You think maybe he's gonna have them iced?"

"Iced?"

"You know. Killed." He runs his forefinger across his neck.

"I know what iced means. What I didn't know is how well-versed you are in gangster lingo."

"I've seen my share of gangster films. *The Godfather, Goodfellas*. My favorite...you know, if they ever do a remake I'd love to sink my teeth into the DeNiro role...or *The Godfather*..."

"I'm sure you'd be awesome in any role you'd get, Travis," I say. But when I look over I can see my sarcasm has flown way over his head. He's far too involved in the moment, his moment, to even consider that I might be mocking him.

"So, what's next?"

"You see what's next, Travis," I say, pointing to the road in front of us. "We're heading home."

"I know that, man. I mean, what's our next move? You've been in touch with Sergio, right? What did you tell him?"

"I told him he'd get back what's his."

"Huh?"

"You heard me. We're gonna make this right."

"I don't understand. How are we gonna do that?"

I shoot him a quick sidelong glance. "I'd say that's up to you."

"Hey, man, you're assuming I have what he thinks I have."

"Or, you know how to find it."

"But I don't. Honest. I don't know anything."

"You think you don't, but you do."

"What's that supposed to mean?"

"It means you've got the answer but you just don't know you have it."

"You're messing up my brain, Pete. How could I know but

not know that I know?"

I smile because I know that irritates Travis. If I can't punch someone, at least I can toy with him verbally.

"Come on, Pete. Stop fucking with me."

It's late afternoon, around four o'clock, and we're just about to cross the border from Alabama into Tennessee, I'm starting to wear down. It's time for a pit stop. Next big city on our route is Chattanooga. That's where I'll stop for something to eat. And I think by now Travis is sufficiently primed he might be able to help with our Sergio problem.

Travis has a taste for barbecue. "You can take the boy out of Texas, but you can't take Texas out of the boy," he says. So, he goes on Yelp and finds a place with high enough ratings to satisfy him.

We've just put in our food order and Travis is sucking on a bottle of Dos Equis.

"We're just about halfway home, Travis. This is as good a time as any to lay our cards on the table."

"Isn't that what I've been doing?"

"A facsimile. I want the real thing. I'm talking about telling me everything about your relationship with Alston and the Albanians."

"I think I've told you everything."

"Humor me. Tell me again."

"Jesus. You don't stop, do you?"

I smile. I might as well have some fun.

"It's simple. Alston hired me to put the moves on his wife. He liked the job I did. Said he trusted me and asked if I wanted to make a little extra dough. I said, sure. I asked him what I'd have to do. Like, did he mean another seduction kind of deal? He said, no. Said he had this big deal brewing. Someone was gonna give him a lot of money to invest..."

"Sergio."

"He didn't say who. I didn't ask. First of all, it was none of my business and second, I didn't give a shit. I didn't want to piss him off. I needed the work."

"Why did he need you?"

He shrugs. "I guess I was going to be his front man."

"His beard."

"Huh?"

"Never mind. How did it work?"

"That's the crazy thing. It never did."

"You're gonna have to be a little more precise, Travis. Tell me everything, whether you think it's important or not."

Our food arrives. A large plate of ribs for Travis. A barbecued pulled pork sandwich with a side of coleslaw for me. I'm not all that hungry, but I squirt a little extra BBQ sauce on my sandwich and take a bite while Travis meticulously tucks a napkin under his chin. Someone might peg us as the Odd Couple, eating out. If there weren't only twelve, fifteen years difference between us, and the fact that we looked nothing alike, someone might think I am taking my son to lunch.

"Okay. So, here's everything. Honest." He raises his hand like he's taking the Boy Scout oath. "Alston tells me he's got this big cash investor. That's very unusual he tells me because it really is cash. Usually, it's just numbers shifted around on paper— you know, like bank transfers. Not this time. This investor wants Alston to take the cash and put it in some business."

"What kind of business?"

"According to Alston, it didn't matter, but I think he was going to sink it into like what I told you about before. Precious metals."

"At the time, did you understand what was happening?"

He has a quizzical look on his face.

"It's called money laundering, Travis."

He shrugs. "He never called it that."

I shake my head. Can anyone really be this dumb?

"Whatever he called it, it's what people do with drug money.

Or money otherwise earned illegally."

"Yeah. I guess that's what it was. I didn't give it much thought. I mean, it wasn't like *I* was doing anything illegal. Like I said, I was just the front man. You know, like an employee."

I take a bite of my sandwich and BBQ sauce squirts out the side and onto my lap.

"Dammit," I say, reaching for a napkin. I dip it in my water glass and try to rub away the stain. I get most of it, but there's still a faint outline on the inside leg of my jeans, like a chalk outline at a crime scene.

"Go on."

"Okay. He wants me to deliver the cash to someone and then get some signed papers."

"Why didn't he do it himself?"

He shrugs, as he strips a bone of what's left of its meat. "I don't know."

"Didn't you wonder?"

"Again, I didn't give it much thought. Come on, Pete. He was going to pay me ten grand to be an errand boy. Was I really going to try to take the thing apart and put it back together again? Would you?"

Yeah. I would. But I'm not an idiot, like Travis. Or at least I'm not so greedy that I don't think about possible consequences. I mean, come on. I've done some stupid things in my life. Especially in the spur of the moment when it comes to controlling my temper. I mean, I'm right up there with the best when it comes to getting myself entangled in something stupid. Or doing something stupid. Which is one of the reasons I didn't even last a year as a cop.

"Tell me about the exchange."

"That's just it. There never was one."

"Come again?"

"We were supposed to meet and he was going to give me the package and I was going to take care of it. But he never showed up."

"When and where was this exchange supposed to go down?"

"We were gonna meet at the bar I was working. But at the last minute he changed his mind. Said he wanted someplace private. So, he was gonna drop by my place."

"Your apartment?"

"Yeah."

"When was that supposed to be?"

Like the sudden darkness that precedes a summer thunderstorm, the expression on his face changes. Like he's just thought of something earth-shattering. Like one of those cartoon lightbulbs goes on in the little bubble escaping from your brain.

It looks like he's about to speak, but nothing's coming out. I fix that for him.

"Travis, by any chance could that be why he was in your apartment right before he left us?"

"Umm. Not exactly."

"What's that supposed to mean?"

"He was supposed to drop by the day before, but he never showed. I thought I'd hear from him, but come to think of it, I never did."

"But it was the next day I found him dead lying in your bed."

He thinks for a moment. "Yeah. I guess it was."

"And only now are you making the connection?"

"Well, you know, I've had a lot on my mind. It just never occurred to me."

I want to call him a moron or worse, but I know that's not going help matters. So, instead I try to be as solicitous as possible. Which believe me, under the circumstances, isn't easy.

"Let me run this by you, Travis," I begin, trying hard as I can to leech the anger from my voice. "He's supposed to drop by your apartment with the 'package,' but he doesn't show. But maybe the next day, when he knows you won't be expecting him, that's when he shows up."

"When you put it that way…"

"What other way is there to put it?"

"Well, then yeah, I guess that sounds right. But why would he do that?"

"Maybe because he was afraid of getting ripped off…"

"By who?"

"Could be anyone…"

"You don't fucking mean me, man, do you?"

I shrug, thrusting my hands out in front of me, which is as good a way of any of saying, *well, duh.*

"But it couldn't be Sergio, right?"

"That wouldn't make much sense. He'd be stealing from himself."

"Maybe one of his people?"

"Possible."

"How we gonna find out?"

"Good question."

"How about an answer?"

"I'm working on it."

"Let's say one of his guys knew about the drop-off and showed up at the apartment to rip him off. He'd have to get rid of Alston, right?"

"He would."

"Which means he's got the money."

"If that theory holds up, probably so."

"What do you mean, theory?"

"Because that's what it is. We don't know for sure. It could have been someone else. Someone who learned about the drop-off and knew he'd be in your apartment alone, with the money."

"My head is starting to hurt," says Travis, as he drops the half-eaten rib he's holding, wipes his hands on his napkin-bib, then sinks his head into his hands.

"I think, for the first time, we're on the same page, Travis."

10
One Step Forward, Two Steps Back

I think all the pieces are laid out in front of me, and yet the big picture is still murky. There are two separate issues which may or may not be connected. First and more foremost, as far as I'm concerned, is where is the money Sergio wants and how do I get it. The other issue, of far less importance to me—in fact, totally irrelevant—is who killed Donald Alston and why. The thing is, these two events might be linked and I might not be able to deal with number one without dealing with number two. In other words, it's very possible that whoever killed Donald Alston also has the Albanian money.

Sergio is only interested in one of these problems. He wants to know where the hell his money is and then he wants to get it back. He has no interest in who killed Donald Alston and, in fact, he may be responsible for Alston's death.

The one who's in real trouble is Travis Chapman. And why I should care about him is beyond me. But at least for now, we're bound together and my fate is wrapped up in his.

First question: Do I think Travis has the dough? Not a chance. If he does, would he be sitting beside me, shaking like a fucking leaf? Would he have high-tailed back home and let himself get tucked in every night by his mother? No way.

All I care about right now is separating my fate from Travis's

238

and getting Sergio off my back. The only way I see to do this is get him back his money. But I can't do that until I find out who has it. I've always been hoping, of course, for the easy way out. That would have been Travis. But it isn't. Which means that suddenly Travis is of little or no value to me unless he can point me in the right direction.

And yet I need to keep him close, because he might be the only connection I have to the dough. One thing that might help is to find out who might have known about Alston's plan to rendezvous at Travis's apartment.

I'm moving forward on one important assumption: that whoever killed Donald Alston has the money. If that's not true, of course, I'm back to square one.

I've got what's left of our trip to get inside Travis's head, a scary place to be, to find out who might have this information.

We're back on the road now, but I'm too exhausted to drive, so Travis is at the wheel. For the first fifteen minutes or so, I stay alert, making sure he's going in the right direction and that his style of driving doesn't get us killed. Turns out, he's pretty good. Probably better than me. He's pretty much tearing ass, generally going five to ten miles above the speed limit, which is fine by me. Eventually, once I'm convinced we're heading in the right direction, I'm hoping I can catch an hour or so's sleep. But it's just not happening. I can't seem to turn off my mind. Finally, I give up and start peppering Travis with questions.

"Who else might have had or has the key to your apartment?" I ask.

"I don't know. Two, three other people maybe."

"Like who?"

"Couple ex-girlfriends. Like that."

"Who else?"

"Maybe a scene partner. My best friend, Kenny. I think I had a key made for him once."

"You never ask for your key back?"

He shrugs. "What are they gonna do? Come back and rob

me blind? Like I've got anything of value, right? Hell, they can take anything they want and I probably wouldn't miss it. Besides, I don't keep track of that kind of shit."

"You're not afraid they'll just show up one night?"

He smiles. "Once Travis is through with a woman, he's through. And so are they."

"Who else?"

"The super."

"Does he live in the building?"

"Nope. He services two or three buildings on the block, so he's got his choice of where to have an apartment. You've been in my place. You think he's gonna choose that dump? Jesus, that building shoulda been condemned years ago."

"Anyone else?"

"Not that I can think of."

"Who knows about the spare key you keep on the door ledge?"

"I don't know. Probably anyone who happened to be with me when I didn't have my key with me and had to use that one."

"Focus, Travis! How many people would that be?"

He doesn't answer.

"Travis! You think I'm asking these questions for my health?"

"I'm trying to think, man. I mean, I've got friends who've seen me use it. And scene partners. We're talking maybe half dozen people. Probably more."

"Alston knew?"

"I think I told him once. So yeah, he knew. That's probably how he got in because I certainly didn't give him a key."

"What about Lila?"

"I didn't give her a key either, if that's what you're asking. Besides, she hated that place. The second time she was there she said she was never going to set foot in there again."

"Does she know about the spare over the door?"

He gets quiet. I interpret this as meaning we're on the edge of a breakthrough.

"I don't know. I guess I might have mentioned it. I mean, we did spend a lot of time together, so it was bound to come up. You know, like maybe I was with her and mentioned that I locked myself out..."

"Did she ever see you use it?"

"I...I don't think so." He hesitates a moment. "Maybe."

"You don't sound positive."

"Cut me some slack, man. You think I pay attention to everything all the time?"

"I know for a fact you don't."

I can see I'm not going to get much more out of him. But I think I've got enough to at least send me in the right direction.

By this time, we're in Virginia. Only five or six hours from the city. I can see Travis is starting to tire. He's turned on the radio to keep himself awake. Time for me to take over.

"Okay, let's hit the next rest stop. We need gas, something to eat, bathroom break, and then I'll take over the rest of the way."

"Good. I've just about had it. I wasn't made for this, man. Have you figured out what we're gonna do when we get there? Where are we gonna go?"

"I'll have everything figured out by that time," I say, lying through my teeth.

Part Three
New York City

"That's a trail nothing but a nose can follow."
—James Fenimore Cooper, *The Last of the Mohicans*

"That depends a good deal on where you want to get to."
—Lewis Carroll, *Alice's Adventures in Wonderland*

1
Home, Sweet Home

Night has fallen by the time we reach the entrance to the Lincoln Tunnel, heading from New Jersey into midtown New York City. The sparkling, impressive skyline of New York beckons. No matter how often I leave, approaching the city, either from the east or the west, always sends chills up my spine. It encompasses the past, the present, and the future with promises of fame and fortune for so many. For me, not so much. For me, it represents reality; a bucket of cold water in the face. Wake up, Pete! Life is about to cut you down to size.

This time of year, only a few weeks before the holidays, is especially beautiful, what with all the festive holiday lights, including Christmas trees lining Park Avenue. No other time in the city magnifies more the difference between happiness and sadness. Between having and not having. Between success and failure.

This time, seeing the bright, flashing lights of the city's skyscrapers only remind me how out of synch I am with reality.

As Travis dozes stretched out on the back seat, I try to collect my thoughts. At the top of my list: now that we're back, where are we going to go?

It's a process of elimination.

We cannot go to Travis's apartment.

We cannot go to my apartment.

We cannot crash at my office, even if it is the start of a weekend.

The idea of checking in to a hotel in New York City just before the holidays? Ridiculous. Even if we could find something, the cost would be prohibitive. Plus, we'd be much too easy to find. I want no record of where we'll be and no city hotel, no matter how bad, is not going to ask for ID. And even if there are such places, we don't have time to scope them out.

How about imposing on friends? I'm sure Travis has some, but I'm not about to trust them with my life. As for me, well, I've spent the past five years losing friends, not making new ones. There's always Philly, the Master of the Real Estate Universe. But he doesn't even live in the city. He's up in some fancy McMansion in one of those Westchester towns, like New Rochelle or Scarsdale. I can just see me and Travis showing up at his door, unannounced.

There's my friend, Teddy, who lives in a nice-sized loft in TriBeCa, but I haven't spoken to him in almost six months, and I have a vague recollection that he leaves town in December in search of warmer climes.

Earlier, just as we made it to the New Jersey turnpike, Travis piped up, out of nowhere, "Do you think maybe we should get in touch with the cops?"

"That would be the worst thing we could do."

"Why?"

"Let me count the ways. First off, there's Alston's murder. In your apartment. You don't think they're looking for you?"

"Maybe. But I didn't do it."

"That doesn't matter. You're the prime suspect. You wanna turn yourself in and have them focus on you?"

"I guess not."

"And do you think you're just going to report to them that you've had some problems with the Albanian mob and you'd like them to protect you?"

"Well, it crossed—"

"Forget about it. The best you could probably hope for is them asking you to wear a wire around them. You wanna do something like that?"

He's silent for a moment. I know Travis well enough to know that he's actually weighing the possibility. The idea of hero not corpse is probably sifting through his mind. I'm sure he's contemplating the Hollywood movie based on his exploits.

I give him time to think, hoping he'll realize what a horrible idea that is.

Finally, he comes around.

"Yeah, I guess that wouldn't be ideal."

I riffle through the imaginary Rolodex in my head, but I come up a blank. There's only one place we can go, and even that is ridiculous.

We emerge from underground and I head east on 42nd Street.

"So, where we headed?"

"You'll find out when we get there."

Traffic is heavy, but I'm not in a hurry. Twenty minutes later, I've finally reached Madison Avenue, where I turn north. Travis, wide awake now, is staring out the window.

"Don't you just love the city this time of year?" he asks.

I don't answer.

"What do you usually do for the holidays?" he asks.

"Nothing."

"Nothing?"

"That's right."

"What about when you were a kid? Didn't you love Christmas?"

"We didn't celebrate it."

"What do you mean?"

"Détente. My dad was Catholic, my mom Jewish, so they decided one negated the other."

"What about presents?"

"I don't remember many presents." That wasn't entirely

true, but somehow playing the victim makes me feel better.

"You're kidding, right?"

"Nope. Too poor to have presents," I lie. Now, I'm really getting into this. I wonder how far I can take it. I suddenly realize playing the victim can sometimes be fun.

When we cross 59th Street, Travis pipes up again.

"So, where we headed?"

"To someone I think will take us in."

"Who?"

I smile. I'm enjoying this, too.

"You'll find out soon enough."

"Come on, man…" he whines.

"Your patience shall be rewarded," I say, wondering exactly when I'm going to spring it on him. I don't have to, once we cross 72nd Street.

"Man, you gotta be kidding!"

I look at him in the rearview mirror. I'm smiling. He's not.

"Are you crazy? She's not going to like this. She's not going to let us in."

"Let me worry about that."

"Oh, man," he says, sinking back into the seat, his head buried in his hands. "She's the last person in the world I wanna see. And I'm pretty sure she feels the same way."

The words come out of my mouth without giving it much thought. But once it's out there, I realize this might be just what the doctor ordered in terms of shaking things up. I don't know why, but it isn't until Travis articulates the likelihood that neither of them will be thrilled to see the other that I realize this might bring things to a head.

"I'm pretty sure I'm not at the top of her guest list, but she's the only one I can think of who might have reason to take us in."

"More like kick us to the curb, man," Travis moans, as I watch him in the rearview mirror sink back into the seat.

In this neighborhood it's not easy to find parking after seven p.m., when everyone has tucked their car in for the night. But luck is shining on me this evening because I'm able to find a spot just off 5th and 88th, near the Guggenheim Museum.

"Are you sure this is such a good idea?" says Travis.

"No. But you got anything better?"

He thinks for a moment. "Guess not. I was you I'd have a backup plan."

"I'm never without a Plan B," I lie.

"You really think she's gonna let us up? I mean, I wouldn't be surprised she hears it's us she calls the cops."

"I don't think she'll do that, Travis."

"How come?"

"I just have that feeling."

"What about the stuff?" he asks.

"The stuff?"

"You know. What's in the duffel bag. You want me to take it out and…"

"I don't think we're going to need it, Travis," I say, trying hard to suppress a grin. Does he really think I'm going to walk into a New York City apartment building carrying a duffle bag stuffed with a shotgun, a pistol, and a baseball bat?

The night doorman has never seen me before, so I know he's not going to give us any trouble. But I keep wondering how I should handle it. Should I call and give her a heads-up? Make up some kind of cock and bull story to get us upstairs? Or, should I just hope that when the doorman calls up she's in the mood to receive us? Something that never occurs to me is that she's not home. I don't know why. After all, there's a fifty-fifty chance she's out for the evening. But if so, I'll just make sure we stick around till she shows.

As we walk east, toward Lila's building, I try to prep Travis.

"Travis, I want you to listen to me closely."

From the look on his face, I can see he's a million miles away. I snap my fingers in front of his face.

"Travis! Are you paying attention?"

"Yeah. Yeah. Relax, man. I hear you."

I stop, face him, and turn him to face me.

"This is important. I need you to be present."

"I'm here, man. I don't know what else you want from me."

"I want you to listen to what I'm going tell you."

"Okay. I'm listening. But it's getting kinda cold. Why can't we talk about this inside?"

"Because we're not going inside until I make sure you don't fuck things up."

"How'm I gonna fuck things up more than they already are? You wanna tell me that?" He shakes his head. "I don't know how the fuck I got myself in the middle of this."

"I know. But it doesn't matter how you got into it, it's how you, how *we*, are gonna get out of it."

"Okay. Okay. I hear you. What's so important?"

"Something doesn't sit right with me."

"What do you mean?"

"I keep trying to put this whole thing together and the piece that doesn't quite fit is sitting up there." I point to the building in front of us, 19 East 88th Street.

"You mean Lila?"

"That's right."

"I don't get what you mean?"

"I keep trying to figure things out, but every time I take Lila out of the equation, she seems to pop right back in."

"Sure, she does. She hired you."

"She hired me to find her husband and I found him. But that was just the beginning. That's what got both of us here. Now."

"So, what are you saying?"

"I'm saying that until I figure out how she fits in...or, if she fits in...we've got to be very careful."

"Careful how?"

"Careful about what we, especially what you say."

He's silent for a moment. I think he's thinking, but I can't be sure.

"Okay. Okay. I think I get what you're saying. Are you telling me you want me to keep my mouth shut?"

"Exactly. But I also want you to pay attention."

"Pay attention how?"

I'm getting frustrated, but I can't let him know that.

"Okay. How about this? I once heard this interview with a bunch of actors and they said that one of the most important things for an actor to do is listen..."

His face lights up. "Yeah. Yeah. That's true. It's not just reciting the lines, it's listening and reacting to your scene partner."

"Exactly. It's the same with improv, right? You can't have a preconceived agenda, right? You have to be *present* and go with the flow."

"Hey, man, I'm impressed. How do you know so much about acting technique?"

"It's not just acting technique, Travis. It's a technique that can serve all of us well. In my job, I have to pay attention. Not just to the big things or the little things, but *everything*. That's what I want you to do up there, assuming we get up there. I want you to just listen and when it's appropriate for you to get involved, I won't even have to tell you. You'll know. But just in case, I want you to not take your eyes off me. I want you to be inside my head. I want you to anticipate where I'm going, and then I want you to go there with me. Is this getting through to you? Am I making sense?"

"Absolutely, man. I totally get where you're coming from and where you're going."

I hear the words, but I'm not so sure the meaning is getting all the way through.

"So, how are we gonna get in?"

"I'm not sure yet. But that's what I'm saying. Just play along with me, no matter what I do or say. Can you do that?"

He nods.

I whip out my phone, find Lila in my contacts, and punch her up. The phone rings a couple times before she picks up.

"Peter. What a nice surprise. To what do I owe the honor?" she says in this sweet, syrupy voice that kinda makes you want to dive into the phone and wind up on the other end.

"I wouldn't call it an honor, Lila, but I need your help."

"Really? How could little ole me help you, Peter Fortunato?"

"I'm in your 'hood."

"Really?"

"Yes. And I'd like to come up and talk to you."

"It's kind of late, honey."

"I know. But it's important."

"Important how?"

"I'm in a little trouble and I need your help."

I'm not sure the flip side of damsel in distress is going to work with someone like Lila—I don't really see her as having a nurturing, caring side. But it's worth a shot.

"I can't imagine how I could help you, honey."

"I was hoping I could come up and let you know exactly how."

"Couldn't this wait till tomorrow?"

"No. It couldn't. I've just got back from a long trip and I think I've got some interesting news for you."

"A long trip? Now, that's provocative. To where?"

"I'll tell you all about it when I see you. I'm just gonna have your doorman buzz and you just tell him to let me up, okay?"

"You're persistent, aren't you?"

"Yes. I am. And it's cold out here," I add, smiling in Travis's direction. He smiles back. He's enjoying this.

"Well, I guess it'll be all right."

"Great," I say, and disconnect before she can change her mind.

"Man, you are really good."

"Let's not get ahead of ourselves."

He begins to walk toward the building entrance—we're still about a half block away—but I stop him.

"She said to come up, right?"

"She did. But I want to give her a little time to think."

"About what?"

"I don't know. But I'm sure we'll find out."

2
Bottom of the Ninth

Lila Alston answers the door dressed either as if she's getting ready for a night on the town or has just returned from one. Her bright red, unruly hair flows halfway down the back of her neck. She's wearing a tight black miniskirt, black sparkly top, and black stockings. When I look down at her feet, I see she's barefoot, though behind her, leaning against the wall, is a pair of black, knee-high, high-heeled boots. Leaning up against the boots there's a pair of black stiletto heels.

It's the first time I see Lila in full makeup and I realize she's even more breathtakingly beautiful than I recall.

I'm tempted to whip out my camera and snap a picture, not just to capture all her beauty in this moment of time, but more to remind me of the expression on her face when she sees Travis standing behind me. Let's just say, he is not someone she is expecting to see again. Maybe ever.

"Thanks for inviting us up, Lila. Hope we aren't interrupting something. You look like you're on the way out."

For a moment the words she has to express what she's really feeling seem locked inside her head, having trouble escaping. Finally, when she's able to compose herself, to put on the face she wants others to see, the face that expresses not what she's seeing or feeling but what she wants others to think she's seeing or feeling, it morphs into a facsimile of a welcoming smile. But somehow, it doesn't look right. Which is because it isn't. At least that's what I'm thinking.

"I didn't realize you had someone with you," she says, staring directly over my shoulder at Travis, as if to make sure it's really him. A split second passes before she refocuses on me. "You might have mentioned it." Her voice is light and airy on the outside but grim on the inside. "Oh, and by the way, I don't think this rises to the level of an invite."

"I didn't think it was important. After all, Travis here is anything but a stranger. Right, Travis?"

He looks at me first, as if asking permission to speak, and I see he recognizes the show has begun and he's expected to play his part. Which, I hope he remembers, is just to shut up and let me do my thing.

"I guess my idea of important doesn't quite match up to yours," she says.

"I'm unpredictable, Lila. Even I don't know what I'm going to do sometimes. Women like that, don't they?" I don't wait for a reply. I don't expect one, either. "How about you invite us in and we can have a little talk?"

She hesitates, but she realizes she doesn't have a choice. Technically, no matter what she says, we are invited guests—or at least I am. Under those circumstances, she can't very well threaten to call the cops and have us ousted.

She waves us in. As I pass her by, I catch the aroma of a sweet, subtle perfume. She's moved away from the lemon scent I've come to associate with her. This one is more sophisticated. More complicated. I look back to Travis, who's a couple steps behind me, and see this lecherous grin he's sporting. The closer he gets to her, the wider and more sickening the grin. If I wasn't there, standing right beside him, I have no doubt he'd be leading the way to the bedroom. In the middle of this thought, I realize there's a good chance Travis has never set foot in this apartment, though from the way he's holding himself, and staring at Lila as opposed to the surroundings, I suspect I'm wrong about that.

Like two obedient Boy Scouts, we line up behind her and follow her to the living room, sunken two steps below the rest of the apartment. Travis doesn't wait to be invited to sit. He spies the big comfortable Eames chair and immediately plops himself down. I expect him to say something like, "First come, first served," but he doesn't say that. He doesn't say anything. He just slumps back in the chair, as if he's settling in for a performance.

I take the couch. Lila chooses a straight-back chair.

"Just for the record," Lila says, "this is an imposition. I'm not a fan of the drop-in and since I have a life, I'm hoping this will be quick."

"Originally, I was going to ask you if we could crash here for the night. But I guess that's out of the question."

She laughs. She's still got that throaty, incredibly sexy laugh. But it's a laugh that cuts through me like a Ginsu knife.

"Oh, that's a good one, Peter."

"I'm just a natural wit," I say, as I settle into the couch.

"Why are you boys here?"

"Well, we got ourselves into a little trouble. Wait. Scratch that. Someone else got is into more than a little trouble."

"That someone being...?"

"Oh, I don't think we have to name names."

"Suit yourself," she says with more than a hint of sarcasm in her voice.

"And what about you?" she asks accusingly, staring daggers over at Travis, who seems to be enjoying the comfort of his chair.

"I'm with him," he says, and my heart skips a beat. Damn! Maybe he's not as dumb as I think he is? Or maybe, he's a little smarter than I give him credit for. Let's face it, if I'd scripted this I couldn't have come up with a better reply.

Her face sours. Maybe she thought Travis would be a weak link. And maybe he's thinking now, not so much. I couldn't ask for a better situation. Lila is off-balance and I'm in charge. Let's hope I can keep it that way.

I decide the time is right.

"We're kinda on the run, Lila."

"What's that supposed to mean?"

"It means people are after us."

"Are they green, by any chance?"

"I'm glad you haven't lost your sense of humor, darling." The word feels strange in my mouth. Even stranger when it comes out. But it fits. Damn it. It fits. I look over at Travis and, sure enough, I can see from his eyes he's paying attention, looking, maybe even thinking, waiting for that cue which might or might not come.

"I think you know the folks who are after us. Or at least you know why they are."

She crosses her long, shapely legs. "I have no idea what you're talking about."

"You want me to take the time to spell it out? Fine by me. I'll start with a little summary to get us up to date."

"I don't have all night. I actually did have plans for this evening."

"Yeah. I could tell. Boots are heels?"

"Excuse me?"

"Never mind. You know something, Lila. I have a very strong feeling that whoever you have plans with will find it well worth his or her time to wait. In fact, if you want to give them a call to tell them you're running a little late, it's fine with me."

She launches daggers at me with her eyes.

"No, thanks. I'm fine for now," she says, so cold it appears like icicles are shooting from her mouth. "But I appreciate you worrying about my reputation."

"What was it Oscar Wilde said about reputation? Oh, yeah, 'One can survive everything, nowadays, except death, and live down everything except a good reputation.'"

"I'm impressed. Not least of all because you think I have a good reputation."

"I wouldn't go that far. But enough of the witty banter. Let's go back to the beginning. You hire me to find your husband. I find him dead as dirt in Travis here's apartment…" I look over at Travis and, lo and behold, he's still paying full attention.

"But it doesn't end there. Because then Travis here," I jerk a finger in his direction, "wants to hire me to protect him."

"Protect him? From what? From who? From me?"

"That's a very interesting question, Lila, and I hope, when I'm finished, it's a question I can answer. Because, actually, it might be coming from more than one direction or one person."

She holds out her hands. "Please. Continue."

I lean back. I'm experiencing a weird sensation. Often, I can feel sleepy and know that there's no way I can fall asleep. I don't even try. But now, here, sitting on this comfortable couch, embraced by the pillows, I am so relaxed that I think if I closed my eyes, sleep would finally come. Weird, right? Because I am totally, as they say, totally engaged. My mind is perhaps sharper than it has ever been, despite the lack of even the semblance of quality sleep over the past few days.

"Just so all my cards are on the table, Lila, I know about Donald hiring Travis and I know why. I also know all about your relationship with Travis and Travis's relationship with your deceased husband. I know that somehow the Albanian mob has worked its way into this triangle."

"Albanian mob? I have no idea what you're talking about. I didn't even know they have a mob. Does every country have their own mob? Is there an Icelandic mob? A Swedish mob?"

"When we're finished here perhaps you can do a little research. A nice addition to your more formal education. But why don't we skip the wise remarks and the digressions and move ahead. And just stop me if there's something you know is wrong, you want to add some information, or if there's something you don't understand. Though I think you probably understand a lot more than I do."

"You think I'm Bonnie to someone's Clyde, do you?"

"In your case, darling, I'm more inclined to think of you as Bonnie *and* Clyde. But that's not where I'm going here. Back to the narrative. Your dear, departed husband decides to start a side business. A dangerous business. But a lucrative business. Money laundering. You know what that is, right?"

She shrugs, trying to look bored. But I know better. She's lasered in to every word I say.

"I can guess."

"Good. I don't want to waste time telling you something you already know. Anyway, he decides Travis here might make a good employee, though god knows why..."

Travis tenses. His face starts to turn red. He wants desperately to say something, to jump to his own defense but must realize him speaking at this point is not part of the script. Point to Travis for self-restraint.

Suddenly, out of nowhere, and for no discernible reason, that sour, bad taste that warns me of disaster ahead, appears. It's creeping up from my stomach, toward my mouth. Why? Why now? I ask myself. I don't wait for the answer but instead, plow ahead.

"You know, Lila, you're right."

"About what?"

"About wasting time. I mean, it's much too precious, right?"

"Er..."

"Sure, it is. How'd you feel if I skipped ahead? That would be good, wouldn't it? I mean, then you could get on with what you're supposed to be doing tonight, and maybe the rest of us can get on with our lives." I turn to Travis. "You'd like that, wouldn't you, Travis?"

Bewildered, caught unaware of where I'm going, he plays his part beautifully and simply nods.

"All this time I knew all the pieces of the puzzle were within reach, I just couldn't figure out how to put them together, so they fit. You know, when you get those thousand-piece puzzles and right there on the cover is what the final product is supposed to look like? That's your guide. Without it, you'd have no idea what you were putting together. No matter how difficult the puzzle might be, the one thing you have is what it's going to look like if all the pieces properly fit together. No cover, no way anyone can put that puzzle back together."

"I have no idea what you're talking about. But there is someone waiting..."

"Of course, you don't. You're not supposed to. It's just me, thinking out loud. And I'm sorry I'm ruining your social life. But this is important because I just realized I know what that puzzle's supposed to look like when it's finished. I have all the pieces. I've just been struggling on how to put them together. And what I never bothered doing, something I should have done a while ago, was to step back and take a good look at that final picture."

"I still..."

"You're right. Why waste your time with my thinking out loud? I'm just gonna put all the pieces together right here, right now, right in front of you and me and Travis and see what happens. Let the chips fall where they may. First off, when we walked in, I noticed that jacket over there, hung over the railing, and two pairs of shoes in the foyer."

I point to the black, wrought iron railing that separates the living room from the foyer.

"I actually have more than two pairs of shoes, Peter."

"I would hope so. But it struck me as rather odd. I mean, wouldn't they be near the closet where you keep your shoes? But hey, I don't want to get stuck on a pair of shoes. Besides, it's not the shoes. It's the jacket. It's a nice jacket, but how's this for a coincidence? I've actually seen that jacket before. Pretty amazing, right?"

"No. Not so amazing, at all. I don't own one-of-a-kind clothing."

"Didn't say you owned it. In fact, I think someone else owns it."

I'm on a roll. I'm not even sure where this is coming from, but it's coming. My sleep-deprived brain? Muscle memory I'm not aware I had? A voice from God? I'll figure that out later. Or maybe I won't.

Travis, engrossed in my tale, can hardly contain himself. As if on cue, he asks, "If they're not hers, whose are they?"

I look over at him and smile. Good work, Travis.

"A woman I met recently, who works in a very high-end women's clothing shop on Madison Avenue. Perhaps you know her? What's her name again? Susan something, right?"

The blood drains from Lila's already pale face. Her makeup, which moments earlier was so perfect, is turning garish, like a clown's. The red of her lipstick is too red. The blue of her eye shadow is too blue.

She's not saying anything, so I will.

"I didn't realize you and Susan Lane were friends. You girls like to swap clothing?"

"Susan Lane? I have no idea who you're talking about," she says, stumbling for words.

"Who is Susan Lane?" asks Travis.

"For your edification, Travis, Susan Lane is the woman who had an affair with Donald Alston while you were having your affair with Lila over here."

"I don't..." Lila stammers.

"Almost finished, Lila. Just a couple more minutes. Here's the way it shapes up. Somehow, you and Susan Lane connected. Maybe you knew her before her affair with your husband. Maybe you met her after. Maybe you had Donald followed and found who he was having an affair with. Or, knowing how you guys operate—will I ever understand the rich? Maybe you even helped manufacture that affair, the same way your husband did with you and Travis." I glance over to Travis and see he's focused on Lila. "Doesn't matter. Somehow, you two connected and went into business together."

"You have quite the imagination."

"Yeah, don't I?" I smile. "Pretty good stuff, right? We're almost finished. So, let's move on to your husband's untimely demise. It's really none of my business but I'm kinda enjoying this so I'll keep going. I figure it could have gone down any one of several ways. You could have killed him. Susan Lane could have killed him. You could have killed him together. Or, it's possible neither of you had anything to do with it and it was the Albanians who did it."

"That's a lot of possibilities," she says, crossing and uncrossing her legs.

"It is. But here's the best part. I don't have to figure out who did it. First off, I don't really care. If all you people turn on each other and think murder is the answer, who am I to stand in your way? What I might care about is why. But there are so many reasons. Jealousy. Hatred. Anger. Greed. In this case, my money's on greed. But again, I don't really give a shit. That's between you and Susan who, I wouldn't be surprised, is waiting for you behind that closed door." I gesture toward the other end of the apartment. "...And the cops."

"And Travis?" she asks.

"Oh, yes. Poor, pitiful Travis who has skin in this game only because whoever did kill Donald Alston decided it was a good idea to do it in his apartment." I turn to Travis. "Sorry about that, Travis. But you know what they say about sleeping with dogs..."

"If none of this matters to you, why are you here? And why don't you just leave?" Lila says. Every last bit of fake sweetness is leached from her voice. She's every stern, angry woman I've ever met. My mother. My teachers. My ex-wife. It doesn't bother me anymore. I'm used to it. But maybe, just maybe, that's what makes me so easy to anger. Maybe one day I'll work on that with a shrink. But I've got better things to do right now.

"Don't worry, Lila. I'm on my way. Just need a minute or two to finish up because there's this other thing. It's the dough your husband was supposed to launder. Evidently, it's disappeared. I have a pretty good idea who has it, but I'm not sure how to get it back. But then, I realize, wait a minute, Pete, you don't have to get it back. All you have to do is tell the Albanians where it is, and they'll get it back."

I take a breath and look at Lila's face. If it's possible, she's turned even paler. Her ruby red lipstick has become the color of Lucille Ball's hair.

"This is my ticket out. And if it helps Travis here, well, I don't really care one way or the other, though I'm sure he does. Right, Travis?"

He's too confused to answer.

"By the way, whatever happened to those guys you hired to follow us down in Texas?"

"Excuse me?"

"The two yahoos who were trailing us and then lost us in New Orleans..."

"I thought those were the Albanians," Travis pipes up.

"I thought so, too. But then I realized they didn't look like any of the guys I met up here. And they really weren't very professional. I'd already stuck them once, so I don't think Sergio would send down a couple amateurs who could be stuck by me again. But if not them, who? And now it occurs to me I probably know who."

"I have no idea what you're talking about," says Lila, in a tone even she can't possibly believe is persuasive.

I start to get up. "Come on, Travis. I think we're done here."

"Done?" says Travis.

"Like stick a fork in it done. We're gonna get outta here and as soon as we do, I'm gonna make a call to my old pal, Sergio, and tell him who has his money."

"Who...?" Travis stammers.

"You wouldn't..." says Lila, shooting up from her chair as if shot out by one of those T-shirt canons they use at sporting events.

"Not only would, but I am."

"What are you going to say?"

"Haven't quite crafted the words yet, but I know what the general idea will be."

I turn toward the front door, as Travis falls in step behind me.

Lila lurches toward me, her hands outstretched. "You can't...No one will believe you..."

I know if she could reach my neck she'd wring the life out of it. Fortunately, I'm quicker than she is. I sidestep her and put my hand up, as if to stop her from getting too close. But if she does I have absolutely no doubt I'd slug her. And I'd enjoy it.

"No one has to believe me, honey. All I have to do is plant the idea in Sergio's head and let the chips fall where they'll fall. One thing he knows, and that's that I don't have it. And all I care about is taking the heat off me."

"...and me," Travis pipes up.

I smile and turn to Travis. "You're so cute, Travis." I turn back to Lila. "Between you and me, Lila, even though I'm starting to think of Travis here as one of those lovable little puppies who can't help having accidents and pissing all over your brand new carpet, I really don't give a shit about what happens to him either. Or Susan Lane. Or anyone else stupid enough or greedy enough to get themselves involved with you, the Albanians, or your dead husband. I hate all of you. All I care about is yours truly and you know what, this bad taste I get in my mouth whenever there's trouble ahead, well, it's not quite as strong as it was when I first got here."

I head toward those two steps that'll lead me out of the living room and into the foyer. At the top of the steps, I stop and turn toward a still stunned Lila.

"It's been fun knowing you, Lila. Any last words?"

"You son of a bitch." She spits out the words as if each one is a bullet. Aimed at my heart.

"Yeah. Well, I'll try working on that. But the truth is, right now that suits me fine."

"You'll be sorry," she screams, her face now turning almost

as red as her hair.

"You think?"

"He won't believe you. I'll tell him you've got the money."

"Tell him whatever you want. But I don't think he'll believe you. He knows I don't have the money. He probably figures Travis here does. But once I finger you, it's going to get him thinking. And once he starts thinking he's going to put two and two together and there's a good chance he's going to come up Lila. But if he doesn't. If he still thinks Travis is holding the dough. What do I care? You guys got yourselves into this. You get yourselves out of it. As far as I'm concerned you deserve each other."

For the first time, Travis speaks up.

"You'd throw me...us to the wolves?"

"You bet your ass, I would. This isn't my problem anymore." I smile. "I'm going to Disneyland."

3
Last Licks

The great Yogi Berra said it best. "It ain't over till it's over."

This, I think, is what over looks like.

No one's happy.

No one's out of the woods.

No one is getting what they want.

No one is getting what they need.

No one is getting what they deserve.

This is often what over looks like.

So yes, Yogi, it is over. Really. Over.

I do not make idle threats. I really do call Sergio. And he's pretty happy to hear from me. I tell him what I know and what I think, leaving out certain unimportant details, of course. By the end of our phone call, he really does believe Lila Alston has what's his. Does she? Probably. But I can't swear to it. I don't have to. I don't know Sergio well, but I have a pretty good idea he knows how to get back something that's his once he knows who has it. I also know that men like him don't have rules about how to get back their property. In other words, if I were Lila I wouldn't count on her gender to give her any kind of free ticket to ride.

If Lila asks me for advice, which I'm pretty sure she won't, I'd tell her to give back the money. That it's not worth it. But I don't think that's what she's going to do. I think she's going to collect Susan Lane, or whoever else was in that bedroom, pack a bag, and scram.

Why not give it back?

Good question. Ninety percent of folks would probably do just that, hoping they can make things whole again. But not people like Lila Alston. People like Lila Alston—let's call them what they are: narcissists—really believe they can beat the system. That's what keeps them going.

Me? I know I can't. Never did. Never could. Never will. I know my place in the world order. I don't have to be happy about it. I just have to know it. My job, at least for now, is to put broken things back together. I only wish I could do it to myself.

But Pete, you might ask. What about this? What if you're totally wrong? What if Lila Alston doesn't have the money? What if you've sealed the fate of this woman with a lie? Will you be able to live with yourself?

Absolutely. In fact, what I'm hoping is that I'll go home tonight and get the best night's sleep I'll ever have.

A boy can dream, can't he?

ACKNOWLEDGMENTS

Thanks to Chip MacGregor, who took a chance on me and thinks I'm a much better writer than I am (shh, don't tell him the truth), Eric Campbell, who's always there when you need him, and Lance Wright, who steers the ship and always manages to get it ashore. Also, a big tip of the hat to Chris Rhatigan, who made this a better book with his sharp eye and editorial suggestions.

CHARLES SALZBERG is a freelance writer who has lived in New York City his whole life. He is a former magazine journalist who's written for *New York* magazine, *Esquire, The New York Times, The New York Times Book Review, Redbook* and other periodicals. He is the author of over two dozen nonfiction books. His first novel, *Swann's Last Song,* was nominated for a Shamus Award. In addition to the Swann series, he is author of *Devil in the Hole,* named one of the best crime novels of 2013 by *Suspense* magazine, *Second Story Man,* winner of the Beverly Hills Book Award and nominated for a Shamus Award and the David Award, and he has novellas in the collections *Triple Shot, Three Strikes* and *Third Degree.* He teaches writing at the New York Writers Workshop, where he is a Founding Member, and is on the Board of MWA-NY.

CharlesSalzberg.com

BOOKS

On the following pages are a few
more great titles from the
Down & Out Books publishing family.

For a complete list of books and to
sign up for our newsletter,
go to DownAndOutBooks.com.

Razing Stakes
The De La Cruz Case Files
TG Wolff

Down & Out Books
February 2022
978-1-64396-245-0

Colin McHenry is out for his regular run when an SUV crosses into his path, crushing him. Within hours of the hit-skip, Cleveland Homicide Detective Jesus De La Cruz finds the vehicle in the owner's garage, who's on vacation three time zones away. The suspects read like a list out of a textbook: the jilted fiancée, the jealous coworker, the overlooked subordinate, the dirty client.

Motives, opportunities, and alibis don't point in a single direction. In these mysteries, Cruz has to think laterally, yanking down the curtain to expose the master minding the strings.

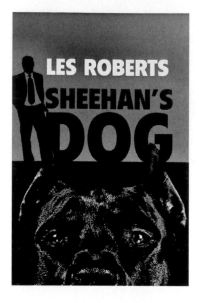

Sheehan's Dog
Les Roberts

Down & Out Books
February 2022
978-1-64396-247-4

Former Irish mafia hitman Brock Sheehan lives quietly on a boat fifty miles from Cleveland. When his long-lost nephew, Linus Callahan, tracks him down and asks him for assistance, he agrees to help. A few days earlier, the nephew got into a bar argument with a multimillion-dollar basketball player just released from prison for running a high-level dog-fighting ring. Then the athlete is murdered, and Linus becomes the Cleveland police department's "person of interest."

Investigating the athlete's former dogfight ring, Brock winds up with a pit bull of his own, which he names Conor. And eventually, with Conor's instincts, he discovers and turns over to the police the real killer of the dog-killer turned sports legend.

Bad Guy Lawyer
Chuck Marten

Down & Out Books
March 2022
978-1-64396-249-8

The only time Guy McCann stops talking is when he's downing scotch. Guy was a hot-shot attorney for the West Coast mafia until he got cold feet and split town, earning a target on his head. Now he's lying low in Las Vegas, giving back-room legal advice to second-rate crooks while pining over his old girlfriend Blair, a working girl with a razor wit and zero inhibitions.

When Blair is committed to a psychiatric ward, Guy is drawn back to the dangerous underworld of Los Angeles. Next thing he knows, Blair has escaped from the hospital and Guy's former mafia associates are on her trail, with Guy caught in the cross-fire.

Hell to Pay
A Diggy and Stick Crime Novel
Andy Rausch

Down & Out Books
March 2022
978-1-64396-248-1

Dirty ex-cops Robert "Diggy" Diggs and Dwayne "Stick" Figgers have found themselves in a terrible situation. After Kansas city drug lord Benny Cordella discovers that they have wronged him, he devises an insane plan: he's going to force them to commit suicide. This, he believes, will send them to hell, where they will track down Dread Corbin, the man who killed his daughter. Of course, Diggy and Stick don't believe this is possible, but they will soon discover that hell is real.

Hell to Pay: Diggy and Stick Book One is unlike any crime novel you've ever read before. It's dark, dangerous, edgy, and laugh-out-loud hilarious. Buckle up for one hell of a ride!